Soor l'Ignorario, Collionario
July 1985

R. L. WOODBERRY

Karari

KARARI

*The Sudanese Account
of the Battle of Omdurman*

by

'ISMAT HASAN ZULFO

*Translated from the Arabic by
Peter Clark*

Frederick Warne

First Published in Great Britain by
Frederick Warne (Publishers) Ltd
London

Copyright © 1980 by 'Ismat Hasan Zulfo
Translation copyright © 1980 by Peter Clark

ISBN 0 7232 2677 6 (hard cover)
    0 7232 2499 4 (paperback)

Set in 11/12 pt. Photon Baskerville,
Printed in Great Britain at
The Pitman Press, Bath
1376·180

CONTENTS

MAPS

vi

TRANSLATOR'S INTRODUCTION

THE Arabic version of *Karari* was first published by the University of Khartoum Press on 1 January, 1973. It was about twice the length of the present volume and was a best-seller in the Sudan.

In translating it, it has been necessary to reduce its length. Some material of historical interest and value has had to be omitted. I have tried, however, to bring out certain features of the story that will be new to most English readers and that bring forward the central theme of the book – the battle of Omdurman as seen from the Khalifa's camp.

There has been the perennial problem of the transliteration of Arabic names. I have kept to no hard and fast rule. In general I have followed the practices of Professor P. M. Holt and Mr Richard Hill in their many writings on the Sudan. I have avoided pressing consistency too far and well known cities of the Sudan appear as Khartoum, Omdurman, Dongola and el Obeid rather than as al Khartum, Umm Durman, Dunqula or al Ubayyid. Illogically I have written Osman Digna, rather than 'Uthman Diqna, though 'Uthman Azraq and 'Uthman Shaykh al Din retain a form nearer to the Arabic written equivalent. When a place name is from a non-Arabic root (such as Fashashoya) I have given it the name accepted by the Sudan Survey Department. I have refrained from adding diacritical marks or marks lengthening vowel sounds. For certain words and phrases that cannot be translated a glossary has been added.

Four people have been of enormous assistance in the

translation. In the early stages Sayed Ishaq al Khalifa Sharif gave me great help. In addition to being an acutely sensitive literary craftsman in a number of languages, he is also a grandson of the Mahdi and is a great repository of Sudanese Mahdist lore. In later stages, Sayed Meccawi Suleiman Akrat made many useful comments which have improved the English. My wife, Isobel Clark, in addition to typing an earlier draft, made many useful suggestions. My biggest debt goes to the author himself, 'Ismat Hasan Zulfo. He read every chapter of the English translation most carefully. We have discussed the text and the battle most exhaustively and any merits the translation has are due to him, any shortcomings my own.

PETER CLARK

Pentlow, Essex.

INTRODUCTION

Mɪʟɪᴛᴀʀʏ knowledge differs from other branches of knowledge in that its theories and principles can only be learned from battles and from practical experience, and of this military history has an unlimited store. We are forever resorting to it for lessons, precepts and theories.

Military history deals with the changing situations of nations, communities and individuals. It is not just a story to be told, but its lasting value lies in its lessons and in the analysis of events and situations. An army is the microcosm of a nation, reflecting the strengths and weaknesses of that nation. Thus, when we study military history we cannot separate it from social and cultural factors. If this is a general practice in the study of military history, how much more is it when we consider the case of the battle of Karari? For in the battle of Omdurman, as it is generally known, or the battle of Karari, as it is locally known, all the men of the town were combatants. Men were soldiers before they were anything else.

The military aspect is the principal theme put forward in this study. It is perhaps the most important aspect of the Mahdist revolution, for that revolution was born by the sword, lived by the sword and perished by the sword. It is not possible, however, for us to ignore the social factors that moulded the circumstances surrounding the battle. Not for one moment was I able to discount these factors and their effect on the military situation or on the battle formation of the Khalifa's army and on the basic military ideas that fashioned the way his leaders plunged into the battle or on the unity or disunity of the ranks of that army – both among the leaders and the men. I was unable to overlook the effect of the economic circumstances that restricted the Khalifa's mobilization, making him hesitate and then plunge into the fateful battle.

If we wish to discuss the Khalifa's planning or his methods of mobilizing his military forces for raids, we must consider the principles and military ideas behind his army's activity. These principles were derived from the experiences of earlier battles. We are thus obliged to pass rapidly over the lessons these battles taught and which impressed themselves on the thinking of the Khalifa's generals. Indeed, to a certain extent the policy which he adopted at the battle of Karari was just a repetition of his policy at Shaykan.

The first three chapters of the book give a quick survey of the Mahdist revolution and the social background of those who people the stage of our drama, deal with the wars of the Mahdist revolution itself, and with the period of the Khalifa 'Abd Allahi, the central figure of our story. We touch on the characteristics of the schism that prevailed during the Khalifa's time, the ebbing of the tide of enthusiasm and the collapse of that unity which was such a feature in the lifetime of the Mahdi himself. We deal with the Khalifa's own personality and its development in the face of events up to 1898. We also deal with the Khalifa's organization – battle formation, chain of command and military activities. Hitherto in accounts of the battle the Khalifa's side has always been neglected. Thus the main purpose of our researches from Anglo-Egyptian sources is to consider the impact of the Sirdar's activities either on the Khalifa or on the course of the battle.

The next three chapters examine the reactions of the Khalifa to the Sirdar's advance to 'Atbara. First we try to explain the international situation and the motives which impelled Britain to agree to, and participate actively in, the invasion of the Sudan. The next chapters discuss the consequences of the Sirdar's advance, such as the reduction of the military might of the Khalifa by at least fifteen thousand men after the rout of Mahmud wad Ahmad at 'Atbara, and more indirectly, the massacre of al Matamma which weakened the morale of many of the Khalifa's warriors.

The major part of the book deals with the battle itself. For this we are forced to adopt a slightly different procedure.

The battle of Karari marked the end of the Mahdist revolution. Those five hours, together with the preceding few days, cover a period in which there are very few documents or reports from the Khalifa's side. Unlike the earlier battles of the Mahdiya, almost all the leaders were wiped out. Thus there were no survivors to explain what had happened.

Evidence from written sources deal with the Khalifa's army in a very sketchy way. They discuss the character of the Sirdar or the heroism of his army, or they discuss the movements and reactions of the Sirdar's forces. The paucity of information or the deliberate neglect of the progress of the Khalifa's army is one of the reasons that has prevented me from relying exclusively on European sources. There is another reason, no less important, that makes me have grave doubts about the accuracy of these sources. There has been a distortion of the truth in order that the record will tally with the official sources of information. These sources have tended to deal with the army of the Mahdiya in a hostile manner. When the British Light Cavalry Brigade made a fatuous charge at Balaclava in broad daylight, exposed to Russian gunfire, and were virtually annihilated, tales and songs were spread glorifying their courage, heroism and sacrifice. When tens of thousands of the Khalifa's army defied a storm of fire while defending their homes, they were denigrated as 'dervishes', 'savages' and 'fanatics'.

This prejudice was not unnatural, for the writers had been enemies of the Khalifa. But when the bias affected the presentation of the truth itself, such as the estimated size of the Khalifa's army or its movements, operations or plans, I began to pay greater attention to a second source. There has been one major source used by historians of the battle of Omdurman – the published and censored reports of the Intelligence Department of the Egyptian army under Wingate, Shuqayr and Slatin. There is some disparity between the information derived from the Field Intelligence diary written in pencil and hitherto unpublished, and the published intelligence reports; between what the generals of the Sirdar himself saw when they clashed with the Khalifa's army and recorded officially in reports, that also have never been published, and the published official reports.

I have also tapped a valuable source of information which has for long been neglected – the oral testimony of survivors of the battle from the Khalifa's side. Obtaining the statements of these people who are scattered over a wide area was no easy task. I travelled thousands of miles and listened to hundreds of people.

I have thus relied extensively on unwritten statements. This raises the question of the legitimacy of accepting oral or traditional evidence.

It is true that the weight and value of a document rests primarily on the fact that the document does not change and is not affected by time, whereas the memory of man is subject to weakness, decay and forgetfulness.

In general it was a matter of comparing and balancing different sources. I have treated all the evidence – oral and written – as if I were assessing legal evidence. I have taken into consideration circumstantial evidence, the great authority of one source rather than another and the effect of the passage of years and natural bias.

This has led me to take a number of precautions before accepting the statements of those who took part in the battle. To guarantee veracity I made them speak on oath – and they were very old men who would hesitate to perjure themselves, fearing divine retribution on the Day of Judgment. I also checked the validity of their testimony in the dating and dis-position of the forces as recorded in the documents and military reports. Their testimony was then recorded on tape as being of historical importance.

It may at first sight appear almost impossible to activate the memory of some old man and make him describe events that took place over seventy years ago. I disagree. I noticed in my wanderings around the various parts of the Sudan that coun-tryfolk – and most of my sources were from the coun-tryside – have a keener memory than townsfolk, with their cares and worries. For the majority of them, moreover, Karari represents an unforgettable experience – in fact the most memorable experience of their lives. The bloodshed of the battle, the sequence and speed of events, the weight of fire that was turned on them, the loss of most of their tribe and comrades within the course of a few minutes – all this made an indelible impression. Indeed some men were so haunted by their memories that they had been unable, according to their sons and grandsons, to refrain from talking about it.

This study is primarily a military study of a battle. But Karari is too important to be the monopoly of military men alone. In our national history it had the grave consequence for us of sixty years of foreign occupation. In world history it represents the climax of the period of imperialism known as the 'scramble for Africa', which enabled Europe to dominate the continent.

We are not yet able to talk of the price paid when 'we achieved' our independence. That is the task of future generations. But we can talk with confidence of the price paid when 'we lost' our independence. It is a great price worthy of a fine nation.

'ISMAT HASAN ZULFO

Omdurman,
May, 1972.

GLOSSARY

Allahu akbar: God is greater.
aman: Peace, a call for a truce.
'amil: regional governor in the time of the Mahdiya, in charge of an
     'imala.
amir: prince, commander.
angarayb: a bed made of wood and rope.
ansar: followers of the Mahdi in the Sudan.
'araqi: alcoholic drink made from dates; arrack.
ardabb: measure of weight, usually corn, approx. 200 lb.
ashraf: members of the family of Muhammad Ahmad the Mahdi.
'asida: pasty porridge made from millet.
baltajiya: soldiers in the Khalifa's army who carried axes.
bashibuzuq: irregular soldiers of the Egyptian regime in the Sudan
     1821–1885.
bayt al-amana: lit. house of security; the Mahdist armoury.
bayt al-mal: lit. house of property; the Mahdist treasury.
dhurra: Sudanese variant of millet.
dukhn: pearl millet, basic diet of western Sudan.
dum: a Sudanese palm tree.
Fatiha: the opening verse of the Qur'an.
furwa: goatskin rug, used for praying on.
'imala: administrative district headed by an *'amil.*
imam: leader in Islamic prayers.
'imma: characteristic Sudanese turban.
jabal: mountain, hill, outcrop of rocks.
jallaba: north Sudanese merchants in southern and western Sudan.
jallabiya: long gown worn by Sudanese men.
jihadiya: black trained soldiers in the Khalifa's army.
jubba: patchwork gown worn by Mahdists.

Khalifa: lit. successor; 'Abd Allahi was the Khalifa, the successor of the Mahdi, but the term Khalifa was also given to 'Ali wad Hilu and Muhammad Sharif.

khalwa: Qur'anic school.

khashkhashan: armed contingent of the Khalifa's personal guard.

khur: river bed, dry in all but the rainy seasons.

Mahdiya: the period of Sudanese history 1885–98.

maqdum: subordinate officer in the Khalifa's army.

mihrab: prayer niche in a mosque indicating the direction of prayer.

mudiriya: term used by Egyptian Government for provincial administrative district.

mulazim: plural *mulazimin;* lieutenant; the bodyguard of the Khalifa.

muqaddam: subordinate officer of the Mahdist army.

muqaddamiya: soldiers commanded by a *muqaddam.*

mushammaratiya: contingent of the Khalifa's private guard.

nazir: head of a tribe.

nuqqara: small war drum.

qadi: judge.

qubba: domed tomb, usually of a Sudanese saint.

rakuba: awning over branches for shade.

rasmiya: commander of 100 soldiers in the Mahdist army.

ratib: prayer book compiled by the Mahdi.

riyal: silver coin, based on the Maria Theresa dollar.

rub': the basic unit of the Mahdist army.

rukwa: small pot used for washing before prayers.

shari'a: Islamic canon law.

Shaykh: old man; courtesy title applied to distinguished old men.

sudd: the barrage of weeds on the Nile impeding passage between north and south.

suq: market.

tabaldi: Baobab tree, common in western Sudan.

tariqa: religious sect in the Sudan.

'ulama, singular *'alim:* orthodox learned men of religion.

ummbaya: hollowed elephant tusk which, when blown, emits a shrill noise.

wad, short for *walad:* a son of.

zaka: taxes prescribed by Islam to be used for alms.

zariba: stockade made of thorn bushes.

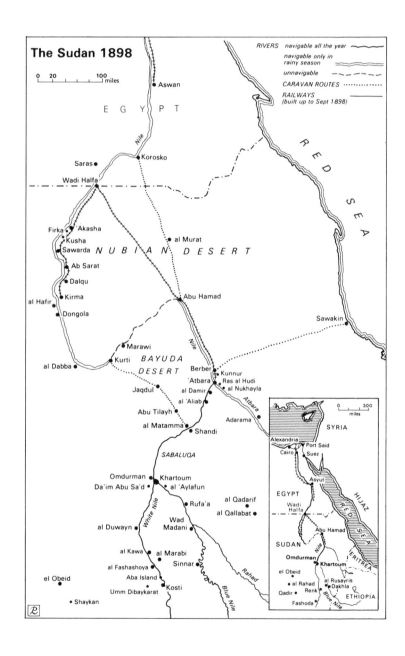

The Sudan 1898

RIVERS	navigable all the year
	navigable only in rainy season
	unnavigable
CARAVAN ROUTES	
RAILWAYS	(built up to Sept 1898)

0   20   100 miles

Aswan

E G Y P T

Nile

Korosko

Saras

Wadi Halfa

R E D   S E A

Firka   'Akasha
Kusha
Sawarda   N U B I A N   D E S E R T
Ab Sarat   al Murat
Dalqu
Kirma
al Hafir   Abu Hamad
Dongola

Sawakin

Marawi   Nile
Kurti   BAYUDA
al Dabba   DESERT   Berber
Kunnur
'Atbara   Ras al Hudi
Jaqdul   al Damir   al Nukhayla
al 'Aliab
Abu Tilayh   Atbara
al Matamma   Adarama
Shandi

SABALUQA

Omdurman   Khartoum
Da'im Abu Sa'd   al 'Aylafun

White Nile   Rufa'a   al Qadarif
al Qallabat
al Duwayn   Wad
Madani

al Kawa   al Marabi
al Fashashoya   Sinnar   Rahad
Aba Island
el Obeid   Umm Dibaykarat   Kosti   Blue Nile
Shaykan

[inset map]

0   300 miles

SYRIA

Alexandria   Port Said
Cairo   Suez

Asyut

EGYPT   HIJAZ
Wadi
Halfa   RED SEA

Abu Hamad

SUDAN

Omdurman   Khartoum
el Obeid   al Rusayris
al Rahad   Dakhla   ERITREA
Qadir   Renk   Blue Nile
Fashoda   ETHIOPIA

CHAPTER ONE

White Ivory and Black Ivory

THE midday sun was going down, casting its waning rays on the long swaying grass. Two men were sitting down, quietly talking together. One was tall, of brownish colour, with powerful eyes and shining white teeth. A few men were gathered around him. The man in official uniform leant forward attentively, interrupting him now and again. Suddenly the tall man leapt to his feet, struck his chest and began to talk loudly. The more he talked the more excited he got. He ended up by saying: 'I shall not go to Khartoum and justify myself in front of the misguided 'ulama. I have been entrusted by Heaven with a divine mission and I must carry it out even if I am opposed by all the difficulties of the world.' The official, alarmed by the vehemence of his words, sought to calm him, but only succeeded in arousing him further. The official gave up and began to glance towards the river where the steamer that would take him north was moored, his objective now being to return safely to Khartoum. The speaker permitted him to go and bade him farewell, accompanying him to the steamer which then set off north.

The scene occurred at Aba Island, 200 miles south of Khartoum, on the afternoon of 7 August, 1881, and the speakers were Muhammad Ahmad, the Mahdi, and Abu Su'ud Bey, sent by Ra'uf Bey, the Governor-General of the Sudan, to persuade the former to come to Khartoum and face the 'ulama, thinking that they might bring him to his senses after his proclamation that he was the expected Mahdi. This was the first time that the Mahdi had declared his claim before a representative of the

I

Government, thereby openly proclaiming his sedition.

Before the Egyptian invasion in 1821 Sudan was not one nation but a collection of independent communities, the great majority of which preserved their primary tribal characteristic – nomadism, moving according to the needs of the shepherd and his flocks. But some tribes had settled on the Nile and were more exposed to the winds of civilization which blew from outside. They had settled on the river, cultivating the narrow strip along its banks and enjoying the blessings of being settled within a tribal framework, without ties except for the bonds of a deep communal religious feeling, and without officers except for the chieftains of their tribes.

In 1821 Muhammad 'Ali, Viceroy of Egypt, sent his son Isma'il Pasha to conquer and plunder these lands. He assembled a well-equipped army which invaded the country and went south, then east towards the Funj capital, Sinnar, which he took without difficulty. The war that followed was one between gunpowder and human muscle, between the sword and the rifle.

The headstrong young Isma'il went from one victory to another. But he was checked by Mak Nimr, chieftain of the Ja'li tribe of Shandi, who was personally insulted by Isma'il. Mak Nimr fought back and killed Isma'il and his attendants.

Troubles now began for the people, for the Defterdar, brother-in-law of Isma'il, who had left him to go west and conquer Kordofan, heard of his fate and headed for Shandi. He crossed the river, but Mak Nimr had left, so he vented his wrath on the unarmed inhabitants, razed the town and slaughtered the people, then continued to pursue Mak Nimr, ravaging the towns and villages on his way. The Defterdar's bloodbaths caused much bitterness towards the Egyptian administration.

Muhammad 'Ali thought that the Sudan was one vast goldmine. When he was disillusioned he looked to the other resources of the country, the most important being slaves, to raise money for his huge army. Hitherto soldiering had been a monopoly of the Anatolian and Balkan Turks. But the Viceroy's campaigns in the Hijaz persuaded him to look for a fresh source of manpower and thus he turned his gaze to the south. A few important men and tribal chiefs used to maintain slaves, but the number was small. It is a mistake to compare them with the slaves in the southern states of America, for example, since their exploitation was not organized. They were treated well and were generally considered part of the family. This had been the case for centuries, but the instructions of Muhammad 'Ali to his generals were to collect as many slaves as possible. Slaves were recruited first from the southern Sudan and from the Nuba mountains, but in time also from northern tribes.

However, the Egyptian occupation led to the administrative unification of the Sudan. For the first time official boundaries were drawn up for the vast expanses which began to be known as the Sudan. Sudan was divided into *mudiriyas*, which were in turn divided into districts, each with a semi-autonomous administration responsible for collecting taxes.

In 1863 the Khedive Isma'il came to power in Cairo. He aimed to established a great empire that would reach as far as the sources of the Nile in the south and would include the whole of east Africa and Ethiopia. At a dance held on the most glorious day of his life – the night of the opening of the Suez canal – he offered the explorer Sir Samuel Baker, who was at the time accompanying the party of the Prince of Wales, the honour of working with him at a tempting salary. Baker's task would be, first, to conquer all of the southern Sudan as far as the sources of the Nile and annex it to Egypt, and, secondly, to put an end to the slave trade in those distant lands. Isma'il thought that the products of the new regions – ivory, gum, leather and grain – would help him to finance other projects. But he was probably less sincere about achieving his second objective. Isma'il filled his army with scores of thousands of blacks and he knew perfectly well where they came from, but he closed his eyes to this source of the wealth and to the shady operations of his agents.

The selection of Baker was a sound one, for it was he who had appealed to the British Government years before: 'Unless England steps in, this promising wilderness will be utterly despoiled by the slave trader and lost forever to Christianity.' His reputation would guarantee the necessary loans from

European countries.

In the next few years Baker established bases on the White Nile and then turned west to Bahr al Ghazal. There he encountered resistance organized by al Zubayr wad Rahma.[1]

A simple trader from the north, al Zubayr had built up a private army of over 15,000 men. In its ranks served many future generals of the Mahdiya. Al Zubayr was a pioneer of the idea of training large numbers of men in the use of firearms – hitherto restricted to the army of occupation. After signing a series of treaties with the authorities, he ruled all Bahr al Ghazal. He developed an astonishing military skill, trained armies, organized and armed units and practised night operations. He set up a headquarters and fortifications and established important tactical principles. He achieved the element of surprise in his night raids and in his attacks on the enemy in unexpected places.

From Bahr al Ghazal he went north and conquered Darfur, a considerable military undertaking. In his advance into Darfur he sought assistance from Khartoum. The Governor-General, Isma'il Aiyub, led a force to take part in the invasion but al Zubayr was able to crush the army of the Sultan of Darfur and to reach al Fashir before the Governor-General arrived. He began to reorganize the sultanate, which he named the *mudiriya* of Darfur. After this a difference arose with the Governor-General. Al Zubayr requested an audience with the Khedive in order to make some complaints. When he reached Egypt he was detained there. He left behind him in Sudan 15,000 trained warriors who included al Zaki Tamal, Hamdan Abu 'Anja and al Nur Anqara.[2]

When Baker's five years were up, the Khedive Isma'il sought the assistance of one of the most famous men of the age – General Charles Gordon. Isma'il reckoned that Gordon's reputation alone would be sufficient guarantee for the European countries and their representatives in Cairo. For Gordon's name carried great weight at that time. His fame as 'Chinese Gordon', the Leader of the Ever-Victorious Army, had spread far beyond the Great Wall of China. He was a veteran of the Siege of Sevastopol in the Crimean War and of other wars in Asia and Africa. His name was worth a whole

4

army.

Gordon was appointed Governor of the province of Equatoria with wide powers allowing him to choose his assistants from among Europeans. They assembled in Cairo and went on to join him in Khartoum. Europeans now appeared as administrators, taking the places formerly occupied by Egyptians.

Gordon completed the work of Baker and surveyed the area of the sources of the Nile. When he finally submitted his resignation in 1876 he left behind him dozens of garrisons.

In Cairo, however, the situation had reached rock bottom. Egypt had got involved in a costly war with Ethiopia and this put a further strain on the Khedive's empty treasury. His financial straits forced him to look in the direction of the Sudan. He enjoined his agent in Khartoum to raise annually £150,000 with £50,000 from the south from the sale of ivory and ostrich feathers. All the resources of the land were absorbed by the improvements introduced by Gordon and by the financing of the invasion of Darfur in which the Government had participated with al Zubayr. The Khedive added a further burden when he ordered the construction of a new railway line from Egypt to Khartoum, provided that the expenses of its construction fell on the *mudiriyas* of Dongola and Berber. When his expenses exceeded the limited resources of the land, he ordered the postponement of soldiers' and officials' pay. In their turn the latter, in order to live, redoubled their efforts in collecting bribes and taxes. The burden fell on the inhabitants: exorbitant taxes for which there was no return, no social services, no justice, no security, nothing but hardship piled on corruption and oppression. The country groaned under the weight of financial burdens and universal despair. Bahr al Ghazal and Kordofan had exhausted their reserves in paying for the Darfur invasion, Dongola and Berber theirs in financing the new railway, while the rest of the country had to raise the annual tribute to Egypt as well as pay for the salaries of soldiers and officials.

Even Isma'il became aware of the economic difficulties that were crushing his southern lands when they were reflected in a falling annual return. The situation needed a man of vigour and decision who would restore peace with Ethiopia and

5

reorganize the administration of the country, including Darfur and Bahr al Ghazal. He must break local private armies and their leaders who still considered themselves independent monarchs. He must expel the corrupt officials who battened on to most of the annual revenue, allowing only a small part to trickle through to Cairo. In 1877 the Khedive offered Gordon the post of Governor of the Sudan. Gordon accepted with alacrity and within a year had succeeded in making peace on the Ethiopian frontier, calming the troubled *mudiriya* of Darfur, establishing good relations with Sulayman, the son of al Zubayr and the governor of Bahr al Ghazal. He stopped work on the railway, thereby saving the great expense of its construction. He then issued a decree proscribing slavery. His plan was to abolish slavery gradually over ten years, during which time all slaves in the Sudan would be set free.

In the second year he began to dispense with the services of senior Egyptian officials and exchange them for Europeans he could trust. But this had serious consequences. We can well imagine the attitude of the Muslim inhabitants when Christians took over control of their affairs, and their feelings at a time when a religious revolution was stirring the country. A stand had to be made.

Then followed the treacherous assassination of Sulayman al Zubayr. With this Gordon forfeited the friendship and loyalty of Sulayman's father, the strong man in exile. One day Gordon would need him but it would be too late. Next Gordon ordered the expulsion of the traders in Darfur and southern Kordofan, mostly Dongolawis and Ja'lis who had long been settled in those lands, had married locally and considered those parts as their second home. Gordon detected reluctance on the part of the officials to execute these orders, so he went himself and ordered the *shaykhs* to carry them out, charging them with direct responsibility for any trader he might find in the area.

There was no place more fitting nor more ripe for revolution than the Sudan in 1881 – a corrupt and oppressive régime supported by a worthless army. The army of occupation numbered 40,000 at this time. Half this number was made up either of Sudanese soldiers who were sent back to the Sudan from

Egypt to serve in the army of occupation after their training, or were soldiers of al Zubayr Pasha, who were attached to the Government army after Sulayman al Zubayr's death.

But, in spite of their numbers, they had little effective fighting capacity, for most of them were irregulars. Reliance on the officials was clearly more effective than on the army, but so long as most of the former were Christians, their position was in jeopardy in the face of a religious revolution. Furthermore there was no training, as most of the soldiers' time was spent on tasks like tax collecting. Discipline was wholly absent. The officers set no example and there was no system of paying wages. Most of the garrisons were either ill fortified or not fortified at all.

An army in this state of morale would not be able to suppress revolution, relying on speedy movement, and with the support of the great majority of the inhabitants.

There were many identifiable causes of the Mahdist revolt, but it is unreasonable to argue that the motives that impelled thousands to die rose from adverse economic or social conditions alone. The appearance of a revolutionary leader with a capacity to inspire and inflame the masses prepared them for acts of sacrifice. The leader was Muhammad Ahmad 'Abd Allah who is known to history as the Mahdi.

NOTES

1 In his memoirs al Zubayr considered himself as the head of an army, and although he never denied that he bought slaves, he claimed he never sold them. We can accept this from the size of his army. However, there are doubts over two points. He did not sell men, but what happened to their families? Some people aver that there is no answer to this question, as he only bought males. Then there is the question of his rapidly gained wealth. Were ivory, honey and gum by themselves the sources of profit big enough to established him in lifelong prosperity? To investigate this question I rummaged among his papers, at present in his old house at al Jaili. A cursory examination of the receipts and account books confirms that the returns from his trading operations exceeded hundreds of thousands of pounds.

2 Al Nur Anqara had the major role in the training of al Zubayr's

soldiers. Al Nur had been a soldier since he was fifteen, when he joined the 'army' of the kings of the Sha'iqi, a semi-regular battalion which the Sha'iqi chieftains formed for service with the Government. He travelled with it to Egypt.

CHAPTER TWO

The Warrior Imam

From early times the idea of the 'Expected Mahdi' had spread in the Islamic world. When he appeared he would 'fill the earth with equity and justice, even as it has been filled with tyranny and oppression.' He would wipe out injustice and its perpetrators and restore glory to Islam after her degradation; he would exhort the people to the ways of God with the sword. Whoever denied him would perish, whoever disputed with him would be confounded.

All who have written about Muhammad Ahmad, the Mahdi, agree that he spent most of the years preceding the declaration of the 'Call' in study, reading and self-improvement. This was broken only by long spells of seclusion and meditation. This time of reading and reflection was the period during which his personality was formed; his resolutions, his plans and even his sermons are in a vigorous style disclosing a refined mind steeped in learning.

Military success is achieved when three elements are present: incentives derived from spiritual or environmental influences, a military mind that generates theories, and material military strength that can apply these principles. We have in the previous pages quickly reviewed the first of these elements. As for the second element, the Mahdi's military aptitude was the fruit of continuous study, mental alertness and natural talent. It is wrong to view the Islamic culture so widespread at the time in these parts in a superficial way and to restrict it only to matters of soul and conscience. At the Azhar University in Cairo philosophy, logic and law were taught. All this filtered through via the *shaykhs* of the *tariqas* and *khalwas* to that ardent student, Muhammad Ahmad.

One source of the Mahdi's military skill was his study of Islamic military history. The story of the early days of Islam was a tale of military glory, so the student of early Islam also studied, willy nilly, military history. The effect on the Mahdi, and his application, at times literally, of the principles of the Islamic wars can frequently be seen. Just as the Prophet migrated, so the Mahdi migrated. In his first battle, the battle of Aba, he had 313 men, rounded up by the boys of the *khalwa*; this was exactly the same number as the Prophet had had in his first battle. Literal adherence to Islamic history also led to the few setbacks. The outstanding strategy that he displayed in the battles of Aba, Qadir, Shaykan and Khartoum excuse and to some extent conceal the awful tactical failings shown in the battle of el Obeid. Principles of strategy change only slightly over the course of centuries, whereas tactical principles are constantly changing as a result of weapons and supplies.

During early exploratory journeys to Kordofan the Mahdi's 'Call' was still secret. He persuaded many tribal leaders of Kordofan and the Nuba mountains to join him. They showed an immediate enthusiasm for the revolution but the Mahdi asked them to wait until the time was ripe. News of this reached the ears of an old enemy, Shakyh Muhammad al Sharif, who reported the matter to the Governor-General, Ra'uf Pasha. At first Ra'uf gave the matter little thought. Then Muhammad al Sharif gave him some of the Mahdi's writings. Ra'uf Pasha wrote a letter to Muhammad Ahmad, suggesting that these letters were forged. But Muhammad Ahmad confirmed that the letters had come from him. A government official, Abu Su'ud, was sent to the Mahdi to bring him to Khartoum and justify his position in the presence of the official government *'ulama*. This was the background to the scene at the beginning of the last chapter. Before Abu Su'ud had reached Khartoum the Mahdi sent a cable to the Governor-General from al Kawa – 'as to the exhortations to the faithful, whoever does not accept them will be purified by the sword.' With that the Mahdi threw down the gauntlet at the feet of the Government.

The Governor-General sent a detachment with one cannon

under Abu Su'ud up the river to Aba. The Mahdi recruited 313 men from the local tribes and from this embryo grew the strongest army in Africa.

The Mahdi's ideas of organization were derived from the *khalwas* and the Sufi *tariqas*. At that time the novices of the Sufi *tariqas* used to assemble on the Prophet's Birthday or on other religious occasions in processions that resembled military parades. The leaders and their disciples were organized under *muqaddams* and would march to the sound of drums, anthems, calls to prayer and cries of *Allahu Akbar*.

The Mahdi divided up his men under five standards, on each one of which was written the name of a holy man. He then divided the whole force into about thirty sections, placing a *muqaddam* at the head of each section.

Abu Su'ud divided his force into two and placed at the head of each an officer of the rank of major, promising promotion to the one who captured the Mahdi.

The steamer moored at Aba at dawn. The soldiers disembarked. The two leaders rushed ahead, vying with each other to be the first to take the Mahdi. They reached the village by different routes at the same time. The right flank thought that the standards waving above the heads of the Mahdi's warriors were the flags that are customarily placed on graves. They advanced until they were very close. When the Government forces realized that this was the enemy the order was given to open fire. But because of poor visibility each flank opened fire on the other. In the midst of this the Mahdi swept in upon them and was able to wipe them out in a few minutes, apart from those few who managed to swim to the steamer. Abu Su'ud ordered the steamer to move off and returned to Khartoum.

What happened in this battle brings out a feature that always attended the early victories of the Mahdi. He exploited to the full the confusion of his enemy, and waited for the right moment to deliver the fatal blow.

News of the Mahdi's victory spread like wildfire in all parts of the country. More tribes sent envoys to this *shaykh* who had inflicted a defeat on the forces of the Government.

But the Mahdi was not a man to allow himself to get drunk on the wine of victory. He moved to Kordofan, out of reach of

Khartoum, and was joined on the way by thousands of men who pledged their loyalty to him. In the timing of the Mahdi's migration we discern a faultless instinct that marked all his decisions. When he migrated from Aba he migrated not as a defeated man, not as one who shunned battle, but as a victor.

In October, 1881, the Mahdi was in southern Kordofan, not far from the strong garrison of Fashoda. The commander of this garrison, Rashid Bey, without waiting for orders, gathered a force of more than 1,200 men and headed for the Mahdi. He took every precaution to prevent news of his advance leaking out, but a woman of the Kinana tribe – Rabiha by name – saw the enemy moving at night and in silence. She hastened to the Mahdi, going on foot day and night without stopping, and told him the news. The Mahdi gathered some 8,000 men. When he heard from herdsmen that Rashid Bey was approaching Khur Maraj, the Mahdi ordered the drums to be beaten. He advanced on the night of 28 December in a battle formation that resembled the array of early Islamic battles. Rows of infantry were made up just like the rows of men in prayer, with horsemen on both wings. They ambushed Rashid and massacred his men. The result was the total destruction of the Government forces.

After the battle thousands more tribesmen flocked towards the Mahdi's base at Qadir. The first directives were issued, organizing units and commands for combat and administrative purposes. In the directive addressed to the rank and file of the army the Mahdi wrote: 'The most important thing is submission to the *amir* who organizes the battle. As the Prophet Muhammad said, "Whoever obeys my *amir* obeys me and whoever disobeys my *amir* disobeys me." I have warned time and again of the need for the brethren to submit to their *amirs* and the *amirs* to their *khalifas* and all to the Khalifa 'Abd Allahi.'

The Mahdi spent the following months in a kind of military training camp, awaiting arrival of the next Government expedition. During these days one of the most renowned generals of the Mahdiya joined him – Hamdan Abu 'Anja, accompanied by Yunus al Dikaim.

A new force, Khartoum's reaction to the rout of Rashid's army, was mobilized at al Kawa from 1 March. After they left Kawa the Mahdi kept them under observation, luring them to lands where it would be easier to crush them. The force, led by al Shallali, reached Jabal Jarrada on the morning of 28 May. They built a huge *zariba* in which to spend the night. Before dawn, the Mahdi gathered 15,000 men and divided them into four, each division to deal with one of the four sides of the *zariba*. They inspected the land around the *zariba*, surrounded it and waited. At first light they all rushed forward.[1] Panic seized the defendants as they tried to collect their wits and their weapons. But it was too late. The attackers pierced the *zariba* and lashed out with their swords at the soldiers. In defiance of the Mahdi's instructions, 'Abd Allahi wisely ordered the enemy's rifles and cannons to be collected and taken back to Jabal Qadir.

The Mahdi's next objective was el Obeid. By occupying el Obeid he would cut off Darfur from Khartoum. Darfur would then more easily fall to Madibbu, the chieftain of the Rizayqat and the Mahdi's ally in Darfur. All Kordofan would then fall into the hands of the Mahdi. He laid siege to the city and waited for some weeks, then attempted to storm it on 8 September. But the loss of thousands persuaded him of the futility of facing direct fire. He revised his policy and retired to await the city's surrender. His patience was rewarded and el Obeid fell in January, 1883. This painful experience guided him in his next battle, Shaykan, and in the management of the siege and occupation of Khartoum.

Shaykan saw the beginning of the development of the Mahdi's army as a regular army. Before their ingenious strategy and planning had made up for primitive tactics. There had simply been one-phase frontal attacks under the leadership of the Mahdi or of the Khalifa 'Abd Allahi with warriors armed only with swords and spears. This led to enormous losses as they attacked in the face of heavy fire. Their compensating weapon had been the element of surprise and superb exploitation of the terrain.

Before the fall of el Obeid the Mahdi rejected the advice of 'Abd Allahi to use firearms. The slow rifles of those days had little effect in his kind of ambush. With swords and spears he had been successful, and in the long run it is success that is the

13

yardstick.

The Mahdi had issued his first directive on the organization of the army at Qadir, dividing it into standards, each under the direction of a Khalifa. The battle formation upon which rested the success or failure of strategic attacks and of tactical deployment was at this time in three parts:

1. The reconnaissance forces, made up of horsemen whose duty was to cut the enemy's supply lines, to guarantee the flow of information during the campaign, to carry out small operations in the form of long-range skirmishes which would lead to serious losses for the enemy and thus lower their morale, to spread propaganda and to impede the enemy's progress by filling in or poisoning wells. All these tasks were assigned to Abu Qarja with more than 3,000 horsemen.

2. The main attacking forces, the vast majority of those carrying swords and spears, supported by horsemen under the leadership of wad al Nujumi. These numbered 30 to 50,000.

3. The *jihadiya*, armed with Remington rifles plundered mostly at Aba and Qadir or from the arsenal at el Obeid, numbered about 7,000 warriors.

The *jihadiya* became the hard core of the new army, thanks to the efforts of their founder, Hamdan Abu 'Anja.[2] They were formed when the Khalifa 'Abd Allahi convinced the Mahdi of the importance of firearms. The men were mostly black soldiers who had been taken prisoner in previous campaigns. Hamdan Abu Anja was a success, with a friendly and paternal attitude towards his men. He supervised the training, the discipline and the arming of the *jihadiya*. It was to sustain the major burden of the wars in Ethiopia and the crushing of internal revolts. Its existence was to prove an embarrassment to the Egyptian authorities who had thought that the revolutionaries possessed no firearms.

In 1882 Britain became responsible for Egypt and its possessions. The Egyptian army was disbanded. Britain's policy at first was one of non-interference in the Sudan and neutrality towards any measures taken by the Egyptian Government. But when the latter sent a large force to crush the revolution and to recover the fallen garrisons, the British Government decided to assist them with some staff officers, led by General Hicks, the Chief of Staff. He assembled a force from the remnants of the old Egyptian army. Some soldiers actually reached the Sudan in chains, which were not removed until after they reached Khartoum.

As soon as Hicks arrived in the Sudan disputes arose between him and the Governor-General, 'Ala al Din, who interfered in military matters.

After completing their preparations, the force set off in early September, 1883, south along the Nile. At al Duwaym they struck west. On 29 September they reached al Marabi and saw the enemy for the first time, but were unable to engage in combat. This was to be the characteristic feature of Abu Qarja's operations: a group of horsemen would suddenly appear and then fade away. No contact was made until Hicks had travelled far to the west. Then skirmishes began and Hicks' men were only able to grab snatches of sleep. At the suggestion of the Mahdi, tribes abandoned the lands on the route after closing up the wells. Hicks thus found himself in an unpopulated and barren land. The army became threatened by drought and morale slumped.[3]

Meanwhile the Mahdi observed Hicks' progress closely. His knowledge of the enemy's position was further improved when a European deserted and joined Abu Qarja. Relying on his information, the Mahdi's plan began to take final shape.

Two courses of action were open to him: either he could wait for Hicks and fight defensively in el Obeid against a weary enemy, reduced and weakened by the skirmishes with Abu Qarja, or he could confront him on a suitable battlefield before he reached el Obeid. He chose the latter course. He based his decision on the information that was brought to him about the shortage of water and the expedition's fearful thirst. He realized that if he was to draw the enemy to a favourable spot, then it was vital to control the only water supply in Hicks' reach – at al Birka. He would then entice him to the chosen battle-ground at Kashqil and confine the enemy to the scrubland of Shaykan. Here the dense thorn bushes were a sufficient curtain for the *jihadiya* of Abu Qarja to advance and attack the enemy with rifle fire, and the narrow tracks would impede the progress of Hicks' vast squares, limit their room for manoeuvre and bring on the desired engagement. Here also the trees deprived them of a field for that open fire which gave their forces effective superiority.

The Mahdi now moved with all his army, numbering over 60,000 men, from his camp outside el Obeid to Fartanqul. He sent ahead a force of 1,000 horsemen under the leadership of Mahmud 'Abd al Qadir. Mahmud took possession of the pool of al Birka, the most vital place in the area, and so forced the enemy to take the al Mulbis road through the forest of Shaykan. The Mahdi ordered his horsemen to make a lot of noise in order to lead Hicks to suppose that a major attack was about to take place. Hicks' army was forced to stop and build a *zariba* while the Mahdi's army was still fifteen miles away. After Hicks stopped, Abu Qarja's horsemen began the huge task of bringing up all the *jihadiya*. The operation was quickly carried out by mounting two or even three men on each of Abu Qarja's horses.

The *jihadiya* climbed the trees on either side of the road and hid among them. As soon as darkness fell they started firing at Hicks' huge square. Meanwhile the assault troops and the horsemen advanced under Wad al Nujumi.

On the morning of 5 November Hicks left his *zariba* after dividing his forces into three squares in the form of an equilateral triangle, placing the defenders in front and the cavalry on the sides to protect them. He and his staff were in front. Within half an hour he found himself hemmed in on all sides, Abu Qarja behind, Wad al Nujumi in front and the *jihadiya* on both sides.

The Mahdi and his *ansar* were now only about 1,000 yards away. When he saw the enemy moving he drew his sword, brandished it and ordered a general assault. His men rushed towards the three squares and in about an hour destroyed the whole force except for 300 men hidden under the dead bodies of their fallen comrades.[4]

The Mahdi returned to el Obeid. The news of his victory over the largest force recruited in the history of the Sudan spread throughout the land. There could be no doubt about his 'Call'. Tribal leaders formerly hesitant hastened to join him. He now ordered the march on Khartoum, his army swollen by thousands.

Two aspects of the progress to Khartoum show up the sound judgment of the Mahdi and the Khalifa. The march took four months, during which time tribal loyalties were consolidated. The Mahdi was now directing a theatre of war extending for hundreds of thousands of square miles. He slowly tightened the knot round Khartoum, sending Abu Qarja to direct the siege of the city from the south, and Shaykh al Ubayyid to kindle the revolution in the suburbs of Khartoum, to occupy al Halfaya and to lay siege to Khartoum from the east. In this way Khartoum became cut off from the rest of the Sudan. He then strove to master the broader scene of the siege by occupying Berber and getting Osman Digna to forward the revolution in eastern Sudan, thereby cutting communications with the rest of the world.

Then, mindful of the lesson of the battle of el Obeid, the Mahdi chose to rest the camels and to wait four whole months.

The second aspect worth noticing is the mechanics of the advance itself. The Mahdi did not advance with warriors only but with all their families as well. He thus took a long time to reach Khartoum. His camps took on the form of temporary settlements and have been described by Slatin and Father Ohrwalder. From al Rahad near el Obeid they advanced to Khartoum in three broad streams. The northern route, where grasslands were scarce, was assigned to the camel tribes of Kordofan and Darfur. The second route, by Tayyara and al Duwaym, was the main route, the one taken by the Mahdi, the Khalifas and the *jihadiya*. The southern route, where grasslands and water were plentiful, was assigned to the cattle-rearing Baqqara tribes.

In February, 1884, while they were in al Rahad, they received news that Gordon had arrived as Governor-General of the Sudan. He had come to evacuate troops and supplies from the Sudan.

Before we proceed to the siege itself, we must stop awhile with Gordon. His death was one of the direct causes of the decision to recover the Sudan, and his name will hover over this book to the end. British public opinion strongly supported the invasion of the Sudan in order to avenge the insult of Gordon's death. In 1884 the force that was sent to the Sudan was unequivocally called the Gordon Relief Expedition. It was sent to relieve a national hero.

Gordon's reputation in British history has been subject to fluctuations. After his death nearly everyone read the famous *Journals*, which he had sent out during the siege. But the veil was suddenly rent from Gordon's public personality when Lytton Strachey examined him in his book *Eminent Victorians*, bringing out all his personal defects; a dishonesty and psychological state verging on madness, an energy that was sometimes demoniac. A glance through the diaries he wrote from Khartoum suggests that his situation, with the Mahdi on his heels, was quite beyond his capacity or imagination. He was incapable of assessing the revolution, of appreciating its dimensions or of understanding its motivations or aspirations. The idea he had of the Sudan in 1884 had not changed since 1876. Gordon was now facing a total revolution, inspired by spiritual forces that moved millions. This was entirely different from the minor disturbances he had met before like Sulayman al Zubayr's revolt, or the problem of the traders and slavers, or even the rebellion in China, which could all be crushed by superior military power. By sending embroidered clothes to the Mahdi and appointing him Sultan of Kordofan, by supposing that some arrangements and a little deception would suffice to win over the Mahdi, he demonstrated his total misjudgment of the situation.

Gordon's position in the Sudan was not that of a mercenary concerned only with collecting his wages. When he was first appointed to the Sudan he refused to accept more than one-fifth of the salary that Baker had demanded. The quest for fame and personal glory was a far stronger motive. As to his personal bravery, his military competence or his Cromwellian toughness, there is neither doubt nor argument. But these merits were swamped by others – clownishness, puerility, opportunism and an ability to distort the truth that amounted to complete self-deception.

Gordon's journals were clearly written for publication. Their frankness, too, makes one think that Gordon had a death wish. It is difficult for a person to bare his soul as much as he did and to make such a mockery of the authorities unless we conclude that he did not expect to meet them again.

The city of Khartoum, at the confluence of the Blue and White Niles, already had a deep ditch twelve yards wide, filled with water and linking the two Niles. Thus Khartoum was surrounded on all sides by water. The Omdurman garrison was fortified by a thick wall with gun emplacements and towers for cannons. When Gordon arrived he immediately set about improving these defences. He constructed a wall, two feet high, to protect the riflemen and built more towers for the cannons. He started planting mines, which he designed himself, and also scattered caltrops at the bottom of the ditch.

Gordon, however, was not the man to be satisfied with purely defensive measures. He began to consider methods of counter-attack.

The Mahdi was still at al Rahad when he heard that Gordon had killed a thousand of Abu Qarja's men. However, he received the news calmly and sent the most famous of his commanders, Wad al Nujumi, to occupy the area south-west of the city and take over command. The shelling of the town began. The Mahdi with all his army arrived on the scene on 10 October, 1884. The final act on the well-known drama of Khartoum began.

When news of the Relief Expedition reached the city tension mounted. Gordon spent much of his day gazing north through his telescope or watching the manoeuvres of the Mahdi's army. His despair was intensified by the demonstrations of starving women and the endless bombardment of the Mahdi. But what really distressed him was the news of the deaths of his second-in-command, Stewart, and his companions who had left the city in August. At first he did not believe the news, but then he received a letter from the Mahdi informing him of their end. Letters written by Gordon, found with Stewart, were enclosed to confirm the news. The Mahdi's letter also revealed his precise knowledge of the situation in Khartoum.[5]

The Gordon Relief Expedition was led by Sir Garnet Wolseley with three British brigades numbering 9,000 men. He left detachments of the Egyptian army and some British troops at points all along the supply line to guard his retreat. With

5,000 men he headed for Khartoum. One contingent followed the Nile to Berber, the other left the Nile at Kurti and cut across the Bayuda desert to al Matamma (Metemma). On 4 January Wolseley's vanguard desert column, under the leadership of General Sir Herbert Stewart, left the Nile heading for the wells of Jaqdul. This was the first time that British troops had been on Sudanese soil, but they did not stay long. News of the Expedition reached Shaykh Muhammad al Khair at Berber. He passed the news on to the Mahdi and was ordered to march to al Matamma at once. The Mahdi also ordered an army under the command of Musa wad Hilu to advance and reinforce Muhammad al Khair.

While Stewart was at Jaqdul preparing to leave for al Matamma, Muhammad al Khair's forces speedily occupied the wells at Abu Tilayh (Abu Klea), the only source of water in the area. Stewart thus had to storm the wells and expel Musa wad Hilu from them. He advanced and there followed two battles – Abu Tilayh and al Matamma. In them both sides suffered heavy losses and both commanders were killed – Stewart and Musa wad Hilu. After this a small group, with not more than twenty British soldiers, embarked on the gunboats and went on to Khartoum to relieve Gordon. All this affected the Mahdi's timing in his decision to storm Khartoum.

When definite news of the arrival of the Relief Expedition reached the Mahdi he realized he had to storm the city to avoid being caught between two fires. Councils of war followed. The last was held on the night of 24 January and most speakers supported the idea of an immediate assault.[6] Most sources agree that Muhammad 'Abd al Karim was the leader of those calling for an immediate attack and that he was supported by Muhammad wad Nubawi. During the council Wad al Nujumi sent from the front line a senior officer who had fled from Khartoum. He was interrogated by the Mahdi who learned of the exact state of the city and the position of the only weak point in the ramparts. Opinion finally settled on making the main attack through this gap. The Mahdi summoned Wad al Nujumi and instructed him to attack at dawn. He then ordered all his forces to be ready for an assault and to move to a rallying point in secrecy where he would join them. At midnight on 25

January the Mahdi himself crossed the White Nile. All the assault forces were waiting for him. He addressed his men who all reaffirmed their allegiance unto death. He charged them to take Gordon alive, saying 'Slay not the man Gordon, brethren, but take him alive and bring him to us, for he is a man of great worth among his own people. Do not kill him because his capture, alive, will be very useful for us. We want to exchange him for two fine men – al Zubayr and 'Urabi.'

On the evening of 25 January, 1885, a brass band had been playing some jolly airs to relieve the despair that hovered over the city. Gordon had dined in solitary gloom and gone to his wing of the palace, remaining there writing until after midnight, before he finally put out the light.

Before dawn the assault on Khartoum began, led by 'Abd al Rahman al Nujumi on a wide four-mile front. He planned and directed the attack from the village of al Gharqan with customary skill. He gave a third of the force – 20,000 men under the leadership of Abu Qarja – the task of covering most of the enemy's front, while he kept the main part – 40,000 men – under his personal command. Tightly packed waves of men surged forward. They concentrated on the opening guarded by a single battalion, which was put out of action as the men poured into the city.

Wad al Nujumi's plan led to the amazingly rapid collapse of the city. The men poured in past the ditch and the first line of defence, then divided into two. One group headed straight for Gordon's headquarters and the other, larger, group turned right to attack the artillery. The defences fell within minutes. An hour and a half after the beginning of the assault Gordon's head had been severed from his body.

Ahmad wad Sulayman hurried to the Mahdi and presented it to him, wrapped in a cloth.

'What is this?' asked the Mahdi.

'This is Gordon's head,' answered Ahmad.

The Mahdi's eyes darkened with fury. 'What deeds are these? Why do you disobey my orders? Why have you mutilated him and cut off his head? What is the use of it?' He averted his eyes and Ahmad hastened to get rid of the head.

Who slew Gordon? Most accounts, including Sudanese,

suggest that the killer was the *amir* wad Nubawi, he whom the Mahdi had publicly charged with the task of preserving Gordon's life.

'Ali al Mahdi, the son of the Mahdi and an historian, investigated this thoroughly. His conclusion is as follows:

'I was told by Shaykh Ibrahim 'Ali Sabir al Maghrabi who was a clerk with the standard of Mirghani Suwar al Dhahab that the man who killed Gordon was Mursal al Hajj Hamuda. This Mursal was standard bearer to the *amir* Mirghani. Ibrahim related to me:

"At dawn our standard reached the Palace. Mursal was near me and saw a man standing on an upper floor looking through the window. It was Gordon, looking at his defeated army. Mursal thought he was armed and wished to shoot before he was himself fired at. He shot the man and he fell on the staircase. Mursal did not know that he had killed Gordon." At once Ibrahim 'Ali Sabir entered the palace, went up to the upper floor to discover that the man hit was Gordon. He was wearing his official uniform with all his decorations and was gasping for breath. 'Abd al Qadir wad Kuku, the *qadi* of Hamuda's battalion, came in and asked me: "Who is this?" I told him, "Gordon". He said, "How do you know?" I said, "I used to know him when he toured Kordofan. He used to shave his chin but leave whiskers on his cheeks." 'Abd al Qadir then took a knife and cut off his head. When Mursal learned that Gordon Pasha had been killed he hid himself, asking those with him to swear to hide the matter. Thus Gordon's actual killer was unknown.

'When Shaykh Ibrahim 'Ali Sabir told me this we sent two men with him to ascertain the truth from Mursal or his chiefs but they did not find him, for he was killed at Karari. When they questioned his chief he was afraid and troubled, saying, "We heard from Mursal himself that he killed Gordon and had erred in so doing." He then asked, "What is your purpose in this?" They replied, "Only to get at the truth."'

The Mahdi was now master of a million square miles. He was leader of the first African nation to be created by its own efforts. From this point one can say that the modern Sudanese nation was born. The nation's assets in terms of spiritual ties and unity of purpose were considerable. There are no ties stronger than those created by the sacrifice of blood.

NOTES

1. Shuqayr describes the operation as a sudden night assault but 'Ali al Mahdi writes of it as a long daytime operation. The comparatively slight losses, not more than 200 killed, support the theory that it was an early dawn attack.

2. Abu 'Anja contributed to the military ideas of the *jihadiya* and bound its soldiers to him with strong personal bonds. He was an engaging man, devout, respected by all, with the courage of a lion. In his youth he used to hunt elephants alone, armed only with a lance. When Abu 'Anja died at al Qallabat (Gallabat) all the camp became one great place of mourning for many days. The vicious character and reputation of the *jihadiya* emerged only after Abu 'Anja's death. The expression 'the conduct of the *jihadiya*' is still common in some part of the Sudan. The Khalifa, mindful of their reputation, always used to pitch their camps outside the cities.

3. Some historians have argued that the thirst was exaggerated, for October is the rainy season. But 'Abbas Bey in his diary, and others who survived, were unanimous about the terrible thirst. I enquired about the rains among the people there. Late October and early November sees a little rain which they regard as a harbinger of a good crop. The rains in 1883 were either particularly light or unusually early.

4. Wingate visited the battlefield at Shaykan twenty years afterwards and thought that even a better equipped, larger and more efficient force would have met the same fate. At one stage there were reports that the Mahdi was proposing to suffocate them by burning the grass around them.

5. Wingate felt that Gordon's greatest blunders derived from his ignorance of Arabic, both spoken and written. This led him to miscalculate the whole matter, and to rely on advisers and translators who misled him.

6. Some of the council were for raising the siege and returning to Kordofan.

CHAPTER THREE

The Call and the State

'THERE was a constructive side to his reign which has received little attention from writers whose gaze has been focused upon picturesque horrors and atrocities which our grandfathers believed were committed only by barbarians. The years of 'Abd Allahi's rule were not merely a period of disappointed hopes and regrets for a transitory golden age, they were a period of organization and skilful balance of forces, reflecting a strong will and an able administrative capacity working within the limits of a narrow experience, and too often failing in action through the inherent faults of the instruments employed.'

P. M. HOLT.

The Khalifa 'Abd Allahi sprang from the Ta'aisha, a sub-division of the Baqqara.[1] He was the eldest son of Sayyid Muhammad, nicknamed Turshayn.[2] When he was born at Abu Ruq in south-west Darfur in about 1846, his father occupied a central role in the spiritual and religious life of the tribe. He was a pillar of the Sammaniya *tariqa* in western Sudan, where the major *tariqa* was the Tijaniya. But a dispute arose between Turshayn and his fellow-tribesmen and he moved to the east, settling in the land of the Rizayqat. He took great pains over the education of his sons. Ya'qub, Harun, al Sammani and Yusuf, but he had difficulty with 'Abd Allahi who had little aptitude for religious studies. Instead he yearned for the glories of the world. 'Abd Allahi grew physically strong, tall, with a

24

complexion the colour of ripe corn, and a face pitted with the marks of smallpox from which he had suffered as a child. From his earliest days he was noted for fearless courage. He joined the Rizayqat in their campaigns against al Zubayr Pasha and was taken prisoner. Al Zubayr would have put him to death but for the intercession of some men of religion. He stayed in the land of the Rizayqat but saw in the victorious al Zubayr the 'Expected Mahdi'. Many others at that time looked to al Zubayr as a national saviour. 'Abd Allahi wrote to al Zubayr, telling him that in a dream he had seen him as the 'Expected Mahdi' and himself as his lieutenant. Al Zubayr sent a stern reply, telling him not to repeat such talk.

After this 'Abd Allahi's family decided to go on a pilgrimage to Mecca. They set off to the east and stayed as the guests of the *nazir* of the Jim'a, 'Asakir Abu Kalam, at Abu Rukba. Here 'Abd Allahi's father died. At that time news was spreading about a strange *shaykh* with a growing reputation as a godly man. He was called Muhammad Ahmad and lived on Aba Island. 'Abd Allahi mounted his donkey and went to meet him. He found him at Masallamiya, building a *qubba* over the tomb of his teacher, Shaykh Qurashi. His first encounter with the Mahdi left a profound impression on him. Small wonder, for even Europeans have recognized that the Mahdi had a personal magnetism that left a lasting influence on all who met him.

'Abd Allahi was the first person to whom the Madhi confided his 'Call', after an oath of secrecy and loyalty had been given. They returned to Aba Island together. There they were joined by 'Ali wad Hilu and others of the Kanana and Dighaim tribes.

Most information derived from European sources still refers to the Khalifa's perfidy, his severity, his malice, his blood-thirstiness, his lust for power.[3] Three men – Wingate, Ohrwalder and Slatin – are responsible for this picture and their writings have been followed by others down to the present day. The Khalifa found himself opposed by a huge propaganda machine that hurled abuse at him which stuck for decades. In this way he resembles other African and Asian leaders who have stood in the way of imperialist expansion.

The Khalifa's personality dominated events over the thirteen years of wars, famines, revolts, conspiracies and invasion. He dealt with matters large and small over thousands of square miles with skill and resolution. His skill in dealing with his country's affairs and in taking the best course amid so many dangers threatening the state is generally accepted. But in reports of his personality, his motives and his basic male-volence, the balance still goes against him.

Let us first clarify a number of points. A great mistake is made in comparing the Khalifa with the Mahdi. Not only was there a radical difference in personality, there was also a great difference in the roles each was to perform. It fell to the Mahdi to stir up rebellion, to nurse it in people's minds and to charge it with spiritual power. After this it fell to the Khalifa to organize the new state. It is a difference of the Call and the State. The expression 'The Mahdiya has become a monarchy,' and 'The Mahdiya has become a state,' were much used by his opponents. He ruled a nation united only after five years of continual warfare. The tribes had long resisted all manner of control. They united only when religion stimulated and co-ordinated their energies, but after the Mahdiya had triumphed and the first wave of enthusiasm receded with the Mahdi's death, tribal animosities began to reappear.

The Khalifa's greatest achievement, which has at the same time exposed him to most criticism, was his insistence on a centralized state and his success therein. At first he had little to guide him save the general framework of Islamic law, the in-herited Egyptian-Turkish state structure and the principles of justice and charity laid down by the Mahdi. The Khalifa devoted his efforts to these ends, taking every advantage of the experience of those engineers and administrators who had served the former régime and had become his prisoners. After ten years he had forged a cohesive state. The men of such a state were hardly the barbarians of European propaganda.

The Khalifa set up a sound fiscal and legal system, with courts throughout the country. The distant lands were brought together by an efficient postal service. The Khalifa constructed a capital and even attempted to rebuild Omdurman on modern sanitary lines by pulling down ill-planned houses and laying out wide streets, ordering the inhabitants to keep them clean and punishing those who refused.

'Abd Allahi's qualities and personality, his capacity to plan and organize, his military prowess and his experience of the world and of men, recommended him to the Mahdi for the second place in the state. He was commander-in-chief and *amir* of the Mahdi's armies at a time when the revolution was tantamount to one long military operation. He was one of the most influential voices in all military matters. His qualities complemented those of the Mahdi.

When we look further we soon discover that, in spite of his pivotal role in the state, the Khalifa – unlike the Mahdi – was never a dictator. The Mahdi's word was considered sacred law, and everybody sought to implement it at once. Nobody ventured to dispute with him or offer him advice. In all that is related of the Mahdi in writing or in oral tradition we seldom find any mention of advisory councils except in military matters. By contrast the Khalifa's own judgment on military matters was often sounder than that of the councils he consulted in order to legitimize his decisions.

It seems as if the Khalifa lacked self-confidence. He found himself the successor of a learned spiritual leader, heir to a religious revolution and head of a state whose *raison d'être* was the reform of aberrations in religious instruction. But he was not learned or steeped in Islamic law. He felt obliged to resort to *qadis* and *'ulama* for counsel. Hence the prominent position achieved by his better educated brother Ya'qub. Nevertheless the Khalifa's capacity for dealing personally with the subtleties of conflicting interests and matters of state stands in favourable contrast to the judgments issued by the *qadis*, the *'ulama* and the advisory councils.

Let us consider some of his policies, first his relations with the Ashraf, the kinsfolk of the Mahdi, then with his creation of a Ta'aisha oligarchy.

In the years after the Mahdi's death there developed a strained relationship between the Ashraf and the Khalifa which reached its peak in 1891 when the Khalifa Muhammad Sharif attempted an armed revolt in Omdurman.

The suppression of the Red Standard of the Khalifa Sharif, the third Standard of all the armies of the Mahdiya, was one of the most important causes of the attempted coup, for this had been the Standard of the people of the north end of the Jazira. It seemed as if the Khalifa was resolved to strip the riverain people of arms. By appointing members of his own tribe to all the major positions of leadership in the state, he helped to strengthen this impression. Many people began to withdraw their support for the Mahdiya as represented by the Khalifa, and there were murmurings both secret and open. Ancient tribal feelings and animosities began to emerge. The factors that had unified the nation were unable to quench the suppressed fire that had long been smouldering. The state lost its cohesion and cracks began to appear.

'Abd Allahi felt isolated in his capital, most of whose inhabitants were from the Nile valley. His sole authority was the Mahdi's decree appointing him Khalifa, together with the report of the Mahdi's nomination of him as his successor on his deathbed. He embarked on measures to reduce the power of the Ashraf. He asked the Khalifa 'Ali wad Hilu to hand over the *jihadiya*, together with the weapons and the copper drums belonging to his Standard. This request was made so that it would appear that his action was not directed at the Khalifa Sharif alone. The Khalifa 'Ali submitted and Sharif was then pressed to hand over the weapons of his Standard, which he did with reluctance.

In 1891, when the Ashraf attempted to take over power, the Khalifa Sharif was condemned and imprisoned. The power of the Ashraf was now reduced and the Khalifa set about creating a new ruling class formed from the Ta'aisha tribe. Within three years his kinsmen were occupying nearly all the leading positions.

At the same time he tried to bring in western tribes to Omdurman, not his tribe alone but others of Darfur and Kordofan. The Khalifa's motives for this were complex. In the first place his aim was to tame the tribes, for he knew only too well their aversion to all restraint. He thus placed them under his direct control in Omdurman and in the Jazira, so they would not be able to scatter into the Jabal Marra, or to the swamps of Bahr al Ghazal, whenever he summoned them to the holy war or sought taxes from them.

The second aim was part of a larger strategic plan – the setting up of a concentration of fighting men, to be always near at hand. For the Khalifa, in the earlier years of his rule, aimed not only at dominating the Sudan, but also Egypt and then Mecca. This was particularly so in the early days of the Mahdiya.

Darfur, with its periodic revolts, was a perpetual headache for the Khalifa. It obliged him to maintain an enormous force there which he was never able to reduce to less than 20,000 men. He sent 'Uthman Adam to Darfur to organize the migration of the tribes to Omdurman. But they resisted all his efforts, and even raided other tribes who had yielded and were beginning to move.

The Khalifa and 'Uthman Adam expected no trouble from their own tribe, the Ta'aisha. The Khalifa supposed that they would hasten at once to Omdurman, to the land of the Nile, the land of ease and plenty and of all good things, leaving behind for ever the rigours of their life of hardship; but to the Khalifa's fury, they refused. He wrote a letter to his people, threatening them with lands laid waste if they continued to ignore his orders. Eventually over 10,000 moved from Darfur, accompanied by their families and their cattle.

The migration of the Khalifa's tribe stirred up fanatical tribal animosities, which were in no way lessened by Ta'aisha haughtiness and villainy. Popular verses and songs current at the time illustrate the feelings of the people of the capital towards the migrants.

In the course of time the Ta'aisha came to dominate the Khalifa. A Council of Elders was formed from its senior men which virtually ruled the country. In most instances this council was able to impose its will on the Khalifa. He in turn became irritated with the behaviour of his tribe, and preached sermons of castigation at them in public, in an effort to win the hearts of the people as a whole.

In 1888 the Khalifa was at the height of his power. All the tribes had submitted to him and his armies had dealt with all enemies, external and internal.

The wars between the Khalifa's state and the Christian kingdom of John of Abyssinia started with small skirmishes which developed into a large-scale clash of arms. But, thanks to the generalship of al Zaki Tamal and Abu 'Anja, they ended in victory. The Ethiopian wars guaranteed the eastern frontier for a long time and destroyed the Khalifa's most dangerous enemy. But the price was high, for he lost his finest units and his best equipment. Furthermore, the wars forced him to maintain a large garrison at al Qallabat (Gallabat) at the expense of other districts.

One of the most serious charges levelled against the Khalifa is that he sent Wad al Nujumi to Egypt to destroy him. The outcome of the unsuccessful northern campaign was far-reaching, for it revealed to the enemy in the north the weakness of the Khalifa's army, even though they chose not to reconquer the Sudan at once. After the campaign there were many murmurings within the country, especially among the people of the North. The thousands who fell into the hands of the Egyptian army provided Wingate, the head of Intelligence, with accurate information about the Khalifa and his army. There was no such flow of information again until after Slatin's escape.

When al Nujumi invaded Egypt to take on the British-trained Egyptian army, his force consisted of about 4,000 soldiers, 300 rifles, ten cannons – and 7,000 women and children. After the first three clashes there was no relief from the pressure applied by the enemy. In more than one letter to the Khalifa he described his army's wretched state. The enemy's gunboats followed them step by step, preventing them from drawing water or gathering dates along the banks.

In a letter to the Khalifa al Nujumi told how some of his army had deserted to the enemy and how the camels had died. Without waiting for a reply he continued his march, clashing with the enemy again. In spite of his weakness he launched an assault, but lost 900 fighting men and 500 women and children. He himself was wounded. He then held a council of war with his generals. Most of them advised a retreat south until supplies arrived, but it seems that al Nujumi bore in mind the insults that would await him in Omdurman. He concluded the council by saying, 'No, by God, I will retreat only as a cold corpse. If we are hungry and thirsty we are after all fighters in a holy war. Let us endure in patience until we triumph either with victory or with martyrdom.' He brandished his sword and went out. His army followed.

Grenfell, the Egyptian commander, wrote a letter that probably expressed al Nujumi's inner feelings. In it he said, 'I know your evil condition and I know that you are the victim of the Khalifa who has sent you and the Arabs, whose mischief he fears, to conquer Egypt; but he only seeks your destruction. He knows that he has sent you on a hopeless mission – and you know this too.' But al Nujumi banished any such thoughts and wrote a defiant reply to Grenfell, sending both Grenfell's letter and a copy of his own to Omdurman.

In the final battle at Tushki, al Nujumi launched a dawn assault against superior forces, causing the Egyptian army to withdraw. Finally, Grenfell, with his three brigades, counter-attacked with a heavy cover of artillery fire until al Nujumi's men abandoned their position and withdrew to the camp of the women and children. Nujumi himself dashed up on his horse, trying to prevent a rout. As he urged his men to stand firm, he was hit by a bullet that pierced his chest. He fell to the ground and died, his sword still in his hand. Grenfell then sur-rounded the women's camp and took them all prisoner.

The last years of the Khalifa's rule were marked by relative calm, and for the first time there was a degree of security. Peace reigned and a measure of prosperity was enjoyed in all parts of the country. These years saw ample rain, and all reports point to good harvests. The threat of famine receded. There was a respect for authority and the rule of law, and the Khalifa and his colleagues displayed capability in the direction of their affairs.

It is true that here and there were echoes of the former violent years. But the Khalifa did his best to achieve prosperity, to the extent that he permitted the resumption of trade with Egypt. Conditions were never as bleak as they were portrayed by those newspapers and books from Europe which claimed that the land was still steeped in the blood of tribal exter-minations. Mustafa al Amin, when he was interrogated by the chief of Egyptian Intelligence in 1892, reported that the Khalifa was 'profiting by former experience and is doing his utmost to establish a more lenient and popular system of government; and his efforts are not altogether unsuccessful . . . Thus a slow but gradual consolidation is being effected and it is not unlikely that when the Egyptian Government does eventually decide to re-enter the Sudan, it will meet with opposition from those very tribes who have been most clamorous for its return.' Support for the Khalifa was 'strongest in Omdurman and its vicinity, and weakest amongst the population immediately in contact with outside influences.'[4]

But the Khalifa's enemies did not allow him to enjoy this stability for long.

The Organization of the Khalifa's Army

The organization of the Khalifa's army into three standards remained in being for a short period after the Mahdi's death in 1885. But when the Khalifa divided Sudan into *'imalas* or administrative regions, he also reorganized the army. His representative or *'amil* became the commander-in-chief of the *'imala*. To enable his army to undertake its civil and military duties – operations against the external enemy, garrisons on the borders and matters of internal security – a new fighting structure had to be created.

In this reorganization almost all the male population of the Sudan was involved. All men were warriors, though some only volunteers in the reserve army. We are thus able to divide the Khalifa's army into three parts:

1—the permanent regional garrisons,
2—the volunteers,
3—the military expeditions.

The garrisons were formed from long-serving regular soldiers living in barracks. The volunteers were in theory everybody else. These two parts combined to undertake military expeditions, ranging in size from those of the Ethiopian wars, involving tens of thousands, to small operations of internal security undertaken by the garrisons alone.

For administrative purposes the country was divided into six *'imalas*. A senior *amir* commanded an *'imala* and was the administrative overlord or *'amil*. Generally the *amir* took military command when operations were on a large scale and most of the district's fighting force was needed. However, when a district became a theatre of war, engaging larger forces, a senior commander of the Mahdiya was detailed to undertake operations. The *'amil's* duties would then be confined to administrative matters, answerable to the military commander.

In Omdurman there were a number of administrative units co-operating with the senior *amir* in the *'imala* on particular matters. This administrative pattern was reflected also in the provinces. Both at Omdurman and in each *'imala* there was a treasury, *bayt al-mal*. Its officials were responsible for provisioning the army, gathering taxes, storing booty and recording the national wealth. The treasury was divided into a number of departments, a granary, a general store, an arms and ammunition store and a compound for the camels and mules that were used for transport.

A judge was appointed in each *'imala*. The senior *amir* in the *'imala* usually kept a number of clerks at this headquarters. During military campaigns clerks were assigned to duties at the *amir's* headquarters. Each administrative base also had a corps of buglers and drummers.

The *amir* of each *'imala* was provided with some artillery and a private guard. Most of the Khalifa's artillery was at Omdurman but Dongola had a battery of six mountain cannons and both al Qallabat and the *'imala* of the west had small batteries. The *amir's* guard consisted of a standard formed from a few hundred *mulazimin*.

The basic fighting unit in the army of the Mahdiya was the *rub'*. Its composition and numbers were not fixed. In general it was never less than 800 men and might total several thousand. The *rub'* of the *mulazimin* in Omdurman and most of the regular and standardized units were between 800 and 1,200 men. Its apparent lack of numerical uniformity went back to the earlier years, when each fighting unit of whatever size in an expedition was divided into four smaller units. Thus each was called a quarter or *rub'*. A *rub'* was made up of three combat units and one administrative unit.

The first combat unit consisted of spearmen.[5] They were the troops mainly responsible for assault and hand-to-hand fighting. They were divided into a number of sections behind a banner (or standard), each section belonging to a tribe or subtribe. The number of such standards varied according to the recruiting capacity of each *amir* or to the number assigned by the Khalifa. The *amir* commanded the standard. He was always mounted and provided with a standard-bearer. A large standard was divided into groups of hundreds. A 'centurion' or *rasmiya* commanded each hundred and the hundred was divided into *muqaddamiyas* of twenty-five men, at the head of each of which was a *muqaddam*. Each man was usually armed with a sword, one long spear and four short spears.

The second element, the *jihadiya*, represented the fire support of the *rub'*. The *jihadiya* was divided into standards, each of one hundred men headed by an *amir*. Each standard was divided into four *muqaddamiyas* led by a *muqaddam*. Most soldiers were armed with Remington rifles. To each standard were attached a number of Ta'aisha as instructors in both religious and military matters.

The Khalifa recruited new soldiers to make up the devastating losses in the Ethiopian wars. They became his most effective fighting force and he distributed them among other units as fire support. He forbade the general sale of black youths; instead they were to be sold to the state at the fixed price of thirty Majidi *riyals*. Each soldier was branded with the letter J on his left hand.[6]

The third element was the cavalry. Most of the Khalifa's mounted forces were from the Baqqara tribes. The horses came from Darfur. A group of horsemen was assigned to each *rub'*. Each man had to find his own horse and so the number of horsemen was never fixed. The horseman was armed with a long spear and a sword which hung down on his left side. If he was on reconnaissance he would carry a rifle and seven belts of ammunition. All wore a red *'imma* and a red cartridge belt.

Except during troubled times, such as the wars in Ethiopia and Darfur, the Omdurman garrison was the Khalifa's largest single military establishment, being many times larger than all the other armies.

In general the Omdurman garrison was the Khalifa's strategic reserve. Its geographical position made Omdurman his stronghold, and thus the place for his higher command, where units of the three standards were assembled, particularly the Black Standard. After the dissolution of the Red Standard, the Black Standard became the one to which all volunteers, especially Omdurmanis, rallied. The garrison was then made up of the Khalifa's direct command, including the *mulazimin* and the private guard, the Black Standard and the Green Standard.

Originally the *mulazimin* were simply a guard belonging to the Khalifa, but they increased in number until they became the main striking force in the strategic reserve. His private guard was then detached and placed under his direct command and he delegated the command of the *mulazimin* to his son, 'Uthman Shaykh al Din.

The Khalifa's private guard was made up of 2,000 soldiers all armed with rifles. They were divided into two *rub's*. The men of the first *rub'* were all armed with Remington rifles. The second *rub'* was divided into a number of sections. There were the *khashkhashan* who carried elephant guns. They were characterized by red waistcoats over their *jubbas*. The *mushammaratiya* were tall, well built men, carefully chosen for their jobs. They were armed with a long spear and wore a *jubba* with their leggings folded up to just above the knee. They did not wear an *'imma*, but instead a two-horned skullcap.

The Khalifa paid great attention to the appearance of his private guard, and supervised the design of their clothes himself.

Attached to the private guard was a detachment of musicians, divided into three sections. A group of brass instrumentalists were mostly prisoners from the former army of occupation. Then there was a band of buglers and other wind instrumentalists who played music of the Fur tribe. Finally there were four men who played the *ummbaya*. The *ummbaya* was made out of a huge hollow elephant's tusk. When it was blown it issued a shrill whistle which could be heard for miles. It was sounded whenever the Khalifa set off for the Parade Ground or for an assembly of his troops.

The Mulazimin

The *mulazimin* themselves were under Shaykh al Din's command, although some of them were veterans of the Omdurman garrison commanded by Ibrahim al Khalil.

After the attempted Ashraf revolt, and after the Ethiopian wars had destroyed the regular force of *jihadiya*, the Khalifa set about recruiting a select group of regular soldiers with a high level of training and equipment. They were recruited from two main sources, from the sons of chosen tribal leaders and from the blacks whose sale had been monopolized by the state. As they grew in number the Khalifa added to them some *jihadiya* from the army of the west.

Shaykh al Din's *mulazimin* were made up of eighteen *rub's*. Most men were armed with Remington rifles. Each *rub'* was commanded by an *amir*. The *rub's* were divided into between eight and twelve standards, each standard containing one hundred men.

The *mulazimin* received a regular salary and had permanent barracks and a treasury separate from the general treasury. Most of the grain of the rich Jazira district that came to the capital provisioned the *mulazimin* treasury. Their weapons were separate from the rest of the Omdurman garrison and they also had their own musical detachment.

The Black Standard

The Black Standard was no ordinary unit. Originally it had comprised the whole of the Mahdiya army. It then became the principal standard of the army. When the army was divided into three standards it absorbed warriors from the west and south, becoming something like a reserve army, whose services could be called on when circumstances demanded. Two factors contributed to this. It was the personal standard of Ya'qub, who was also the overall commander of the whole army. It was he who issued mobilization instructions to the reserve. It thus became more than just a regional standard and people from the Jazira and the north were added to it, as well as people from the west, its original recruiting area. All the irregular elements came under its command, regardless of tribal origin. The Black Standard became the recruiting centre. As a result the *rub'* was not its dominant organizational unit. Instead the size and armament was decided according to the recruiting capacity and zeal of the tribal chiefs, ranging from thousands to a few dozen. Furthermore as the Black Standard was strictly an assault force, with the *mulazimin* the fire support for the whole garrison, there was no need for all the varied support elements that existed in the other standards.

The standards of the Black Standard were divided according to tribes and sub-tribes. Each standard was subdivided in the usual way into groups of hundreds and *muqaddamiyas* if it were large enough.

The Black Standard did not have its own treasury, arms store, administrative unit or clerks. As Ya'qub was its commander the treasury of the whole army was its treasury and his clerks acted as the Black Standard's clerks.

The Green Standard

The Green Standard, like the Black, was poorly armed. Recruiting was on a tribal basis and was confined to a few tribes in the White Nile area. These tribes were organized into three main divisions, the Dighaim, the Kanana and the Lahiwiyin. There was also the standard of the Dighaim horsemen.

Each Friday the Omdurman garrison used to hold a review on the Parade Ground. Whenever the Khalifa wanted a review he ordered the great drum to be beaten at dawn. When they heard its noise the people hastened to the mosque to say morning prayers and to read the Mahdi's prayer book. The standard bearers then went to fetch the standards. Each man would rally to his standard and then all, whether on horse or on foot, would march to the Parade Ground, chanting *'Allahu Akbar'* and 'There is no God but God.' The *jihadiya* came from their barracks and stood at the far south. To their left was the Black Standard, then the Green and then, before its dissolution, the Red Standard. At the far north the *amirs* would wait on horseback, each with his own standard. There were Ya'qub, the Khalifa 'Ali wad Hilu and the Khalifa Sharif. The *ummbaya* would be sounded and the army of the *mulazimin* would emerge with their rifles, led by Shaykh al Din on horseback, followed by his *rub's*, one by one in rows of six to twelve men. Before each *rub'* was its standard, its *amir*, its horsemen and drums. Then came the Khalifa, surrounded by his private *mulazimin* with their rifles on each side of him. The *baltajiya* marched in front, the *mushammaratiya* behind. At each side were the *khashkhashan*. Amid them all rode the Khalifa. This procession continued until it reached the *mulazimin*. Then the Khalifa would proceed to review the whole army.

Reserve Army

When a reserve force was summoned to Omdurman it would spend some time in camp training, reading the *ratib* and participating in the Friday parades. The men would then return to their homes and fields.

There were two ways of calling up the reserve. First, they would be summoned to Omdurman and added to the Black Standard before being sent to join the various campaigns. The Khalifa naturally preferred this way, for it satisfied his desire for centralization and placed his soldiers under his direct control. The second way was by local recruitment undertaken by the commanders of those areas which were then theatres of war. This was the course adopted in operations of internal security, such as in Darfur. The Khalifa used to write the recruiting instructions himself and send them to the *amirs* of the reserve army in order to strengthen the orders issued by the *'amil*.

The Chain of Command

At the summit of the pyramid of command was the Khalifa. He

was the supreme commander and was responsible for matters of policy and grand strategy. Operational planning took shape after conferences, of which the most important was an annual conference held in the Islamic month of Rajab and attended by the commanders of all the major units including the provincial garrisons. During the conference the general lines of the forthcoming campaign season would be laid down. Regular war councils would follow up and finalize the details of these campaigns. There were other conferences at irregular intervals. The Khalifa decided on the participants who were usually the *amirs* and those tribal leaders whose lands were war zones.

The Khalifa's brother, the *amir* Ya'qub, was the executive director of military policy. He was responsible for the day-to-day running of the army. Orders relating to provincial commands or the garrisons were issued by Ya'qub. General instructions were issued in his name although the most important orders were reserved for the name and seal of the Khalifa. All administrative officials, central and regional, were subject to Ya'qub's authority.

Among the most important of these officials were the *amir* of the Khalifa's artillery, the trustee of the treasury, the official in charge of the camel post, the commander of the artillery factories and the secretary of the armoury, *bayt al-amana*.

The Amir of the Khalifa's Artillery

Most of the Khalifa's artillery was stored in Omdurman and Ya'qub used to detach batteries to the provinces according to campaign needs. The returns of Yusuf Mansur, the *amir* of the artillery, show that the artillery was divided up into eleven batteries with six guns of different types in each battery. The commander and crew of each battery were Egyptian and the total strength was six Krupps, eight ten-barrel *Mitrailleuses* and eighteen other guns of various types.

The Trustee of the Treasury

The resources of the treasury, *bayt al-mal*, were available for all state expenses. The greater part of its income, however, was devoted to the needs of the Omdurman garrison and the administrative units in the capital. The central treasury was in charge of the payment of wages to the soldiers, the distribution of the products of the workshops and of maintenance materials. It stored everything except firearms. The secretary of the treasury had a number of assistants. He was responsible for storing and distributing grain to the Omdurman garrison, for adjusting deficiencies of grain in the provincial treasuries and for financing military expeditions setting out from Omdurman.

Camel Post

The official in charge of the camel post was Karrar Bashir al 'Abbadi. The camel post was charged with the delivery of official correspondence, but army concerns took the lion's share. The transport squadron was divided into two troops with seventy camels between them. The *muqaddam* of the first group with forty was Karrar himself. Al Tayyib 'Abd al Karim was the *muqaddam* of the other.

Ammunition Workshops Supervisor

The ammunition workshops were in three groups. The Khalifa took advantage of the chemical expertise of an Egyptian doctor, Hasan Zaki, and appointed him overseer of ammunition production. He supervised the various processes of production. In one factory gunpowder was sifted and extracted. A former pharmacist, al Sayyid 'Abd al Wahid, was the superintendent of a similar factory at al Halfaya. There was a third workshop at Kutum in Darfur. A second factory in Omdurman was for refining gunpowder. A former major in the army of occupation, 'Abd al Sami Salib, was in charge. Lastly there was an ammunition factory, directed by Hasan Husni, a former lieutenant in the army of occupation.

The Armoury

The secretary of the *bayt al-amana* was Qamar al Din 'Abd al

Jabbar. The *bayt al-amana* was the arsenal in which were stored the small arms, the cannons, the ammunition and the raw materials for manufacturing ammunition. It was divided operationally into stores, a clerical department and a section responsible for repairs. The last section was in two parts, one directed by Balula Jadd al Rafiq, a former mechanic in Bahr al Ghazal, the other by al Sayyid Barnawi.

In the provincial headquarters the military and civil administrative officials under the *amir* and *'amil* respectively answered to Ya'qub. Whenever a senior *amir* went to the provinces to lead a campaign he usually took administrative units with him. His general staff consisted of a standard-bearer, the *amir* of his personal bodyguard, the secretary of the provincial treasury, the judge of the *'imala* and the commanders of the provincial artillery and of postal service camels.

The chain of command in the *'imalas* went down to the leaders of the *rub's* and the commanders of small garrisons in which the military force of the *'imala* was distributed. The *amir* of the *rub'* was responsible for running things in his combat and administrative units. Under him were the *amirs* of standards and then the *muqaddams*. Although the *muqaddams* were the lowest link in the chain of command, they enjoyed a wide measure of military and administrative authority, extending beyond that of a platoon commander, for they were responsible for feeding and training, as well as for leading their men in the field.

Training

The Khalifa attached great importance to training. He issued scores of decrees to his commanders stressing the ideological training of the holy warriors. In the army of the Mahdiya training depended, as in any other army, upon reasonable intervals between active service, but after 1881 the armies of the Mahdiya had little opportunity for training on a regular basis. Furthermore, by relying to a large extent on irregulars who were not available for continuous military service, he exacerbated his training disabilities. Thus there was a great difference in the quality and training of different units in the Khalifa's army.

Training in the Omdurman garrison was in two stages. There was first the basic training received by those who joined up as raw recruits. Then there was the regular training cycle undergone by established soldiers. There was no clear distinction between the two, except that in the first period of training there was an emphasis on religious guidance, especially for the pagan *jihadiya*. The Khalifa's mosque and the space surrounding it was full, in the periods between prayer times, of thousands of soldiers reciting the Qur'an or the *ratib* or drilling under the eyes of their instructors.

The daily training of the more experienced soldiers in the Omdurman garrison, especially the *mulazimin*, was devoted to the use of firearms and took place in the area east of the *qubba*.[7]

The Friday parade was not just a military review, but was a sort of weekly drill with cavalry charges, manoeuvres and troop movements, with the Khalifa and Ya'qub ordering the men to advance, to wheel and change direction.

Seniority and Rank

Seniority in the Khalifa's army rested on two factors. The first related to the ordinary chain of command: the leader of the *rub'* was naturally senior to the leader of a standard and the *muqaddam* was senior to the ordinary soldier. There was a further criterion of precedence among the individual soldiers, which depended upon priority in accepting the Mahdi's Call. This was generally honorary and became significant only in the summons to attend councils or in leading the faithful in prayer. The Khalifa advanced individuals rapidly; most of the leaders of the original standards sank to subordinate positions and the leadership fell to young *amirs* of the Khalifa's own kin.[8]

The outward marks of rank depended on the size of the standard and whether its *amir* possessed a drum. All *amirs*, furthermore, were horsemen. 'Abd al Rahman al Nujumi was regarded as the senior *amir* in the army. After his death his place was taken by Osman Digna.

Apart from the *jihadiya* and the *mulazimin*, ordinary soldiers in the army only received rations during campaigns. Rations were issued to each unit *en bloc* from the treasury. Senior *amirs* received various gifts in the form of money, slave girls, or horses. The commanders of the provincial garrisons distributed gifts to lesser *amirs*, which were an official charge on the provincial treasury.

Regulations and Discipline

The Islamic *shari'a* law was the guiding rule for moral conduct, but the development of the army and its emergence as a separate entity made it necessary for there to be a military code covering the soldiers' behaviour. Grave misdemeanours, if they were outside the jurisdiction of the *qadi* of the *'imala*, were referred to the chief *qadi* in Omdurman and a board of investigation would look into the charge. On such an occasion the *'amil* would be instructed to send the defendant to Omdurman. Sentences varied according to the standing of the defendant and the gravity of the charge. Crimes of humble soldiers, mostly committed by volunteers, were generally confined to desertion. Major crimes, like highway robbery, were punished by imprisonment. Lesser crimes such as absence from the camp and entering the city without permission were subject to flogging. Senior *amirs*, when accused of corruption or abuse of power, were cashiered or sent to Omdurman to be *mulazimin* under the direct eye of the Khalifa.

Records

Surviving inventories refer precisely to activities of the Khalifa's troops, down to the rawest recruit and the last bullet, to the minutest expense or military infringement.[9] Records also survive for the reserve army. In them are mentioned the names of each individual private soldier. Other returns follow the same pattern with families' servants and, in the case of migrants, livestock. Yet other returns give the daily production of the ammunition factories and a complete account of its distribution and whether it was for ordinary issue or for campaigns and emergencies.

During campaigns returns of the slain and wounded were sent back by name on a sheet of paper with the words, 'List of the martyrs and wounded among the Ansar who were in the attack of . . . in the course of their combating the enemies of God.' There then followed the names of the dead and the wounded. Those who died from natural causes were also added.

Supply

The system of supply was carried out on broad lines laid down by the Mahdi in various decrees relating to the organization of the army. The details changed to keep pace with military expansion. There were two standard procedures – central and regional.

The centralized method was generally adopted for large campaigns that set out from Omdurman and were financed by the principal treasury. If the army was vast, the treasury would provide the commander with cash so he could purchase his needs through contractors.

The decentralized system was adopted in the provinces. The *'imala* treasury would be filled with grain gathered in the district. This income in kind was derived from the *zaka* tax imposed on all inhabitants. In the remoter provincial areas, each garrison had a grain store built some way from the soldiers' lines. The major source here was the crop harvested by the soldiers or their families. The geographical position of fertile areas which could meet an army's needs influenced the dispositions of the forces and at times, indeed, defined the shape and objective of a campaign. At the appropriate time of the year units moved to more fertile areas. This factor also helped to determine the siting of garrisons. Each garrison had lines of defence, behind which was the settlement where the warriors lived with their families. On them fell the major task of cultivation. Behind the settlement stretched the fields and some miles further back was the grain store. The cultivation of *dhurra* in the east, *dukhn* in the west and palms in the north was assigned to the wives and children.[10] Hence the importance of building the settlements away from the front lines.

The Khalifa's ammunition factories produced one hundred boxes of ammunition each month, with 144 bullets in each box. The Khalifa also inherited a large amount of ammunition from the army of occupation. However, he realized that his extended military operations would soon use this up, so from the beginning he faced the task of manufacturing ammunition locally.

Requests for ammunition were presented by the commander of each military district with a written explanation of his needs. The request was forwarded either to the *bayt al-amana* in Omdurman or to the headquarters of the *'imala*. The commanders of the outlying areas received whatever ammunition they needed. A fixed amount was kept in the provincial stores for use in sudden operations until further supplies arrived from Omdurman. For larger operations the amount needed was estimated according to the number of warriors and what each rifleman could carry. In addition pack camels on the march could carry more and a reserve stock would be kept in a central pool. The amount allocated naturally depended on the number of rifle-bearing soldiers, on the number of cannons and the nature of the anticipated enemy.

The nature of the provisions led to a decentralized system and a dependence on local sources, but it was a different matter with ammunition for there was only one source, Omdurman. Thus a reliable transport system was necessary. The means for this were camels or steamers, or a combination of both. Camels were the principal vehicle for land transport, although the Khalifa tended to be very cautious about using them to carry ammunition.[11] The steamers, as well as transporting men and artillery, used also to tow barges and rafts bearing ammunition.

Perhaps the weakest point in the Khalifa's military organization was the maintenance and repair of equipment. The main reason for this lay in the limited number of trained technicians. Repairs and maintenance were concentrated in the capital to the detriment of the provinces, where there was no opportunity for thorough overhaul or competent maintenance. Machines and tools were restricted to the workshops of the capital. The mechanics of the boat repair workshop, which was in Khartoum, maintained high technical standards to the end. They were able to assemble a complete Nile steamer, which arrived in separate parts from London, after the fall of Khartoum. Indeed only one steamboat was out of action throughout the thirteen years, in spite of their continual use.

1 Until recently the writing of Slatin had a great influence on the world's view of the Khalifa and the Mahdiya. Slatin was apparently well treated in captivity and the Khalifa in no way used him ill beyond having him closely observed. He cannot be censured for his treatment of Slatin. In *Fire and Sword in the Sudan* Slatin sometimes stated the truth but he did not state the whole truth. He was anxious to exonerate himself from the charge of perfidy. Slatin was being less than honest when he said that the Khalifa kept him merely in order to humiliate him and to brag that the former governor of Darfur was now his servant. From his own account and also from the accounts of others it seems that his position was rather that of military adviser than that of servant. He himself mentions the gifts given him by the Khalifa in the form of slave girls. He even offered one of his own relations as a wife.

2 Turshayn in the Baqqara dialect means an ugly bull and referred to his strength and resolution.

3 By contrast the Sudanese historian Muhammad 'Abd al Rahim considered that he was 'a wise and conscientious man, pious, noble and heroic, who feared not adversity and whose conduct was beyond reproach.' He noted in particular the Khalifa's concern for justice and respect for education.

4 The same report draws attention to the large number of men from northern tribes – Mahas and Dongolawis – who had migrated to Egypt at the beginning of the Mahdist revolution – and who now sought permission from the Egyptian authorities to return home.

5 The *amir* Ya'qub used always to call them lancers, distinguishing them from the *jihadiya* and the cavalry. Most lancers were from the tribes; the roll-call sometimes calls them nomads.

6 This measure was taken to make it easier to catch deserters, most of whom were from the ranks of the *jihadiya*. The Khalifa was constantly worried about the loyalty of the *jihadiya*. He thus stressed the importance of their induction until their loyalty was sure.

7 The Khalifa forbade the use of live ammunition not solely – as Slatin says – from fear of insurrection – but lest it all be used up. His ban applied to the regions as well as Omdurman and also to its use for hunting.

8 The Khalifa's military leaders and provincial rulers were remarkably young. Most of the active military commanders were in their early twen-

ties. 'Uthman Adam was twenty-two when he took command of the *'imala* of the west. Ibrahim al Khalil and Shaykh al Din were in their early twenties. Muhammad Bishara and Mahmud wad Ahmad were both twenty-six or younger in 1898.

9   The varying colours of ink shows that the register was kept continuously. One difficulty with the records is that they are mostly not dated. We have to guess the dates from internal evidence.

10   Returns show that most soldiers had wives and many were accompanied by servants. Some returns were submitted in the form of a list of soldiers without their womenfolk.

11   The main supplier of camels were the Shukriya and the Mahiriya tribes. The main tribe for cameleers was the Kababish, but their hostility to the Mahdiya inevitably weakened the Khalifa's transport system.

CHAPTER FOUR

The Lion and the Lamb

NINETEENTH century imperialism was no new phenomenon, for Europe had been discovering and colonizing the rest of the world for four centuries. But the new field of operations was Africa.

Economic factors were one of several causes for this new fever of imperialism in the 1880s and '90s. The race for the Nile basin manifested several motivations in the four competitors in the race – Belgium, Italy, France and Britain.

Belgium was the smallest of the four. Under the ambitious and autocratic King Leopold II, Belgium concentrated on the exploitation of her African empire in order to safeguard her economic future. The Congo was not enough and Leopold coveted the lands to the east. An agreement with Britain in 1894 recognized the sources of the Nile as a British sphere of influence while conferring upon Belgium the right to the territory bordering the Congo and on the greater part of Bahr al Ghazal. Thus the way to the sources of the Nile was closed to the real rival, France, whose only direct route from her possessions in West Africa would be bound to lead to clashes with the Khalifa.

However, the French offered Leopold the southern part of Ubangi, the present-day Central African Empire, in exchange for a corridor to the Nile basin by a route to the south of the Khalifa's armies. Leopold amended his agreement with Britain and signed a Franco-Congolese agreement in the same year, though still affirming his respect for 'the claims of Turkey and Egypt in the basin of the Upper Nile'. Under European international law Sudan was still considered as an Egyptian possession and European countries did not recognize the Mahdist rule. Turkish and Egyptian rights were a cloak for British rights as neither the Sultan of Turkey nor the Khedive Tawfiq had any say in the allocation of spheres of European influence.

Italy had penetrated Africa in the east, occupying the port of Massawa in 1885 and constructing a series of military forts as far as Kasala. All Eritrea was under her control.

The Ethiopian Emperor, Menelik, who had come to the throne with Italian support, concluded a treaty with the Italians, giving them some territory, concessions and privileges. But a French envoy persuaded Menelik to drop the Italians, and French weapons and money then began to pour in in return for mining concessions and the right to build railway lines in the country. Menelik used the money to pay off Italian debts and the arms to get rid of them. He renounced his treaty with them and began to provoke them in small military engagements. On the morning of 1 March, 1896, the two armies met in a great battle at Adowa. A vast Ethiopian army, armed with modern rifles and quick-firing guns, inflicted an overwhelming defeat on the Italian army.

France was seeking to approach the Nile basin under the Emperor's cloak as well as from the west. Anglo-French rivalry in the Nile valley went back a long time. It was through French eyes that Egypt, in the time of Napoleon, first looked at Europe. It was French help that Muhammad 'Ali and the Khedive 'Isma'il sought in their efforts to modernize Egypt. De Lesseps, the builder of the Suez canal, and his experts were French. Financial backing for the canal was French. When Britain invaded Egypt in 1882 France did not realize that the occupation would last for decades.

France felt that whoever controlled the sources of the Nile controlled Egypt's fortunes. She sought to use control of the sources of the Nile to put pressure on Britain to review her occupation of Ottoman and Egyptian possessions.

In the last years of the century French expeditions from the west quickened an interest in the African interior that resembled the excitement of the 1850s and '60s when Burton, Speke and Baker sought the sources of the Nile.

When Britain invaded Egypt in 1882 her aim was to put internal affairs in good order and to prevent the 'Urabi revolt from threatening her interests. When matters were straightened out she would withdraw. Her aim was not permanent occupation. Nor was it initially an exclusive occupation; in 1882 she invited France to participate in the invasion.

Britain did not want to get involved in Egyptian problems nor in Isma'il's huge scattered empire. As for the Sudan, British policy was confused and British involvement half-hearted. Britain was unwilling to get involved in these remote lands. The Government ignored British public opinion which had called for the relief of Gordon, and had been slow to send the Relief Expedition.

The death of Gordon aroused much concern. The defeat of the white man in Africa was a shock to racial pride but by 1887 British public opinion had turned away from the Sudan in shame.

Then the Egyptian Intelligence Department began to issue reports to the British War Office about the weakness of the Khalifa's state and the dire straits of the people. Wingate succeeded in smuggling Father Ohrwalder out of the Khalifa's capital, soon to publish his book *Ten Years' Captivity*.[1] Slatin's more famous book, *Fire and Sword in the Sudan*, followed. These publications stirred public opinion in Britain and suggested that a reoccupation would bring with it the restoration of honour. It would also help to realize the imperial dream of laying a railway from Cairo to the Cape. After the occupation of Kenya, the only piece missing from British control was the stretch of land extending from Halfa to the Nile sources, from Kasala to the Kingdom of Wadai – the Khalifa's empire.

Britain was guided by Cromer's advice. In 1889 it was considered important to recover the Sudan for the sake of Egypt's security, and that the existing state of affairs was satisfactory only so long as the Khalifa did not threaten Egypt directly or the waters of the Nile, so essential to Egypt's existence. The appropriate time for recovery would be when the Khalifa's military power was on the wane, when the Egyptian army was ready, and when the Egyptian budget could bear the expense of such a costly campaign.

When the Egyptian budget revived, attention was paid to the rebuilding of a modern army to deal with internal security and to protect the southern border.

In December, 1882, the old Egyptian army that had fought with 'Urabi was disbanded and a new army established. Compulsory military service began by lot. Within months there was an army of 6,000 at the head of whom were twenty-six young British officers and a group of British non-commissioned officers for training. Among the officers were Kitchener, MacDonald and Hunter.

In 1894 Kitchener was appointed Commander-in-Chief, or 'Sirdar', of the Egyptian army. By 1896 there were in the Egyptian army eighteen battalions of infantry including six (the 9th to the 14th) Sudanese battalions. Each battalion, which had 759 men armed with Martini Henry rifles, was composed of six companies. There were nine cavalry companies, all Egyptian. Each company had 100 men, armed with rifles, swords and long lances. In addition there were eight camel corps, four Sudanese and four Egyptian. Each man carried a rifle. There were also six artillery batteries, two armed with quick-firing nine-pounder Maxim Nordenfeldt cannons. The rest had eighteen-pounder field cannons. One battery of horse artillery was armed with twelve-pounder Krupp cannons.

All the senior officers above company commander were British except for the 5th and 6th infantry battalions which had Turkish and Circassian officers. At the time of the invasion the total strength of the army, apart from the railway battalion, was 20,000 men.

From 1888 the Egyptian army gained confidence in itself and its modern equipment, whereas the strength of the Khalifa was on the wane. The battle of Tushki destroyed the myth of the Khalifa's invulnerability, and Wingate's reports began to record the decline of the Khalifa's empire.

In the early 1890's reports of the success of French missions in their advance from the west were published in the French press. Gradually France's ultimate ambitions in the Nile basin became clear. Cromer began to take the French threat seriously and confirmed to London that the solution to the problem lay not in Cairo but in a direct confrontation with France.

It was up to the British Government to decide. Doubts about French ambitions were expressed in Sir Edward Grey's remark that the advance of a French mission towards an area long regarded as a British sphere of influence would be considered 'an unfriendly act'. As month followed month Cromer began to incline more and more towards the adoption of a forward policy to safeguard the Nile basin by reconquering the Sudan.

Meanwhile another project was revolving in Cromer's mind – the construction of the Aswan Dam. To this he had applied all his financial acumen and had called on the assistance of every available engineering skill. The dam was a project that would help the Egyptian budget, exhausted by its debts. But the reconquest of the Sudan would consume the fruits of his economy and impose severe retrenchment once more.

Cromer's office in the Residency saw regular visits from two men. One was Kitchener, demanding that Cromer persuade London to underwrite an invasion of the Sudan. He outlined the French and Belgian threats to the sources of the Nile. After he left there would enter Garstin who would sing the praises of the Aswan Dam. At first Cromer gave his support to the dam.[2] But Garstin's happiness was not to last long. On 13 March, 1896, the British Government decided to occupy 'Akasha, a deserted and worthless station 130 miles south of Saras. Salisbury explained that the reasons for the advance to Dongola were a desire 'to help the Italians at Kasala, and to prevent the dervishes from winning a conspicuous success which might have far-reaching results'.

This sudden change in policy was caused by Menelik's victory over the Italians at Adowa. As General Baratieri was making his fateful advance to Adowa the chancelleries of Rome and London experienced a flurry of activity. In London the Italian Ambassador explained that the Italians would have to evacuate Kasala if they did not receive prompt support from Britain. The natural place for such support would be an advance south-west from Sawakin (Suakin) to draw the attention of the Khalifa away from the Italian garrison at Kasala. But the War Office objected on the grounds that such a relief expedition would in time itself need a relief expedition. The British answer was to offer a show of force, a small scale demonstration, in order to relieve the pressure on the Italians. It would have limited aims and would avoid provoking the French. Cromer objected in principle to a show of force, arguing that the inevitable withdrawal would be considered as a victory for the Khalifa, not only in Omdurman, but throughout the Near East.

Thus instructions were sent to the commander of the British occupation forces in Egypt, General Knowles. There were to be two separate operations: first, an advance to and occupation of 'Akasha, and then an advance towards Abu Hamad, south of the wells of al Murat, in the Nubian desert between Halfa and Abu Hamad, the base of the 'Ababda tribe, allies of the Egyptian Government.

The instructions were sent to the Commander of the British occupation forces in Egypt, who passed them on to the Sirdar, by-passing Cromer. Cromer protested that the preparations and the expenditure should be his responsibility.

Salisbury's answer was to make the Sirdar directly responsible to Cromer. He explained in his long telegram to Cromer of 13 March that the aim of the operation was to assist the Italians but that the Nile was chosen as a theatre for operations rather than the east of the Sudan because of the importance of the Nile to Egypt.

But support for the Italians would be of no value unless the Khalifa realized that the invasion launched against him was in earnest. So Salisbury informed European ambassadors in London that troops had begun to advance to Dongola. He apologized to Cromer for the fact that the invasion was to start before the Egyptian economy was in order. The haste was made necessary by the Italian defeat. It was neither in the interests of Europe nor of Africa, said Salisbury, to stand idly by while Africans crushed Europeans.

For long it was known that French arms were pouring into Ethiopia. There was suspicion of cooperation between the Khalifa and Menelik before Adowa, but this increased when it was learned that the French were pushing on to the Nile basin from the east. There emerged the spectre of an alliance of the Khalifa, Menelik and the French. Such an alliance would dash the dreams of recovering the Sudan and securing British control over the waters of the Nile for ever.

NOTES

1   Mr Gasim Bedri, in his thesis, notes the large number of publications in England on the Sudan after Gordon's death in 1885. The number declines and then rises again in 1898 and 1899.

2   Cromer had always been, as he said, 'afraid of the soldiers getting the bit in their teeth and running away with one . . . I have persistently put forward the objection to the adoption of a forward policy . . . The Sudan is worth a good deal to Egypt, but it is not worth bankruptcy and extremely oppressive taxation'.

CHAPTER FIVE

The Sirdar Advances

THE Khalifa was well aware that an invasion was being planned. According to Muhammad 'Abd al Rahman he had his spies and observers in Cairo who used to scan the daily newspapers, cut out stories of army movements, diplomatic negotiations, ministerial meetings and everything relating to the reconquest of the Sudan. These were sent in envelopes among invoices which Sudanese merchants in Egypt sent to the Sudan. After going through them the Khalifa would give instructions to his commanders on the frontier according to the information received.

From the beginning of 1896 the Khalifa was active. At the feast of Rajab, on 13 January, he held his usual annual council of war, attended by the senior *amirs* and the provincial *'amils*, and announced his intention of recovering Kasala.

In Dongola Muhammad wad Bishara was Governor, replacing Yunus al Dikaym who had been removed after complaints from the people of Dongola of his oppression. The Khalifa warned wad Bishara of the probablity of an advance by the enemy. He made some major adjustments to the disposition of his forces in the area. Of his four *rub's* he kept one in Dongola and sent one to reinforce Hamuda Idris, commander of the Sawarda area in the far north, where there were already two *rub's* – half wad Bishara's available forces.

On 15 March, before the main force came south from Cairo, Colonel Hunter, commander of the southern frontier region, ordered a small task force to advance and occupy 'Akasha, the first point inside Sudanese territory. They found 'Akasha deserted.

The Sirdar spent three months after the occupation of 'Akasha gathering his invasion forces on the southern frontiers. He called up his reserve and established a supply line along the 825 miles from Cairo. The railway was mainly used for transporting his soldiers, and Cook's steamers towed hundreds of barges bearing cases of ammunition and rations. There was also a small flotilla of native sailing boats. By the end of May the Sirdar had mustered 9,700 soldiers. There were three brigades, under Major Lewis, Major MacDonald and Major Maxwell. The force comprised ten battalions, five Sudanese and five Egyptian. Colonel Hunter was the commander of the infantry division. There were also seven squadrons of cavalry and eight of camelry. The artillery was made up of one horse battery, two field batteries and one Maxim battery.

Twelve years earlier, when Major Kitchener was an intelligence officer at al Dabba, he had spent much of his time surveying the Dongola district, studying the flow of the Nile, its rise and fall. He felt that the only solution to the problem of a guaranteed rapid supply line would be a railway. On his return to Egypt he insisted that this was the best way of circumventing the obstacle of the cataracts. It would also avoid slow camel transport.

At Firka (Firket) Hamuda Idris was in charge. He first distributed his forces in the area between Sawarda (Suarda) and Firka and then, in compliance with Muhammad wad Bishara's instructions, concentrated them all in Firka at the end of March.

Wad Bishara had an efficient intelligence system which brought him news of the Sirdar's visit to the frontiers in February. He relayed the news to Omdurman and requested reinforcements.

Hamuda was slack and news of the advance to 'Akasha reached wad Bishara in Dongola before it reached Hamuda at Firka. Wad Bishara had little confidence in this commander who failed to reorganize the defences in the district and had repeatedly to be urged to take the initiative. Wad Bishara sent a rousing address which was read to all the troops. When, after a month had passed and Hamuda had still not stirred, wad Bishara reported him to the Khalifa.

Letters from wad Bishara to Hamuda, dating from the two months after the Sirdar's occupation of 'Akasha, reveal the former's organizational ability and gifts of leadership, but also show up the latter's inadequacy. Hamuda was slow in sending detailed information about the distribution and intentions of the enemy. By 17 April the stage had been reached when wad Bishara informed Hamuda of the enemy's plans and urged him to cut the Sirdar's lines of communication and the railway. Four days later wad Bishara expressed his anxiety to Hamuda about the speed of the advance of the railway and said that Sukkut would be taken within a few weeks.

Hamuda finally moved. He attacked the Sirdar's caravan on 1 May as it was approaching 'Akasha. Hamuda's force surprised some of the Sirdar's reconnaissance force, but a withdrawal and a subsequent dispute with the commander of his *jihadiya* persuaded wad Bishara to dismiss him. Accordingly he wrote to the Khalifa seeking permission.

Meanwhile, as the mobilization of the necessary forces and reinforcements was being completed at Dongola, wad Bishara sent the *amir* 'Uthman Azraq north to take command of the garrison at Firka. He was the most suitable choice for a situation that required positive action. The Khalifa approved Hamuda's dismissal and agreed to the appointment of 'Uthman Azraq at once.

There was general satisfaction at the appointment of 'Uthman Azraq. His infantry consisted of one standard of the Habbaniya tribe with 332 warriors under the command of Hamuda Idris, one standard of Dongolawis, 441 strong, under the command of Karam Allah Kurkusawi, and one standard of Ja'liyin, 245 strong, commanded by Muhammad 'Abd al Halim. All these were armed with swords and spears. There were also two groups of *jihadiya*, the larger group commanded by Yusuf Anqara and consisting of 400 men, the smaller group, under Dudu Badr, containing 210 men. In addition there were 250 horsemen led by the *amir* Jubayr and a contingent of camelmen with 110 porters bearing 720 rifles and fifty boxes of ammunition.

57

At the beginning of June the Sirdar issued a proclamation declaring his war aims. In it he warned the people of the Sudan against the 'Call' of Muhammad Ahmad, the 'so-called Mahdi. It ought to be clear to you now that this "Call" is not of the Mahdiya at all but is a bloody revolution that has engulfed a tyrant monarch who has now taken command, 'Abd Allahi the Ta'aisha. This man has banished every *amir* not of his tribe and has appointed his kinsmen who now oppress you.' The Khalifa had broken up the truth of Islam, dishonoured people, oppressed the poor and destroyed old families. 'He was once a wretched penniless individual. He now lives in new-built palaces, has taken the peaceful women of the faithful and indulges himself in secret with all that delights and gratifies him.' The declaration went on to enumerate *amirs* who had been executed or imprisoned, individuals who had been insulted and tribes that might have a grievance against the Khalifa. 'When the noble and benevolent Khedive 'Abbas Hilmi II saw that the crimes of this tyrant were increasing daily, compassion for the suffering believers possessed him and he decided to rescue them. He sent his conquering armies to destroy the foundations of the Ta'aisha state and to establish a lawful government based on justice and righteousness, to rebuild mosques and to see to the spread of right religion. . . . In his name I expect that I will see you shortly in obedience and submission to the government of the Egyptian Khedive'. The proclamation was signed by Kitchener as commander of the Sudan expedition and Sirdar of the Egyptian army.

On the afternoon of 6 June the Sirdar set off south from 'Akasha by the two roads that led to Firka – the desert road and the Nile road. The main force, the infantry, went by the direct Nile road with the objective of taking Firka by storm. All the mounted forces went by the desert road, forming a broad arc round Firka and occupying the positions behind the garrison ready to block the line of retreat to the south and east.

The river column was made up of an infantry division, two field batteries, two Maxims and a field hospital, all under the Sirdar's command. The desert column comprised a battery of horse artillery, 800 cavalrymen armed with sabres, a camel corps with 620 rifles, the 12th Sudanese battalion, two Maxim guns and a medical unit.

The Sirdar's infantry stumbled among the rocks until, late at night, they stopped at the village of Sarkamattu, three miles from Firka. The mounted desert column, meanwhile, crossed the desert and approached Firka.

The village of Firka was in a position that offered clear defensive advantages. It lay between Jabal Firka on the north-east, a range of broken mountains that came down to the houses on the south-east and the Nile on the west. A *khur* separated Jabal Firka from the southern mountains. The houses of the village stretched parallel to the Nile for about a mile, to a depth of three hundred yards. However, these advantages could turn to disaster if the position was stormed.

'Uthman Azraq's plan of defence was to make use of the natural defences round the village. He took his decision some days before the battle, after holding a council of war attended by all the *amirs*. The council organized the defence, allotting a defensive position to each unit in the event of an enemy assault. The defence of the southern mountains was assigned to Karam Allah Kurkusawi with the standard of the Dongolawis, the eastern mountains and the *khur* to Yusuf Anqara, Dudu Badr and Hamuda Idris with the *jihadiya* standard, the Habbaniya and the horsemen, and the north to Muhammad 'Abd al Halim with the Ja'li standard to cover the narrow passage between Jabal Firka and the Nile. According to Muhammad 'Abd al Rahim, Muhammad 'Abd al Halim objected, saying that he only had seventy-two rifles and that the bulk of the Egyptian forces would probably come by the Nile road. Hamuda told him, 'If that happens then I am ready to help you.' Muhammad answered, 'One should not expect to turn to help even to one's brother at such a terrible time.' Hamuda was furious at this and grasped his beard with both hands, saying to him, 'If I do not help you at a time like that, may God destroy this.'

The advantages of Firka's position, however, were to rebound on the defenders. Their plan relied on moving forces from their quarters in the village to occupy the assigned defence positions after due warning from observation posts on Jabal Firka or the eastern mountains. These hills, with their commanding peaks, were ideal for observation. But negligence on the part of the sentries that dawn enabled the Sirdar to take command of the situation. Firka thus became a beleaguered village after the Sirdar's riflemen had occupied the mountains and were able to direct their fire at the village.

In the early hours of the morning the silence was broken by the sound of the *nuqqara* which reached the ears of the Sirdar. He thought that his silent night advance had been discovered and ordered a halt. But the sound of the drum soon died away; it was the call to dawn prayer. After their prayers they assembled in their standards on the banks of the river, sat in groups and read the *ratib*. After the drums had stopped, the Sirdar resumed his advance on the village. Lewis's brigade reached the narrow passage and his cavalry began to debouch into the wide space surrounding the village. Only now did the sentinels on the mountain-top observation posts realize what was happening. They fired a single shot. In confusion the defenders seized their weapons and rushed to their defensive positions. The Nile column arrived at the same time as the Desert column and the surprise was total. The Sirdar's artillery and riflemen occupied the left shoulder of Jabal Firka and directed their fire over the heads of the advancing infantry, concentrating on the warriors and the *jihadiya* as they ran to their stations.

The *jihadiya* and the Habbaniya standard rushed towards the eastern range of mountains, the standards of the Ja'liyin and the Dongolawis to the narrow passage in an attempt to halt the advance of the Sirdar's brigades, but it was too late. The first brigade, led by Lewis, was approaching the Nile just as the *jihadiya* and the Habbaniya began to assemble. MacDonald's brigade was able to dislodge them, so they withdrew towards the village. The horsemen, led by Hamuda Idris and Yusuf Anqara, failed to check the attackers after the third brigade appeared. Their attack petered out as most of the horsemen fell. Hamuda and Yusuf Anqara were among the casualties. Hamuda thus fulfilled his promise to Muhammad 'Abd al Halim that he would assist him under any circumstances. The brigades of MacDonald and Maxwell wheeled towards the village.

'Uthman Azraq's horse fell under him as he charged forward to reorganize the defences. He saw at a glance that he was engaged in a losing battle as a consequence of the sentinels' negligence against an enemy whose strength was far superior to his own. It was now his duty to save as many of his men as possible. One of 'Uthman's soldiers, Muhammad 'Abd al Rahim, recalled that 'our resolution slumped: 800 had died, 450 fell prisoner, the rest of us fled. We made our way between the river itself and the bank. The army attacked us from the bank and directed their fire on us. Thus we fled. When we reached the *khur* we found the way blocked with soldiers. We attacked and managed to force a channel through the hail of fire with our swords.'

As the Sirdar's brigades advanced towards the village 'Uthman Azraq was feverishly occupied in organizing the retreat. He first took the families across the river on the nine boats that had been moored to the bank behind the village. He then collected all the survivors and the wounded from the Firka garrison and retreated with them to the south. 'Uthman himself did not cross until the night of the 8th after making sure everybody else was over. He then reassembled the forces at Kadin where the garrison's granary had been and sent for reinforcements from Abu Fatima. He rallied the men after sending the families on to Dongola, and sent out horsemen to make a reconnaissance.

The reconnaissance informed him that a large mounted force was advancing towards Kadin. 'Uthman burnt all the grain and slipped away just a quarter of an hour before the enemy arrived and then joined Muhammad wad Bishara at Dongola.

In the action at Firka the Sirdar lost twenty dead and eighty-three wounded.

Muhammad wad Bishara received the news of the defeat with great forbearance. He now prepared for a decisive encounter with the enemy. His scouts kept him informed of their whereabouts while he himself sought the best place to meet them. He wrote to the Khalifa, requesting the prompt dispatch of the promised reinforcements.

The Khalifa sent Musa'd Qaydum to Dongola. More relief

was promised which would be led by 'Abd al Baqi 'Abd al Wakil.

The site finally selected by wad Bishara for the encounter with the enemy was al Hafir on the west bank. At the end of June he sent a complete *rub'* as an advance force to build fortifications at al Hafir and at Kirma on the east bank. The Nile here was 600 yards wide – the greatest range at which his cannons could be trained on the enemy gunboats. Three forts were built in which the six cannons would be under shelter. Between the cannons and around the forts trenches were dug for the riflemen. Palm trees richly laden with dates offered sustenance and also provided a protective curtain. 'Uthman Azraq, with most of his force, was to cross to the east and deal with the enemy infantry, thereby cutting them off from their river fleet.

The months after Firka were full of anxiety for the Sirdar. Misfortune seemed to deny the legend of his lucky star. His next objective was Dongola and he resolved to advance there with the largest force available and with his new, fast armoured steamers through the narrow boulder-strewn third cataract, where the Nile is only forty feet wide. The railway line was to be extended to Kusha (Kosheh) south of the cataract; there the separate parts of the steamers would be assembled. They would be launched in the Nile and wait for the river to rise to enable them to advance to Dongola.

The Sirdar had small margin for emergencies, but now cholera crept swiftly along his line of communication from Halfa to the camp at Kusha. It took a toll of 788 men, including 640 soldiers. After he had brought this epidemic under control the Sirdar crossed the desert from Kusha to Ab Sarat, avoiding the westward loop of the Nile. At Ab Sarat the infantry brigades were plagued by thirst and sunstroke. News of this desert journey reached London and the British press attacked the Sirdar, accusing him of negligence and cheese-paring and holding him responsible for the suffering of this 'death-march'.

In northern Sudan for two months of the year the wind suddenly changes direction from the south to the north against the current of the Nile. Much of the Sirdar's supply lines relied on local sailing boats and on this two-month prevailing wind. For two or three days the north wind assisted them but, suddenly and unexpectedly, it changed direction to the south, thus throwing the Sirdar's calculations into further confusion.

Then another blow struck. The Sirdar was very pleased with the steamer *Zafir*. This was a strongly armed gunboat with cannons and machine guns and was equipped to transport infantry. It also had thick armour plate, so that it could come close to the enemy. The camp at Kusha watched it being assembled and marvelled at its capacity. It was then lowered into the water to loud applause. The men listened with swelling hearts to the roar of its engine. But within minutes there was silence. One of the main boilers had exploded. After investigating the problem the engineers said that they needed a new one. The delay meant that they could not use the gunboat until after the rise of the Nile. It was out of action for the year and had to be left behind at Kusha.

Muhammad wad Bishara was aware of the Sirdar's misfortune and wrote to the Khalifa requesting permission to advance north and attack him while he was vulnerable, but it seems that the Khalifa told him to wait for reinforcements that were on their way.

The Sirdar resumed his advance. His infantry and cavalry marched on the eastern bank while the river fleet was negotiating the rocks of the second cataract. Each steamer was towed by rope and chains by the Sirdar's men who dragged the boats over the cataracts. Altogether it took a week to get the flotilla across.

On 5 September the forward party reached Dalqu (Dulgo), the site of the final concentration before Kirma. The Sirdar did not join them with the flotilla until 12 September. The 4th brigade also arrived, fresh from Cairo. The army reached Kadirma on 13 September, al Ghariq on the 14th and on the 15th made the first contact with wad Bishara's mounted patrols. On the 18th the Sirdar occupied the village of Sardik, only four miles from Kirma. At night wad Bishara's drums could be heard. Before dawn the following day the Sirdar advanced on Kirma in an assault formation on a wide front. He headed for the fort at Kirma but, on arrival, found it deserted.

Muhammad wad Bishara had great problems in facing an enemy twice his size with the most modern and lethal weapons yet produced by European arsenals. Even after he was joined by Hamuda's remnants after the battle of Firka, his force never exceeded 5,600 warriors. He also had to offset the negative attitude on the part of his own generals.

Under wad Bishara and his deputy, Musa'd Qaydum, the Dongola garrison consisted of four *rub's* without firearms, a section of *jihadiya*, a section of *mulazimin*, some horsemen and some artillery. The artillery was made up of six mountain cannons and one Nordenfeldt machine gun. The gunners, mostly Egyptians or former *bashibuzuqs*, were commanded by an Egyptian, 'Ali Rayqun. The army was assisted in reconnaissance and communications by 260 cameleers and a number of guides. Finally wad Bishara possessed two small steamers, one armed with a cannon.

As he prepared to move north, the *amir* 'Abd al Baqi 'Abd al Wakil arrived with reinforcements from Omdurman. These consisted of a *rub'* of *jihadiya* and 500 men armed with swords and spears. They all set off in expectation of imminent battle. Wad Bishara travelled by the small steamer, loading all his artillery on it. At al Hafir he sent for 'Uthman Azraq who was at Kirma in charge of the eastern defences. A war council heard a report from 'Uthman Azraq about the enemy's overwhelming superiority in numbers and weapons. After some discussion opinion settled on dealing with the two parts of the enemy's strength separately – the steamers first and then the infantry. Wad Bishara ordered the withdrawal of all the defensive points on the east bank on the evening of 18 September. Under cover of darkness 'Uthman Azraq's forces crossed the Nile and joined Muhammad at al Hafir.

Wad Bishara deployed his forces in preparation for an ambush. He ordered trenches to be dug and forts to be built. The Sirdar's artillery took up their positions and opened fire on wad Bishara's defences but there was no response. Four gunboats, under cover of land cannons that had been sited by the Sirdar, came towards the narrow straits where wad Bishara had concealed his artillery. The cannons of the steamers fired on the forts and the Maxim guns at the trenches. As soon as the steamers came into view the concealed cannons opened fire. Two steamers were hit. Then the riflemen among the palm trees fired at the decks of the steamers, causing a number of enemy casualties, including the commander of the flotilla himself, Commander Colville. This action surprised the Sirdar, who never expected such a small, ill-armed force to show such defiance.

Exchange of fire continued for several hours. The Sirdar's army was standing helplessly on the eastern bank, watching the battle raging between the river fleet and wad Bishara's men. The flotilla tossed about, buffeted by the cannons that did not let up all day.

On the west bank a score of flags fluttered over wad Bishara's ranks. The cries of *Allahu Akbar* drowned the noise of the battle while the smoke of rifles covered the river for more than a quarter of a mile. In the face of the relentless fire wad Bishara was forced to withdraw to the heart of his infantry, safe on the eastern bank.

The Sirdar realized that his armoured flotilla was not enough to deal with the enemy artillery, or even with their ancient rifles. Wad Bishara had deployed his cannons and riflemen in a most effective manner. Any attempt by the Sirdar to bring his infantry across the river would involve heavy losses so he decided to advance directly to Dongola, past the defences of al Hafir, without attempting to silence their cannons. He then moved his land artillery until they were opposite wad Bishara's positions and opened fire. Under this cover the steamers slipped through towards Dongola.

Like other generals of the Mahdiya, Muhammad wad Bishara was particularly aware of the importance of supply lines. He reckoned that the Sirdar would follow his steamers, cross to Dongola and take possession of the city, but would not leave a large hostile force behind him to threaten his rear.

Before sunset a shell struck wad Bishara's tent, wounding him as he wrote a report to the Khalifa; 'Uthman Azraq was also wounded. When night fell, wad Bishara withdrew his army to the south, leaving a long trail of wounded behind him. He decided to make a stand and defend Dongola. But the steamers were already bombarding the city. He moved to a small village to the north and fortified it in preparation for meeting the enemy.

At midnight on 22 September he held a council of war with his *amirs*. He issued instructions for a final defence but was interrupted by Hasan wad al Nujumi who proposed withdrawal. 'My lord,' he said, 'if a man undertakes a trading enterprise and then realizes that he is losing, he has no alternative but to withdraw.' Wad Bishara replied, 'Yes, indeed.' Hasan went on, 'If this is the case with a man who trades in money, what would you say to a man who trades in souls? . . . They have an army on the land and on the river. Do you not think that if our fighting them is a losing enterprise, then we must remove ourselves from them?' To this wad Bishara replied, 'I think that death is preferable to dishonour and flight. If we are resolute we can fight them here until either we are victorious or we die an honourable death.'

On the morning of 23 September the Sirdar advanced towards the city of Dongola on a broad front. Wad Bishara came out to meet him. But his *amirs* suddenly seized his horse, bound him and turned back with him. They had already arranged for the army to withdraw from Dongola. They travelled with wad Bishara, still tied up, until they reached al Dabba (Debba) and from there crossed the desert to al Matamma.[1]

The Sidar entered Dongola without meeting any resistance. Thus the *mudiriya* of Dongola formally fell. The Sirdar at once set about organizing its administration, treating it as a province subordinate to the Egyptian Government. He continued his advance by steamer, occupied al Dabba on the 24th and Marawi (Merowe) on 26 September.

The Khalifa's military losses in the Dongola campaign were of comparatively limited value, but the Sirdar's success raised the morale of the invading army. In spite of its superiority it had entered the battle in low spirits, on account of the terrible reputation of the Mahdiya's victorious armies.

The Khalifa now decided to make preparations for a decisive battle. This was to be the battle of 'Atbara.

1　There are conflicting reports about wad Bishara's retreat from Dongola to al Dabba. 'Ali al Mahdi has told the full story of the conspiracy, led by Musa'd Qaydum, 'Abd al Baqi 'Abd al Wakil and others. In the letters sent by wad Bishara to the Khalifa from al Matamma giving details of the events of the previous few days, wad Bishara declined, even though he was exposed to the charge of cowardice, to incriminate others and told the Khalifa only under pressure and after excuses. 'Your servant . . . does not need to take up the time of his lord with complaints about the integrity of the brethren with regard to what he suffered from them.'

The withdrawal affected his reputation, for there spread in Omdurman songs that accused wad Bishara of fleeing from the field of battle.

CHAPTER SIX

The Artery of Iron

THE railway line followed the invading army step by step in the Nile campaign. In terms of medals, glory and casualties the harvest of the campaign amounted to very little. But Kitchener's lasting achievement, the desert railway, still survives after all these years.

After Dongola fell, the Sirdar obtained permission to take a short leave, went to London and persuaded the British Government to let him continue the advance to Omdurman. He returned to Marawi in December, 1896. His main problem was his long supply line. He had three alternative routes. The first was to advance from al Dabba across the Bayuda Desert to al Matamma and then to Khartoum following the route of the Relief Expedition in 1885. He would rely on camels in the desert crossing while the steamers followed the Nile.

The second choice was to extend his maritime supply lines to Sawakin and then by land to Berber.

The third possibility was to rely entirely on his river supply line, though he would still need to use camels where the fourth and fifth cataracts obstructed the passage of the steamers.

A fourth plan exercised the Sirdar's imagination. This was to extend the railway line from Aswan to Kusha, then to the east from Halfa across the desert directly to Abu Hamad and then south to Berber. His railway line would thus extend from Cairo to 'Atbara. The final advance during the Nile flood would be with combined river and land forces.

The Sirdar sought the technical advice of military and engineering authorities. The engineers unanimously declared that such an extension of the railway was impossible. The military experts deemed the idea crazy. The Sirdar ignored them and resolved to go ahead.

The railway line began to be built from Halfa over the desert at the rate of half a mile a day. The rate improved after workers and equipment were transferred that had been employed on the Kirma extension.

Through sandstorms and the scorching desert sun the line inched forward. The means of its growth, wood and iron, and the means of the workers' life, food and water, were alike transported on trolleys. The iron track became their only link with the outside world. Any interruption of the iron artery would mean their perishing in the desert of thirst and hunger.

Abu Hamad, the final objective of the desert railway line was now the northern limit of the Khalifa's domain, but he placed no great value on the town.

The Abu Hamad garrison, under command of the *amir* Muhammad al Zayn, was not strengthened beyond its 800 men – 250 of the *jihadiya*, 150 cavalry and 400 armed with swords only. They had no more than 300 rifles among them. Muhammad al Zayn's instructions were to stand firm if the advance was by infantry only but to withdraw to Berber if the advance was by both steamers and infantry.

By the end of July the railway line had crossed half the desert on the way to Abu Hamad. Muhammad al Zayn was not content with a passive defensive role and sent out raiding parties. Some clashed with the Sirdar's scouts to the south-west as they approached from Marawi. Others harassed the battalions of railwaymen in the north.

On 27 July the Sirdar instructed Colonel Hunter, commander of the infantry, to advance and occupy Abu Hamad. Hunter's force consisted of the 3rd Egyptian battalion, the 9th, 10th and 11th Sudanese battalions, a squadron of cavalry and an artillery battery. In addition, 140 'Ababda tribesmen led by 'Abd al 'Azim Husayn Khalifa joined them from al Murat. Hunter moved from Marawi on 29 July and was in sight of Abu Hamad on 6 August.

The mud houses of Abu Hamad stretched along the river for 600 yards to a depth of 150 yards, sloping down to the river and overlooking a plain that inclined gently to the east for 200 yards. On a small hill, some thirty feet high, on the far side of the plain were three sentry towers that had been built in Gordon's time.

When the scouts reported the enemy's approach to Muhammad al Zayn he realized from their size and weaponry that he was too weak to attack, so then he decided to dig in in the outskirts of the town.[1] He dug trenches between the towers and extended the defences to the east. The small number of his firearms and men did not allow him to cover every approach from the eastern plain, but his position was too important to abandon altogether for if the enemy occupied it they would be able to destroy the town with their cannons and machine guns. Muhammad al Zayn thus conceived a defensive plan in two stages. The first stage had as its objective a large number of enemy casualties in the eastern plain. His men would then withdraw to the town itself and fight the enemy house by house and street by street. He knew in advance that he would be fighting a losing battle.

At dawn on 7 August Hunter approached Abu Hamad on a broad front from the east, after describing a wide arc in the desert. The 9th Sudanese battalion was on the right, then a battery of cannons, then the 3rd Egyptian battalion and then the 10th and 11th Sudanese. The cannons opened fire at 0600. Muhammad al Zayn ordered the *jihadiya* to hold their fire. For several critical moments, as the enemy advanced towards them, they showed remarkable restraint. When the enemy was only 100 yards away, Muhammad al Zayn ordered his men to open fire. The defenders rained bullets on the attacking soldiers, but the few slow-firing Remington rifles were not enough to check the broad onrush of the assault. He then ordered a retreat to the second line of defence. Each defender barricaded himself in a house and awaited the enemy. Soon the attackers had crossed the open ground and a terrible battle took place within the houses and alleys, lasting for two hours. Hunter was eventually able to occupy the town and the way was opened up for the railway to Abu Hamad.

The enemy suffered twenty dead and sixty wounded in the battle of Abu Hamad. For the defenders, however, there was devastation: 500 dead and 300 wounded as well as the capture of their brave commander.

The railway reached Abu Hamad on 31 October, 1897. This was a great triumph for the Sirdar and a moral defeat for those who had scorned his idea. After this the line began to push forwards towards Berber. When the *amir* al Zaki 'Uthman, the Khalifa's Governor in Berber, heard that Abu Hamad had fallen, and that the Sirdar was advancing towards him, he sought help from the Khalifa in Omdurman and from the *amir* Mahmud in al Matamma. But before his letters were received his soldiers had mutinied and he withdrew to the south and joined Mahmud at al Matamma.

As soon as the Khalifa was persuaded that he should evacuate the whole of Dongola, he decided to rally his forces for a final decisive encounter. However, the only military forces able to stand up to the enemy were the Omdurman garrison and the army of the west. He wrote to the *amir* Mahmud asking him to come to Omdurman urgently. They consulted together and Mahmud returned to the west to recruit all men capable of bearing arms and march them to Omdurman.

Mahmud spent almost a year recruiting men in Darfur and Kordofan. The central part of the Baqqara belt became the main recruiting area. As soon as the roads were dry enough after the rainy season he brought his army, and behind them a vast number of women and children, eastwards. Many deserted as they moved away from their homelands.

The Khalifa now decided to send Mahmud's army north because he thought that al Matamma would be the site of the coming battle, on account of its strategic position at the meeting point of all the roads leading to Omdurman. He believed at this time that Kitchener would follow the path of the Relief Expedition and cut across the Bayuda Desert to al Matamma. The Khalifa knew, as indeed everybody in Omdurman knew from experience, of the brutal nature of Mahmud's army – Baqqara, *jihadiya* and western tribes, who were accustomed to take what they wanted by force. He also knew the pride of the Ja'li and was apprehensive of a clash between the two. He therefore decided that al Matamma should be evacuated in order to accommodate the army. So 'Abd Allah wad Sa'd was summoned to Omdurman and ordered to effect the evacuation.

While Mahmud was in Omdurman he received a letter, dated 23 June, 1897, from his commanders in the north reporting that 'Abd Allah had refused to evacuate al Matamma. He also heard that 'Abd Allah had defected from the cause of the Mahdiya and was resolved to fight against them.

Mahmud saw that this revolt would have a serious impact on the very existence of the Mahdiya in the north, as well as threatening his lines of communication. He ordered his commanders not to enter al Matamma and to do nothing until he arrived. He then hurried there, sending a group of scouts ahead to arrange a meeting between him and 'Abd Allah. This caused further delay and annoyed the Khalifa, for he wished Mahmud to suppress this lesser opposition swiftly in order to concentrate his energies on the main enemy. He criticized Mahmud's delay and ordered him to crush the movement at once. 'Tales and unfavourable rumours have been reaching us,' he wrote to Mahmud. 'Some say that you have become a scribbler and are corresponding with 'Abd Allah guaranteeing his safety when he is not worth it. Some say that 'Abd Allah has barricaded himself in his town and that you are unable to reach him. Some say that the menfolk have threatened to come and see you. All these reports and rumours are caused by your neglecting to deal with him. When this reaches you resolve the army's problem at once and despatch the traitor by your spear.'

Mahmud dallied no longer and made for al Matamma with his army at full speed.

'Abd Allah gathered his tribe together in the town and told them that he was determined not to leave al Matamma but to resist Mahmud's army.[2]

He then prepared to deal with Mahmud from within the houses of the town. Most of the guns were facing south, the direction from which Mahmud was expected to come. Their fire would be directed from embrasures in the walls of the houses.[3] About fifty of the enemy fell in the first few minutes. But the unequal battle was soon settled. Mahmud stormed the houses and the massacre of al Matamma began. The issue, according to Mahmud's own estimate, was decided in a quarter of an hour.

When Mahmud camped his army on the banks of the Nile he left 2,000 corpses in the town.

For months on end they waited in al Matamma, suffering from hunger. Mahmud submitted plan after plan to the Khalifa as the Sirdar's steamers relentlessly advanced from Berber to harass him. He himself complained to the Khalifa of his inability to control the behaviour of his huge army, or to prevent them from pestering the local people. He ultimately sent all the womenfolk back to Omdurman by steamer.

There followed a long series of complaints about the behaviour of his army, about depredations and desertions. He requested reinforcements and also rations for his men. His letters teemed with ideas and plans for dealing with the invasion.

Mahmud was convinced that the enemy would come by the desert route from al Dabba to al Matamma. He therefore refrained from moving north lest a desert march by the enemy cut off his contact with Omdurman. He was not alone in this idea, for the Khalifa shared the same conviction. Memories of the Relief Expedition were not far from people's minds and some of the Sirdar's forces were still scattered between al Dabba and Marawi.

When al Zaki 'Uthman in Berber sought help and reinforcements or, failing that, permission to join him at Matamma, Mahmud wrote to the Khalifa for advice. He suggested that he move north to defend Berber and the Khalifa gave his consent. Here for the first time we find the Khalifa considering the possibility of the Sirdar coming by a route other than the desert route. He ordered Mahmud to advance at once and to engage the enemy there. Reinforcements would be sent from Omdurman. Mahmud spent the next two months waiting for the arrival of those reinforcements.

On 7 August, after Abu Hamad fell, Mahmud wrote to the Khalifa to say that he would relieve Berber at once, but it took him more than ten days to get his army across the river. The Khalifa ordered him to set out at once. On 21 August Mahmud reported the mutiny of the Berber garrison and the evacuation of the city. He apologized, feeling personally responsible for the fall of Berber. He went on to admit quite frankly that his army did not want to go north. The Khalifa tried to reassure his young cousin, assuring him of his absolute confidence in his courage and loyalty.

Although the fall of Berber was a serious blow to the Khalifa, he at once worked out a new plan. The alternative to Berber was the Sabaluqa (Shabluka) area, an area that offered much the same defensive advantages as the rapids near Berber. Furthermore the problems of supply would be easier because it was nearer Omdurman. The Khalifa suggested to Mahmud that he make his stand there. Mahmud rejected the new plan. Any withdrawal from al Matamma towards Omdurman would, he thought, have a most harmful effect on the morale of his men and would lead to further desertions.

Finally the promised reinforcements arrived, under the most illustrious surviving commander of the Mahdiya, the *amir* Osman Digna. He brought 4,000 men, a force that had been involved in continuous campaigning in recent years. Mahmud had asked him to join him at al Matamma but Osman Digna made no attempt to do so until personally directed by the Khalifa. But the extra numbers only added to Mahmud's troubles, for now there was the problem of a divided command.

The Khalifa also wrote to Mahmud counselling tact in his dealings with Osman Digna, who was the senior *amir*. 'He accepted the call of the Mahdiya before you.' Osman Digna had long been a commander and an independent ruler in eastern Sudan. He was not used to taking orders from anybody except the Khalifa or the Mahdi.

There was soon a dispute between the young commander and the old warrior. After the start of the march in February towards the Sirdar, now at 'Atbara, Mahmud clung to the Nile and received the brunt of the shells fired from Kitchener's steamers. Mahmud's plan was then to advance alongside the river and to attack the Sirdar directly at 'Atbara. Osman Digna, on the other hand, suggested an indirect approach: they should leave the Nile at al 'Aliab, describe a broad arc, cross the River 'Atbara, and then advance on the Sirdar. His proposed route would avoid the attention of the steamers. The army would be able to rely for provisions on the *dum* trees that covered the area. Mahmud referred the dispute to the Khalifa who backed Osman Digna. So they left the Nile at al 'Aliab and struck east to the 'Atbara.

Mahmud's march was exhausting. At a single stretch they covered forty miles in thirty hours, suffering from both hunger and thirst in the desert crossing. As they approached the 'Atbara a new dispute flared up between the two *amirs*. Osman Digna thought that they should move further to the east until they reached Adarama. This would place the enemy in a difficult psychological position. The Sirdar would be reluctant to advance south to Omdurman, leaving behind a large force that might threaten his flank and his line of communication. By advancing up the 'Atbara Kitchener would have to abandon his flotilla, his strongest arm. Mahmud, however, did not listen to Osman Digna. Nor did he refer the matter to the Khalifa. Instead he turned left towards the enemy. When he reached al Nukhayla (Nakheila) he selected his defensive position, but again there was controversy. Osman Digna had explained to Mahmud that a position near the main course of the Nile and near 'Atbara would make it easy for the Sirdar to surprise them after a long march of a single night. A defensive position among the dry *dum* trees would expose them to the danger of fires from the explosions of the Sirdar's shells. The position on low ground was furthermore most vulnerable.

Mahmud ignored Osman and built a *zariba* facing north-west with one side of it just touching the dry River 'Atbara. It was a *zariba* of thorns surrounding an almost circular area of 1,000 yards diameter. It was covered with *dum* trees, grass huts and tents. Fifty yards inside it, trenches were dug for the riflemen. Embrasures were built for the seven cannons, distributed round the circular defences.

Mahmud distributed his forces in the following way: Al 'Ata Usul's and 'Abd al Qadir's *rub's* were in the forward position in the north-west where an attack from the enemy was expected. Then, going in a clockwise direction round the *zariba*, there were two cannons, then 'Ali al Sanusi's *rub'*. On the east was al Bishara Rayda and Muhammad Fadl Allah with two Krupp cannons. Furthest from the place of expected attack was Osman Digna. To the west of him was al Fadl Adam and Salah Abu with a mounted cannon between them. Then the *rub's* of Muhammad al Zaki 'Uthman, Muhammad wad Bishara and 'Isa Zakariya. And so back to al 'Ata again.

The minor role assigned to Osman Digna is explained either by him refusing to take a major part in a battle he already feared was lost or by Mahmud deliberately giving him a subordinate position out of pique.

Mahmud paused, full of anxiety. He heard news of the advance of the steamers to the south. They had reached Shandi where his grain was stored. The enemy occupied the town.

Intelligence reports reached the Sirdar that the Khalifa was preparing a great army in Omdurman. Kitchener felt that his recent victories were but bait to draw him south into a trap, especially now that the Nile was low.

His first plan was to wait until the Nile rose before he began his march to Omdurman. He had missed the chance of the 1897 flood because the railway had not yet reached Berber. But now the Khalifa was taking the initiative. Wingate's intelligence sources made it clear that a huge army was mobilizing in Omdurman. The personality of the commander, Mahmud, and the massacre at al Matamma indicated that this time he would have to face a real battle. In spite of overwhelming superiority in equipment, firearms and supplies, his confidence in his army began to waver and he requested London to send further military assistance, however small. London agreed to send one brigade.

After he had occupied Berber, Kitchener was content to wait for the railway line and to advance with it. He constructed a workshop at 'Atbara for the steamers which were brought by rail in parts, and there repeated his successful experiment at Kusha of by-passing the cataracts and the rapids. The troops were assembled at Kunnur near 'Atbara. Very quickly 'Atbara grew from a small administrative post to a huge military camp of 16,000 men. When it was reported that Mahmud had left the Nile for the desert the Sirdar decided to go forward and occupy Ras al Hudi on the 'Atbara at the point where it was expected that Mahmud would reach the river. Then the Sirdar hesitated. He went so far as to seek Cromer's advice as to whether he should attack Mahmud or wait to be attacked. Cromer replied testily that the decision was his and that he was the fittest man to judge the situation.

Not content with the accuracy of the information Wingate provided about Mahmud's *zariba*, the Sirdar sent some of his own staff – Hunter, Maxwell, commander of the Sudanese brigade, Long, commander of the artillery, and Broadwood, commander of the Egyptian horse – on a reconnaissance on the Thursday morning, 5 April.

Scouts informed Mahmud of the advance of a force of the enemy's cavalry and he quickly improvised a plan to deal with them. Mahmud aimed to lure the cavalry into the front of the *zariba* where the *rub'* of 'Ali al Sanusi lay hidden by a sudden depression and where another group of horsemen were concealed. The enemy cavalry would then be surrounded.

The cavalry vanguard looked down on the *zariba* and saw before them horsemen taking up their positions. Mahmud's cannons opened fire from the *zariba* but the commander of the artillery seized the opportunity to record its exact position. The artillery followed the horsemen, who turned to their right and then more horsemen from the *zariba* appeared. Cannons and machine guns opened fire and 'Ali al Sanusi's *rub'* suddenly emerged from its hiding place. The pincers began to close in on the Sirdar's cavalry. They were not able to make good their escape until their cannons and machine guns had opened fire. This checked the assault, but not before they had lost ten dead and seven wounded.

The Sirdar started the advance from his camp on the evening of 5 April. He stopped at 2100 after covering half the distance. He resumed the march at 0100 and was joined by his mounted forces at 0200. At 0300 he stopped, as the dim lights of the *zariba* could just be seen.

The Sirdar's brigades took up a broad assault formation in the shape of an arc more than 1,500 yards long. The horsemen guarded the left flank. Maxwell's Sudanese brigade was on the right, MacDonald's Sudanese brigade in the centre and Gatacre's British brigade on the left.

Kitchener's assault plan was basically simple. After an initial bombardment by the heavy artillery, the assault troops would go forward in two sections. The first section would tear down the *zariba* with their hands, under cover of the cannon and rifle fire. This would force the enemy to keep their heads down as the *zariba* was being opened up. The detachments behind them would then storm the *zariba*. The first part was made up of up to ten companies from each brigade spread out in a long line, one man deep. Behind them were the hand-to-hand fighters, prepared to rush through the gaps. The Sudanese brigades had ten companies each in the broad front line, and the British had eight. Most of them carried blankets to put over the thorns of the *zariba*.

As the first grey streaks of dawn filtered through the *dum* trees, Mahmud was busy organizing his position. Riflemen rushed to the trenches. Behind them massed those with swords and spears. Men were moved to strengthen the *rub'* of al 'Ata Usul. On the left the gates of the *zariba* opened up and the horsemen, led by Bakhit al Namuri, trotted out. They deployed to the left. Mahmud withdrew to the centre of the *zariba* to direct the battle.

At first light the Sirdar's five batteries and all his machine guns opened fire on the *zariba*. The bombardment continued for an hour. Trees, tents and men were blasted. The defenders endured it stolidly, ducking down inside their trenches until the enemy bore down on the *zariba*. With great restraint they held their fire until the enemy were 300 yards away. The defenders' fire was effective and steady in spite of the heavy bombardment to which they were subjected. The *rub'* of al 'Ata Usul was able, in the moments the assaulting force took to cross the fifty yards between the *zariba* and the trenches, to fell many of the Sirdar's soldiers. Gaps in the *zariba* were opened up and a mass of troops poured in. Hand-to-hand fighting broke out and the battle was fought trench by trench, hut by hut. The defenders were driven down. They fell back and returned fire. The *rub'* of al 'Ata Usul which had borne the main brunt of the assault was totally destroyed. The fighting lasted for more than an hour, a ferocious business taking place in a circle only 1,000 yards across, but with 16,000 men, shoving and pushing, bayonets raised high, dripping with blood.

Of the defenders, 7,000 were buried where they fell, refusing to yield an inch. The trenches were filled to the brim with dead.

The 11th Sudanese battalion advanced to Mahmud's head-quarters with casualties falling one after another in the face of the defenders' fire. They killed the guard at the headquarters and found Mahmud with his *furwa* laid out, facing Mecca and awaiting death. He was taken prisoner.

The assault forces finally reached the river bed on the other side. Only about 4,000 men escaped from Osman Digna's forces. The Sirdar lost less than 600 dead and wounded.

The defeat at 'Atbara had far-reaching military con-sequences. In the first place the Khalifa lost no less than 11,000 soldiers, killed or injured, or who deserted to distant parts of the country and did not return to Omdurman.[4] Many rifles and a battery of cannons also fell into the hands of the enemy. Secondly the morale of the Khalifa's army in Omdurman was severely shaken, after the survivors of 'Atbara arrived and described the enemy's weapons and especially the new, lethal machine guns.

Morale was further shaken when details of the massacre at al Matamma spread up and down the country. Some of the Khalifa's army began to work against him. Groups of 'Friendly Arabs' who defected and fought in the Sirdar's ranks were formed. Most of them were Ja'liyin, who wanted to avenge their tribe that had been decimated.

The Khalifa did not feel confident of the loyalty of the people in the area north of Omdurman. This and the difficulty of provisioning any large force in the north persuaded him to abandon the region.

After the battle the Sirdar summoned the captive com-mander. The *amir* Mahmud was brought to him in chains. A tall Arab, graceful and fine featured, he stared proudly before him without turning to right or left.

The Sirdar, on horseback, asked him: 'Why did you come here to burn and kill?'

Mahmud answered: 'I obeyed my orders as you obey yours.' He answered the other questions calmly and coolly, winning the respect of all who witnessed the encounter. When he was finally dragged from the Sirdar, he shouted in his face, 'You will pay for all this at Omdurman. Compared with the Khalifa, I am but a leaf.'

1 Shuqayr relates that a letter reached Muhammad al Zayn from his wife in Omdurman urging him to stand firm. She told him that the women of Omdurman were lampooning wad Bishara in their songs for his rout at Dongola. 'I will not live with you,' she said, 'amid such scorn and censure.' Muhammad al Zayn was thereby persuaded to fight till death or victory.

2 The expression that 'Abd Allah used when he refused to leave al Matamma was 'Nimr's escape from Shandi still lacerates my soul' – a proverbial saying. The flight of al Mak Nimr from Shandi and the army of the Defterdar still evoked memories.

3 Mahmud in a letter to the Khalifa (24 June, 1897) described the manner in which 'Abd Allah wad Sa'd fought, saying that 'Each one of them was fighting individually, . . . in accordance with the precept that "If you die protecting your women and children, then you are martyrs indeed".'

4 'Abd Allah Ibrahim, in his thesis, reckons the number of dead and wounded was much more than the 3,000 claimed in the intelligence report. He alleges that Kitchener deliberately concealed the figures, for he feared press attacks against him. He did not want the slaughter at 'Atbara to mar his triumph at Berber. He was aware of the storm of public opinion at the time over the Armenian massacres and feared that the Radicals, who had opposed the Sirdar's campaign from the start, would make trouble. Kitchener's primary aim in fighting the battle was to destroy Mahmud's army and to prevent it from returning to Omdurman to fight him again. He had no wish to gain possession of any strategic position, as had been the case at Abu Hamad.

CHAPTER SEVEN

The Commanders

Osman Digna (1841–1926)

Osman Digna was the only commander at Karari who inflicted an effective and painful blow on the enemy with the trap he laid for the 21st Lancers. To the end Osman Digna was the Mahdiya's expert in placing successful ambushes, in impeding and penetrating the solid ranks of the British. His activities forced Britain to garrison Sawakin with two brigades for fifteen years after they had withdrawn from the Sudan.

Osman Digna came from the Diqnab tribe, Anatolian in origin. Their Kurdish forbears migrated from Diyarbekir to Sawakin many centuries earlier when the town was directly subject to the Ottoman Sultanate. In his youth he studied Islamic Law, theology and astronomy. For a while he practised his family's trade, but his political feelings led him to oppose the Turkish occupation. Often Sawakin merchants could be seen murmuring against the Government openly in the *suq*.

His hatred of the occupation reached its peak on a trading expedition to Darfur. On their way back they were suddenly attacked by Government forces who impounded the whole caravan. They released the merchants, restoring their merchandise to all except Osman Digna. He had been insolent in his replies to the authorities and for this he was detained for trial. But that night he took advantage of the confusion that reigned in the camp, as a result of a heavy rainstorm, to slip away.

He fell into the hands of the Government a second time and

all his property and that of his family was confiscated. One day when he was sitting in front of his shop somebody began to talk of the Mahdi. Osman Digna listened to him and was eager to learn more. At the end of the conversation he left his shop, still open, and gave it no further thought. He set off west for el Obeid where he met the Mahdi to whom he pledged his allegiance. The Mahdi straightway appointed him *amir* over Eastern Sudan.

But fanning the flames of revolt in Eastern Sudan was not as easy as that, for the tribes were divided in their allegiance. In the south they owed allegiance to the Mirghaniya sect. In the north, their allegiances varied. Osman Digna showed a letter of appointment to the Shaykh al Tahir al Majdhub at al Damir, a man of great religious influence in the east of Sudan. He gave Osman Digna a warm welcome and extended his protection to him, giving him the support he needed.

One of Osman Digna's great skills was keeping his army cohesive. His penetration of the English squares was remarkable, but his withdrawal and his resumption of the struggle elsewhere was more practical. During his interrogation under arrest, Shuqayr asked him, 'Why did you always leave the battlefield and not fight on to the end?' He replied, 'In order to fight again. Had I done what you suggest, I would have had to make my army last for ever in the first battle. I was in twenty battles and was victorious in eight and was defeated in eight. If I had remained on the field until after I was quite sure I had lost the battle, then I would not have achieved my long-term aims.' This iron resolution remained with him until the last moments of his life.

It is clear that Osman Digna was aware of the importance of psychological factors in warfare and how to exploit them. When his soldiers were tired after continuous battles and long marches, he used to spread rumours that the English were fleeing and had been defeated, thereby rallying his men and rekindling their enthusiasm.

He was famous for his oratory, and never tired of delivering fiery speeches to his men. These speeches used to last five or six hours.

Osman Digna's reputation attracted stories. He had the

capacity for great physical endurance; this is recalled by many people. He would often walk for hundreds of miles carrying his weapons and also the weapons of those of his men too weary to walk. He was also known for both overeating and being able to fast.

His loyalty to the Mahdi and the Khalifa was absolute and he used to display literal obedience to their orders, while the Ta'aisha *amirs* argued with the Khalifa. By contrast he awaited his orders, which he would then carry out without delay or argument, and at times literally. When food was ready, for example, and the Khalifa called on those present to eat, they would all eat and then begin to talk, but Osman Digna continued to eat until the Khalifa bade him, laughingly, to stop eating.

It is also said that when the Khalifa concluded his council of war and sent each of the *amirs* to make their way to the front, saying 'Quick march', Osman set off and carried on walking until his entourage caught up with him some miles from Omdurman, having searched for him for a long time. His object was to demonstrate that orders were given to be obeyed and not debated.

His submissiveness did not prevent him from offering his opinion whenever he found fault with the Khalifa's instructions. He declined the *'imalaship* of Dongola after the death of al Nujumi, explaining that he was a stranger there, unused to the atmosphere of dissension in the north. He preferred to deal with the front at Sawakin and felt that he alone could manage the headstrong Beja tribesmen. He also challenged Mahmud wad Ahmad on the way to 'Atbara and submitted only after receiving a personal order from the Khalifa.

Osman Digna was aware of the effectiveness of attacking the enemy from the rear. He quickly learned the strong and weak points of the enemy and where to concentrate his fire. He displayed these characteristics repeatedly in his campaigns in the east.

He also appreciated the hidden weakness in a square's rear line. For whenever he directed his strong first assault at the rear side and penetrated it, the enemy found themselves between two lines of fire. They were confused, not knowing whether to change direction and to direct their fire inside the square or whether to join up with the front line. Osman's tactic was the quickest way of getting to the animals and administrative units inside the square. The front line would find itself isolated. When this muddle occurred the force lost its cohesiveness and would split into small groups which were destroyed, one by one.

Osman Digna's tactics were best suited to a particular kind of terrain and to certain circumstances. They were most effective with a moving army. He used to launch his attacks when the enemy were on the march or while they were leaving a fortified position. The rough Red Sea Hills with their narrow passes enabled him to achieve the element of surprise necessary for the success of his sudden swoops and for preventing the defenders from realigning their forces.

Because of its sensitive position Sawakin was always defended by the British themselves. Osman Digna thus faced many British generals and gained for himself valuable battle experience with well trained armies. He was the Khalifa's most experienced commander.

After his capture Osman Digna lived on to the age of 85. He spent most of his later years under arrest at Wadi Halfa. He allowed Shuqayr to interrogate him but nobody else. To the end he maintained an unbending faith in the Mahdi's Call.

The Amir Ya'qub (1855–1898)

'Woe, woe unto him who takes on Ya'qub with evil intent.' So said everybody who lived at the time of the Khalifa's rule in Omdurman, for Ya'qub, the Khalifa's brother, was the second man in the state, the power behind the scenes and the engineer of the Ta'aisha oligarchy.

Although a Ta'aisha, Ya'qub was noted for his popularity with the people of Omdurman. He was kind, soft-spoken and tactful. He was proverbial for his charity. His seeming lack of tribal prejudice led him to intervene in disputes and to redress ills that his tribe had caused. He did his best to reconcile the tribes of the west and the riverain tribes. He was also the most cultured of the Khalifa's relations. Their father had interested himself in the education of the second son and had planned for him to take over his religious position. His administrative efficiency was apparent when he took on the job of the Khalifa's Chief-of-Staff. He kept a complete record of every individual in the force – the *amirs*, detachments and their personnel, arms returns and ammunition production. Furthermore he was the *amir* of the Black Standard.

It is to Ya'qub that credit is due for transforming revolutionary troops into an organized army. The Mahdi had laid down the broad lines of the army organization at Qadir. The Khalifa reorganized it so that it could defeat Hicks and lay siege to Khartoum. But Ya'qub was the man who transformed the basic administration.

Ya'qub was responsible for internal security and for the protection of the capital against conspiracies. In this he was excellent as *agent provocateur* and as foiler of plots. As an innovator he was tactful and in the advisory councils and the Council of Law used to take a back seat when important matters were discussed, not talking much, stimulating other people to express their opinions. His forte was not public debate, but rather discussing matters with his brother in the long hours of night when they settled things together. Another council would then ratify the Khalifa's policies.

Ya'qub was a man of personal humility, wholly devoted to his brother. This sometimes took the most self-effacing forms. He used to be seen standing at the Khalifa's door all night waiting until the Khalifa came out to dawn prayers. This was because the Khalifa used often to summon him after evening prayers and forget to tell the doorman to leave the gate of his private wing open. Ya'qub preferred to wait until sunrise rather than knock at the door after the Khalifa had retired.

Ya'qub had taken part in the battles of Shaykan and Khartoum. His responsibilities regarding the organization of the army over a long period kept him in close touch with the soldiers. On the other hand his military judgment was poor and his experience limited. This was a consequence of the iron curtain imposed on the country by the Khalifa for thirteen years. Both brothers failed to appreciate the technical developments in the armaments of European states and of the modern

Egyptian army.

The last days of the Mahdist state saw a partial decline in Ya'qub's influence, coinciding with the emergence of the fortunes of 'Uthman Shaykh al Din, the Khalifa's son. This was particularly noticeable after Shaykh al Din was removed from his post as *qadi* to take over the leadership of the *mulazimin*. Rivalry then developed between Ya'qub and his nephew. The feud spread to the Black Standard and the *mulazimin*. 'Uthman began to filch the cream of the soldiers and weapons of the Black Standard. He even did this during the parades, relying on his father's influence. Ya'qub felt that a tactful silence would be less embarrassing to his brother than protest.

'Uthman Shaykh al Din (1873–1899)

'Uthman Shaykh al Din was the Khalifa's eldest son. From his childhood 'Uthman lived in Omdurman. He underwent none of the rigours of life in the country and was not toughened as the rest of his tribe had been. Even his accent was that of an Omdurmani, free from the Baqqara dialect.

His father paid much attention to his education and upbringing and chose learned men of the Sudan to teach him. He was indeed an intelligent young man. When Shuqayr visited his house after the fall of Omdurman he found a huge collection of books, the choice of which pointed to a person of learning and taste. As a young man he was ordered by his father to join the Council of Law. This helped to mature his judgment.

He is also said to have spent most of his time with the people of Omdurman rather than with his own tribesmen. The elders were annoyed at this and recommended his transfer to the army.

'Uthman tried his father sorely. The Khalifa did his best to control him, and arranged an early marriage to a daughter of his brother Ya'qub. But marriage did not keep him away from dissolute company. His nocturnal adventures and his parties were the talk of Omdurman. His father heard all and was furious, ordering him to be placed under house arrest near his own residence.

'Uthman was young and frivolous, but in general his faults

met with paternal indulgence. For it seems that 'Uthman charmed everybody, including his father, with his delightful manners and his gravity in dealing with public matters. But he lacked any direct military experience. Unlike the *amirs* of his age, such as Ibrahim al Khalil, or Mahmud wad Ahmad, he neither led a military mission nor undertook the administration of a separate region.

This was no drawback at first since the original purpose of the *mulazimin* was to protect the Khalifa and to guarantee internal security. But when their strength increased, and most of the best firearms were added to them, the force became qualified to undertake military tasks against any external enemy and it needed a more experienced general than 'Uthman Shaykh al Din, whose only qualification was being the Khalifa's son.

Unlike many of his comrades, Shaykh al Din's culture was contemporary. This enabled him to appreciate world politics beyond his country's frontiers. He was flexible, even advocating a policy of exploiting conflicting imperialist interests and of cooperation with France.

Ibrahim al Khalil (1874–1898)

This young *amir* who led the first attack against Kitchener was, apart from Osman Digna, the ablest military strategist in the field. Ibrahim al Khalil, in spite of his youth, had a mature judgment which did not always meet with ready ears. But his ideas were of the utmost relevance during the Khalifa's successive war councils in the last months before the battle of Karari.

Ibrahim al Khalil was born in the land of the Rizayqat and was a cousin of the Khalifa. Before he was ten years old the Khalifa summoned him to come with his brothers Mahmud, Isma'il and 'Abd al Rahman, to live with him. He supervised their education himself and they grew up as companions of his son, 'Uthman Shaykh al Din. Ibrahim became the most modest and genial of the Ta'aisha *amirs*. He grew up free from tribal prejudice and mingled only with mature men of learning. As a soldier, he devoted the energies of his youth to training and improving his mind. Notwithstanding his youth he was soon admitted to the Khalifa's advisory council.

When he was twenty he commanded a campaign to suppress a rebellion in the Nuba mountains. This he did with startlingly quick success in spite of the rugged nature of the mountains and the strength of the rebels.

After Ibrahim had proved his mettle, the Khalifa gave him the leadership of the al Kara army. In spite of the experience of the Kara garrison Ibrahim continued to supervise, in person, their training, which started daily immediately after morning prayers and continued until sunset in the open ground east of the Mahdi's tomb. Many times Ibrahim with his tall slouching figure would inspect his soldiers while the Khalifa could be seen sitting in the afternoon on his *angarayb* fingering his prayer-beads, watching these training sessions. From time to time he would summon Ibrahim and draw his attention to some point. The latter would go off and rectify any fault at once.

There are two important aspects of the personality of Ibrahim al Khalil. The first is that, in spite of his balance and maturity, he would not suffer fools gladly. When the suggestion he put forward for defending Sabaluqa was under discussion and other speakers denigrated his ideas, he did not try to impose his opinion. Instead he stormed out of the council. On another occasion violent exchanges flared up between him and 'Uthman Shaykh al Din on the eve of a battle, when the subject of a night attack was discussed. Perhaps it was his impetuousness that led him to attack so desperately at Karari, belying his reputation for tactical efficiency.

Secondly there developed a bitter enmity between him and his cousin, Shaykh al Din, which almost precipitated armed conflict between the *mulazimin* and the Kara garrison on one occasion.

'Uthman Azraq (1845–1898)

> '. . . wicked Osman Azrak, faithful unto death.'
>
> Winston S. Churchill, *The River War*

The task of keeping watch on the northern frontier fell to

'Uthman Azraq. Reports of the Egyptian Intelligence devoted long pages to his activities. Much money and effort was spent in resisting the dozens of lightning raids. His military record boasts no fewer than a hundred raids within the Egyptian borders.

'Uthman Muhammad 'Isa, known as 'Uthman Azraq, was born in el Obeid where his Dongolawi family had long been settled. He originally worked as a cameleer for the government postal services between Khartoum and Darfur.

'Uthman's outposts in the north were always busy stopping caravans smuggling arms and war materials from Egypt to the Khalifa's enemies, or confronting formations of the Egyptian enemy emboldened by their victory at Tushku. But 'Uthman was not concerned with defensive policies alone. The methods he adopted in his raids reveal an instinctive understanding of the strategy of the indirect approach.

He would set out with a mounted force and go many miles in a direction opposite to his objective. When darkness fell he would change direction and make for his objective, surrounding the enemy as they relaxed their vigilance. For these methods he needed a quick, light-moving, mounted force. He and Wad al Nujumi were perhaps the only major commanders of the Mahdiya to grasp the possibilities of cavalry. 'Uthman's past as a professional cameleer and horseman was clearly relevant in his refining of the principles of lightning attacks.

To 'Uthman also goes the credit for the only damage caused to a gunboat belonging to the invading army. When he took part in the battle of al Hafir he stood behind one of the cannons aiming at the gunboat *Firka*. Three times it missed in spite of the short range. 'Uthman suspected that the Egyptian gunner, Sulayman al Damyati, was missing deliberately. He got off his horse and struck him with the flat of his sword. As the man raised his left hand to protect his face 'Uthman struck him with the blade, lopping off half the man's hand. He swore that if the gunner missed again his head would be severed from his body before the shell touched the waters of the Nile. He raised his sword in readiness. The Egyptian, blood pouring from him, fired his fourth shell. It struck the gunboat a direct hit in the boiler.

Aware of 'Uthman's efficiency and courage, at Karari the Khalifa exempted him from the general practice of army high command. Usually the influence and efforts of each *amir* in collecting troops and horses alone determined the strength of his command. When 'Uthman reached Omdurman after his withdrawal from the battle of 'Atbara his men numbered no more than thirteen. But the Khalifa detached a large part of the *mulazimin* with their firearms from the command of Shaykh al Din and placed them under the command of 'Uthman Azraq. He gave him a training ground far from Shaykh al Din and the force became a separate command in itself. Perhaps the Khalifa was attempting somehow to remove from Shaykh al Din's damaging control the complete responsibility for all the *mulazimin*.

H. H. Kitchener (1850–1916)

The young Kitchener spent his childhood on the Irish estate of his father, a retired colonel. Colonel Kitchener ran his household like a regiment, and duties were like military drill. The English family of Kitchener felt itself generally superior to the Irish people, and the boy was rarely allowed to play with Irish boys of his own age. As a result Kitchener grew up showing characteristics of haughtiness towards others and a capacity for concealing his feelings. Another feature of his personality was a detached coolness. When he pushed forward on horseback amid the carnage of Omdurman the only thing that moved him was the soldiers continuing to fire their rifles after an attack had been parried. His comment was, 'Oh God, what a waste of ammunition!' Kitchener was a general of robot-like efficiency with a fine calculating mind, a man almost without amusements or private life.

When he joined the Egyptian army Kitchener was an obscure officer, with nothing to distinguish him from his colleagues but his proficiency in Arabic, his knowledge of which qualified him for setting up an advanced post at al Dabba during the siege of Khartoum.

Throughout the years of the campaign he never confided in any of his officers, not even Wingate. But he did reveal his misgivings to Baring (later Lord Cromer), though even with Baring he exercised great caution. Wingate had repeatedly to bully Kitchener to accept information necessary to help him plan ahead.

Kitchener's service with the Engineers and his early training in administration qualified him for the command of a campaign in which the administrative aspect – the supply of water and the extension of lines of communication – was the major aspect.

The conduct of the Nile campaign was characterized by deliberation and caution, irreproachable from a logistical and administrative point of view. The British press which had raged and fumed at Wilson for his three-day delay at al Matamma in 1885, attributing the fall of Khartoum to this delay, now praised Kitchener for taking two years to get himself to Omdurman.

As Sirdar of the Egyptian army and the youngest general in the British army, Kitchener suppressed the graft and corruption which had raged in the army and succeeded in taking to the battle of Karari an army whose soldiers differed completely from those of Hicks fifteen years earlier.

Kitchener's strategic skill was particularly displayed at Karari when he saw MacDonald's brigade in difficulties. His reactions were prompt and he immediately deployed his brigades to cope with the danger. The manoeuvre succeeded and he prevented MacDonald from being cut off.

The most marked defect in the personality of Kitchener as a commander was a nervous indecisiveness. Wingate revealed afterwards that Kitchener used to suffer agonies when he had to take an important decision. He would endure several days of mental torment. He would make one decision and then some hours later would countermand it and make another. Finally he would be inspired with the right answer and his features would light up as if a heavy load had been taken off his back.

F. R. Wingate (1861–1953)

Wingate was the mastermind of the campaign. His influence could be perceived behind the slightest decision; he was behind events from beginning to end.

Wingate was an unusual kind of intelligence officer. He was not content with just analyzing events and writing reports, he also moulded and adapted them to his own ends. His influence extended indirectly, reaching as far as higher imperial policy drawn up in London. His capacious mind took in all branches of knowledge. He was noted not only as an intelligence officer but also as an historian, sociologist and as a first rate administrator.

His appearance was rather unassuming, in contrast to that of Kitchener, with his tall figure and famous moustache.

As we have seen, Cromer did not support a policy of intervention in the Sudan because of the material expense. However, Wingate presented him with a *fait accompli* by publishing three books that succeeded in winning British public opinion to his side, and by sending intelligence reports to the War Office in London. These reports were composed with great skill and were aimed at persuading influential people to accept his views. When Cromer became aware of the trap that Wingate had prepared for him, it was too late. People were mentally attuned to the reconquest of the Sudan. Cromer then went along with the course of events and gave the green light for the invasion.

If you browse through the thousands of pages of reports that Wingate prepared and sent to London over twelve years, you notice the careful long-term planning. From the beginning he foretold the decline of the power of the Khalifa. His work helped to dispel the fears of the legendary power of the Khalifa. He demonstrated this by figures derived from the interrogation of Slatin which showed that the Khalifa's military power was not insurperable.

Wingate's book, *Mahdiism and the Egyptian Sudan*, written in 1891, abounds with accurate, detailed information and testifies to there being an impressive spy network not only in Omdurman but even, at times, in the very house of the Khalifa. He succeeded in recruiting vast numbers of Sudanese to his service.

In 1889 he drafted the letter that Grenfell sent to Wad al Nujumi revealing his complete familiarity with the course of politics in the Sudan and which attempted to undermine al Nujumi's faith in the true purpose behind his being sent to Egypt.

As the campaign advanced the number of agents increased. After the battle of al Matamma, Wingate was able to take advantage of the natural desire of the Ja'liyin for revenge.

Wingate used to spend his time, in the years of the campaign, in his tent. Scores of people would go in and out – mostly prisoners and agents. In the evening he would remain by himself, sifting through the information and preparing a final report. At about midnight he would take his papers to Kitchener and the two of them would be together until the small hours.

Among the British triumvirate round whom the story of the Mahdiya turns – Cromer, Kitchener and Wingate – it is Wingate, as the specialist in the Sudan, who is the political anchorman. It is he who censors and edits the information that must go to Cromer, to the War Office and to the foreign and colonial ministers in England.

CHAPTER EIGHT
The Soldiers

'No white troops would have faced that torrent of death for five minutes but the Baggara and the blacks came on.'

G. W. Steevens.

A soldier must be a fighter and, as such, a tool which has been steeped in moral courage, enabling him to disregard death and also to adapt instinctively to the military milieu. Here lies the role that environment plays in producing different types of soldiers. This was the case with the Khalifa's forces at Omdurman. They won the respect of their enemies, while losing well over half their men in five hours. If the measure of soldiers is boundless bravery that heeds not death, we find the Khalifa's men not only heedless of death, but even regarding death as something desirable; as indeed it was, for their reward was Paradise.

To realize this one has only to note the words of survivors or the last words of the commanders and men who fell on the field of battle. The expression 'I went in search of martyrdom,' was said without affectation. This determination to die raged among the Khalifa's troops to such an extent that it contributed to the destruction of his army and perhaps allowed the enemy to pay an extremely low price for their victory. Rank after rank plunged forward, one after another, to be destroyed in the same place and in the same way. If they had seen the fruitlessness of a suicidal assault and retraced their steps to attack in a different way, it might have forced the enemy to pay a higher price.

Precipitate leadership was one cause of this phenomenon. Ibrahim al Khalil, Ya'qub and 'Uthman Azraq all charged at the head of their men, to fall the first victims of the enemy's fire. They never had a chance to stem the rush of their soldiers to certain death. Another cause was the men's own background. Quite apart from the spiritual Call, a man was traditionally a fighter before everything else. This is the case even today as we see in the folklore of the Sudan.

A great man in the Sudan was distinguished, not by wealth or success, but by personal bravery. Society was still mainly tribal. Girls, when they listened to songs at harvest time or on wedding nights, or even at funerals, used to sway to songs glorifying individual heroism.

Among the Khalifa's men there was a wide divergence in quality. The quality of the soldiers in the Black Standard, recruited from the tribes of the west, differed a great deal from that of the army of al Kara or the *mulazimin*. This was for reasons that went back sixteen years. In the garrisons of the *mulazimin* the soldier received training and regular discipline. Others had no such opportunity. Yet others received the very best and most valuable kind of training – actual battle experience.

The *mulazimin* were the best soldiers. They included the army of al Kara, former *jihadiya* of Abu 'Anja, who had received regular training under Egyptian rule as well as battle experience under able commanders. They were the only one of the Khalifa's units to receive continuous, regular training. They also received regular pay and daily rations. They were devoted to the military life, unlike other standards that were filled with irregulars, who lived with their own people most of the time and served in the militia only when summoned to war.

The Black Standard had in its ranks irregulars who were fighters only. Most of them had come to the battle straight from the fields. Few were experienced. Many veterans from the highly populated areas of Kordofan and Darfur and especially the Rizayqat had fallen in the continuous warfare in the west. Others had been killed at 'Atbara. The gaps in the Black Standard were filled by the people of Omdurman from all trades and tribes. However, there were still many from the Baqqara and other western tribes. For such people warfare and hunting were daily occupations. If they could find no reason for fighting, they would invent one. Craftwork and manual labour was – and still is – the role of the women.

The Green Standard was made up of tribesmen from the White Nile. Although the first soldiers of the Mahdi after the fall of Khartoum, they did not take part in the great campaigns of the Khalifa. Indeed they entered the battle with no more expertise than their fathers had had when they took part in those early battles.

By contrast Osman Digna's men, in general Beja, and in particular Hadendowa, were quite different. The tribes of the east, even in their local and individual fighting, were accustomed to seizing a surprise initiative. They used to infiltrate the enemy ranks and were swift at slipping away. These tactics offset their disadvantages – their numerical weakness, the quality of the British enemy they were dealing with, the rigours they suffered in total warfare, agonizing marches and heavy losses. The force from the east had had most contact with British arms and were thus most familiar with their fighting, their tactics and their firepower superiority.

One of the major objectives of the years of training was to prepare the men to obey, promptly and instinctively, their young commanders on the battlefield. Most of the young *amirs* and centurions were from leading tribal families. This guaranteed a traditional basis of loyalty and was the result of Ya'qub's deliberate policy in the appointment of the commanders.

The soldiers were physically extremely fit. On the day of the battle the infantry's speed exceeded that of the cameleers and cavalry of Broadwood among the rough stones of Karari, when they pursued them for three miles to the north and then returned over the same ground, to join in the closing stages of the battle. Their slender frames, their supple muscles, their acclimatization to the rigours of life, an absence of luxuries and also their light equipment all contributed towards their physical fitness.

Strangely enough this high standard of physical fitness was the result of a meagre and simple diet. The rations of the

Khalifa's army were almost totally based on *dhurra* in different forms. They seldom ate meat. Perhaps the only luxury was tea and there was not much of that, for few tea-makers were left in Omdurman. Instead utensils for preparing tea were taken with them to the battlefield.

Generally the Khalifa's soldiers wore a short patched *jubba* that extended to just below the knee, drawers and sandals. Some went barefoot. They used also to wear a turban. Each usually carried a sword and four short spears. The *mulazimin* carried rifles. Some carried a *rukwa* – a leather pot for water for ritual ablutions. Wealthier soldiers took their slaves with them to carry their *rukwas*, food and tea-making utensils.

Most *amirs* and commanders carried shrouds with them. These were made from a strip of cotton cloth folded up to form a bag. This meant that they were going to the battle intending to die. A few of the richer *amirs* wore chain-mail armour as worn by the Crusaders.

The English soldier was experienced in nineteenth century warfare. At Omdurman he played a limited role in the battle. His superb training, superior equipment and arms, enabled him to behave like a cool machine. The English section bore the brunt of the first assault. Their battalions fired their rifles at the army of the Mahdiya as if they were at a target practice rather than on a real battlefield. When MacDonald called for their assistance in dealing with two successive attacks, they rapidly got into formation and fired their volleys with studied accuracy.

The Egyptian soldier was basically a sturdy, physically agile Egyptian peasant. His performance contrasted greatly with that of Hicks' soldiers, whom the Baqqara horsemen had been able to put to flight.

The soldiers of the Sudanese battalions were the heroes of the enemy's side. It was MacDonald's brigade that saved the situation and bore the brunt of a three-pronged attack from the Khalifa's army, from different directions within the course of half an hour, without yielding an inch. Three of his battalions were Sudanese and one was Egyptian. Churchill was absolutely right when he said of them: 'To the faithful loyalty of a dog, he added the heart of a lion. He loved his officer, and feared nothing in the world.'

97

CHAPTER NINE

The Weapons

THE state of the Khalifa's weapons reveals most vividly the isolation of the young state from the rest of the world. More than half the Khalifa's army was armed with swords and spears. The manufacture of swords was carried out in Omdurman and many specialized in it. The scrap metal, usually old railway lines from the north, was melted down in the ironsmiths' *suq*.

Each soldier had four spears, the main one being between eight and ten feet long. This spear was the principal weapon for assault. The short spears were hurled from close range before the assault with the main spear.

The Khalifa entered the battle with about 15,000 rifles which ranged from the muzzle-loading infantry rifle to the Remington and the Martini Henry, of which last there were about 2,000. There was also a shot gun, called the *khashkhashan*, used for hunting elephants. The Remington was still considered a modern rifle, for it had a grooved barrel and was breech-loaded.

The rifles represented the real fire support of the Khalifa's army. His artillery played no great role in the battle. Furthermore, the qualities of the rifles were reflected in their performance only when they were in top condition and well-maintained, with ammunition carefully designed to suit the weapons. But the Khalifa's rifles, indeed all his weapons, suffered from two defects – a technical failing in their condition, and a tactical failing arising from the methods of individual and collective deployment.

It is well known that the Khalifa's soldiers in general never maintained their rifles at all, although they needed double the usual maintenance because of the poor quality of the gunpowder.[1] The rifles were mostly looted from the soldiers of Hicks, from Khartoum or from the Abyssinian wars, so most of them had not been maintained for years. They were not oiled to protect them from damp or from residual matter in the barrel. Consequently they lost much of their accuracy. Dust and dirt gathered over the firing pin. All this reduced the weapons' efficiency. Most of the rifles were smooth-bore models that had been made at the beginning or in the middle of the century.

Most of the soldiers used to shorten the barrels of their rifles with a saw to make them easier to carry.[2] The effect of this on accuracy and range can be imagined. Nobody knew how the catastrophic consequences of this came to be overlooked by the Khalifa and, more especially, by those who had been officers and soldiers in the former army of occupation.

One of the reasons for the victories of Abu 'Anja and al Zaki over the Ethiopians was the superiority of their weapons, both in their longer range and greater accuracy. Their rifles were still in good condition. But that was in 1888 and the subsequent ten years of neglect had told on the weapons.

The ammunition was all of local manufacture.[3] The quality was not good, although the actual manufacture of it was a considerable achievement on the part of the Khalifa. Its manufacture was not much bound by technical considerations.[4] There were no qualified engineers to supervise the precise amounts of the ingredients for each cartridge.[5] Most of them were foremen from the Egyptian régime and the allocations of material for filling each cartridge were made either from recorded stipulations or by guesswork.

The Mahdiya inherited large quantities of raw materials for the manufacture of ammunition but the continuous wars used most of them up.[6] Ya'qub was aware of the dangers of the situation and kept a large amount in reserve, giving instructions that it be saved, for he feared that it would run out. He then began to think about local production and succeeded in extracting saltpetre from the mountains of Darfur. At first the quality was excellent and the quantity abundant. But Darfur was far away and Ya'qub looked for a source nearer to Omdurman. Finally Shaykh Makki and his Fallata tribe succeeded in extracting saltpetre from the dust of Halfaya al Muluk. But there were no miners sufficiently methodical to exploit it, nor was there the necessary equipment. Saltpetre was brought from various districts to factories at Tuti, al Kamlin and Omdurman. Specimens were brought to Omdurman for testing but the quality of the saltpetre was not the same as that from Darfur, and was inferior to the store inherited from the former régime. Thus carelessness in mixing the ingredients, together with the poor quality of the raw materials, had a deleterious effect on the Khalifa's fire at Karari.[7]

The tactical failing at the collective and individual level can be dealt with briefly. There were few rifle bearers who were concerned with taking precise aim – or any aim. This was due to lack of training, but there were other reasons no less important. The tactical theory of rifle fire held by the Ansar, derived from many battles, was that rifles and small arms were not considered a weapon for killing the enemy or for inflicting losses. They were used for providing fire support for the major role of the bearers of swords and spears, the assault force, allowing them to advance and engage the enemy at close quarters.[8] This meant that it was important to fire as many rounds as possible. They were fired from the waist by soldiers standing or running, not from the shoulder. Rarely was anybody seen lying on the ground to make the best use of his rifle, or looking for cover and a firing position that would afford protection as well as enable him to take aim. Misuse of rifle fire resulted from the prevailing idea of rushing forward to seek martyrdom without considering any other factor. A soldier felt that he would be exposed to the charge of cowardice or fear if he were to lie on the ground and take aim.

The rifles formed the main firing element in the Khalifa's army, but it was necessary to coordinate the fire for most effective use. The best way would have been for them to fire volleys. To guarantee their effectiveness it would have been necessary to put the rifle-bearers into separate units rather than as individuals within a mass of sword- and spear-bearers. The merging of the two forces prohibited their effective use, and kept riflemen out of the front line. As a result the rest of the soldiers were in danger of injury from their own rifle fire.

As for machine guns, the *Mitrailleuse* was the main type used. The other machine guns – Gatlings, Gardeners and Nordenfeldts – were kept in the *Bayt al-amana* but were used neither at Karari nor at any other battle of the Mahdiya. They were complicated to use and the crews were killed when the guns were captured. There was no ammunition and it was difficult to manufacture it locally.

The mountain gun was the main piece of light artillery in the nineteenth century. It was light and one mule could pull it. Its raised angle of fire enabled it to accompany the infantry and to provide them with cover in any kind of terrain. The Khalifa acquired most of his artillery first from the Hicks expedition and then, after the fall of Khartoum, during the campaigns with Ethiopia. The Khalifa had thirty-five guns.

Most of the Khalifa's artillery was antiquated. All the guns, except for the Krupp (of which the Khalifa had eight) were smooth-bore and muzzle-loaded.[9] This did not help the accuracy of the fire, although the cannons were better maintained than the rifles. Most of the cannon crew and the commanders of the batteries were Egyptian, soldiers of the former army of occupation. As old trained professional soldiers they were conscientious about maintenance. But the fatal flaw in the Khalifa's artillery lay in its locally-made ammunition. The Khalifa's workshops were unable to make ammunition for the modern Krupp cannons and his army continued to use ammunition looted from Hicks and Gordon. When Ya'qub saw that it had nearly run out he ordered the Krupp cannons not to be used.[10]

The Khalifa's workshop was able to produce only one kind of ammunition, and this was highly explosive. Most shells were manufactured locally from light copper. This gave the cannon a loud explosion, but without the lethal shrapnel effect.

The explanation for this lies in the theory of artillery held at the time. The Khalifa's army borrowed its ideas from the army of occupation. Throughout the century, it was held that artillery was intended for bombarding fortified places. It was not seen as an element of fire aimed at killing the enemy. This belief determined its use and effect. There were no more than two or three splinters at one explosion, which was more convenient for breaching a wall than for killing enemy infantry.

But by 1898 things were different in modern armies. A new kind of gunpowder had already been produced which exploded a dense quantity of shrapnel, directed primarily at the destruction of enemy personnel. This enabled the British fleet and artillery to have such a devastating effect at Karari. The Khalifa's artillery, however, was mostly booty from Hicks' army in 1883 and the campaigns of the 1880's. Similarly his forts were constructed to an out-of-date design for artillery. They were based on the experience of the years of fighting. As a result the commanders placed little reliance on artillery. The important element of fire in their eyes was, first and last, the rifle, and they took only fire cannons on to the field of Karari.

Most of the cannons were placed in the forts to strike at the enemy's armoured steamers with their mobile artillery: these were regarded as 'fortifications'. The Khalifa thus deprived his forces in the field of valuable fire cover.

The main problem with the ammunition was the weakness of the explosive charge, that came from the locally manufactured gunpowder. As a result most of the shells were unable even to reach the Nile steamers, and those shells directed at Kitchener's *zariba*, as a cover for the assault of Ibrahim al Khalil and 'Uthman Azraq, exploded long before they reached the *zariba*.[11]

The fire-power of the Anglo-Egyptian force that struck at the Khalifa was the largest concentration of firearms ever seen in Africa up to that time. Kitchener's weapons – his rifles, even the artillery of his armour-plated gunboats – demonstrated the enormous development of the war industry in the last twenty years of the nineteenth century. His weapons were similar to those used in the First World War.

The Lee-Metford MK II rifle was the most modern rifle produced by the factories of Europe, and was introduced into the British army in 1895. With modifications and improvements it survived for more than half a century and saw service in two world wars. Its novelty lay in the introduction of a bolt and magazine mechanism for loading it with eight or nine bullets, in contrast to the old models that were one-by-one muzzle- or breech-loading rifles. There was also more grooving, which gave greater accuracy. Furthermore, the charge was smaller, made of cordite instead of saltpetre. This guaranteed a speed of over 2,000 feet per second. The bullets travelled more than 2,500 yards and the marksman had a good chance of hitting any target he could see with his naked eye. The lighter weight also enabled the soldier to carry much more ammunition.

The introduction of this rifle greatly increased the value of the fighting infantry, especially in defence, as they were particularly effective behind stockades, and were able greatly to reduce the impact of the massing of enemy infantry and cavalry in attack. The ratio of attackers to defenders would have to be three to one to ensure a successful assault if the defenders had this rifle. A platoon, when ordered to fire, would break up into small detachments. The first detachment would all fire their rifles simultaneously, then the second group, then the third. Meanwhile the first group reloads, takes aim and fires again. All this would happen in quick succession.[12]

Hiram Maxim produced a machine capable of destroying tens of thousands within a few hours. European nations were working on the new idea of the one-barrel machine-gun. It would have all the advantages of the older machine-guns, with several barrels packed together for a large volume of fire, but at the same time enable the crews to take continuous precise aim. It would also have greater range, if it became possible to pour fire horizontally on a wide front of attacking enemy. This had previously been very difficult with the older machine-guns whose aim had to be continuously readjusted.

The entrenched defenders' volume of fire was able to paralyze a direct attack. A successful assault would thus have to be made either under a strong cover or at night.

For greater effect and range the machine-guns were arranged in batteries, each containing six guns.

Although the Maxim was light compared with its predecessors, its bulk made it a solid defensive weapon. It was thus not possible to deploy it quickly to intervene decisively, according to the demands of the development of the battle.

Kitchener overcame this drawback by installing a large number of them on the fast-moving Nile steamers.

Cannons by now had rifled barrels. When a spring was introduced the recoil was absorbed and the barrel returned to its original position without the need to take aim again. In older guns the recoil had made them slide several yards.

The greatest development in artillery efficiency related to ammunition. The effect of the artillery, particularly over long distances – that is, more than 400 yards, the smallest range for case shot – was slight on enemy concentrations. Most casualties were inflicted as a result of the force of the explosion or blast. The shrapnel effect was very slight. But with the introduction of cordite, a single shell was able to produce a great number of splinters, causing havoc among infantry by itself, quite apart from the explosion. Henceforward the effectiveness of the cannons increased to match that of the rifles and machine-guns. The effect was greatest over distances of more than 300 yards.

There were three kinds of ammunition fired on 2 September. First, there was canister ammunition or case shot which consisted of a tin can filled with bullets, which exploded at the expiry of a time fuse or on impact. Its effect on masses of infantry was devastating. It was not often used because of its short range. Secondly, the high explosive shell, which was the most frequently used, because it covered a long distance, produced a large number of splinters and had great explosive force. It was thus possible to use it against infantry or against fortifications as case shot.

The 5.5 inch Howitzer cannon made up Kitchener's heavy artillery. The main role assigned to these cannons was the bombardment of the city of Omdurman, should the Khalifa remain there and fight within its streets. The Howitzer had a long range for its heavy shells, and lyddite was used for the first time. Its charge held an enormous amount of TNT. These factors made it ideal for striking at fortifications and buildings. The Howitzer was drawn on a carriage by horses or mules and the whole lot was loaded on a steamer. It was these Howitzers whose fire was directed from the east bank of the Nile towards the walls of Omdurman and the Mahdi's *qubba*.

The employment of this great mass of fire-power necessitated the transport of huge quantities of ammunition over thousands of miles. Herein lay Kitchener's achievement and administrative ability. First the steamers stumbled along the cataracts. Then workshops were set up for the assembling of the steamers that were transported in parts by railway to avoid the cataracts.

The effect of the steamers' tactical and fighting value also became clear during the decisive hours of 2 September. The mobile flotilla with its cannon and machine guns resembled the self-propelled artillery of today. It had speed and great flexibility in concentrating fire in any position. Furthermore most of the steamers that took part in the battle were armour-plated.

Without the flotilla Kitchener would not have been able to assemble so great a force on the day of the battle. The Nile steamers assumed great historical significance. Gordon had been the first to draw attention to their effectiveness during his first mission to the Sudan as Governor of Equatoria. He did what he could to study the river, its courses and the *sudd*, in order to provide the necessary information for the specifications of the four steamers he commissioned from London.

Kitchener's river fleet included a number of steamers of the same type as those that took part in the Relief Expedition. There was also a new type constructed in London in the late 1890s.

The flotilla consisted of ten fighting steamers armed with artillery and machine-guns and five transport steamers.

The newest model, *Sudan*, made in 1898, was armed with two Nordenfeldt cannons and one quick-firing 12-pounder cannon. The gunboats *Melik* and *Sheikh* each had one 5-inch Howitzer and four Maxim machine-guns. Each of the armoured steamers of the 1896 model, *Fateh, Naser* and *Zafir*, was armed with one quick-firing cannon, two 6-pounder cannons and four Maxim machine-guns. The steamers of the 1895 model, *Tamai, Hafir, Abu Klea* and *Metemma*, were each armed with one 12-pounder cannon and two Nordenfeldt Maxim cannons.

Each steamer was commanded by an officer of the Royal Navy and had a crew of two engineers from the Royal Navy, two junior British naval officers and a platoon of infantry. The older models had eleven gunners, the more modern twenty-three.

NOTES

1 Muhammad wad Bishara, however, in his letters to his commanders, showed concern for the maintenance of his weapons.
2 Most of the four hundred rifles taken from the battlefield and now in the Khalifa's house museum, Omdurman, have had their barrels sawn off.
3 Some bullets, taken from the battlefield and now in the Khalifa's house museum in Omdurman, are not regular and are not tapered uniformly. They are of unequal size and the lead is welded crudely.
4 Ordinary soldiers were not satisfied by the standard of armaments. When some veteran *jihadiya* soldiers who had been used to Remington rifles and relatively modern Martini rifles, were given ancient muzzle-loaded rifles, the word would spread around, 'The damn thing falls to pieces in my hands'.
5 Dr Hasan Zaki, Ya'qub's officer most qualified in the use of chemicals, was not an expert in munitions.
6 The following chemicals were found in the *Bayt al-amana* after the battle, all raw materials for the manufacture of ammunition:

> 15,000 oz. lead
> 20,800 oz. potassium nitrate
> 6,549 oz. sulphur
> 2,533 oz. tin
> 421 oz. sulphuric acid.

7 At the battle some bullets went over the heads of Kitchener's soldiers into the *zariba* whereas others fell before even reaching the *zariba* though fired by the same rifles from the same place. The ammunition taken from the time of the occupation was much better, though older, than the locally produced stuff. Yusuf Mikha'il, showing that Shaykh al Din appropriated all the good war material, says that he 'took modern arms and old ammunition'.
8 The armies of the Mahdiya, in all their wars – even in assaults – were never seen to use the bayonet.
9 A Krupp cannon, taken from the battlefield, is now placed in front of the town hall at Omdurman. Its barrel is rifled, but its weight and size show that a large number of camels and mules would have been needed to draw it – quite apart from the ammunition.
10 Seventy-five cannon shells were found in the *Bayt al-amana* after the battle
11 This was the view prevailing among most historians. But if we consider what Slatin said, that the Khalifa's shells did not have a range of more than 500 yards, it is most probable that Ya'qub sensibly made use of the

old shells that had been taken from the army of occupation. In the first assault of 'Uthman Azraq, shells reached more than 2,500 yards and fell 500 yards short of the river.

12 The main improvement of the Maxim was in its method of automatic reloading, making use of the explosion of gas imprisoned in the closed part to force the catches in front and behind to reload the barrel. This was instead of using a little wheel that had to be turned by hand. The explosive nature of the new white gunpowder, cordite, made this possible and the user was able to concentrate on taking aim and moving the piece horizontally instead of spending time reloading.

Some small-arms ammunition used at Karari was of the dumdum kind. The dumdum was an ordinary bullet whose tapering head was cut in the form of a cross. It shattered the bones and caused internal damage, leading to terrible wounds. A bullet would enter the body in front causing a small burn, but when it came out at the back the wound would have expanded to a circle 12 inches in diameter.

The use of the dumdum was banned internationally, even in hunting, after the battle of Omdurman.

CHAPTER TEN

Mobilization

AFTER the Khalifa heard the news of the defeat of Mahmud wad Ahmad, he began to prepare for the decisive battle. He reckoned that the enemy would reach Omdurman between the middle of August and early October during the period of the Nile flood, which would assist the progress of the flotilla. The Khalifa relied for his information on his intelligence scouts under their commander, the *amir* 'Abd al Baqi 'Abd al Wakil, who sent regular information.

The Khalifa was faced with three alternatives in dealing with the enemy. First, he could meet them between Omdurman and 'Atbara; secondly, he could face them in Omdurman itself or, thirdly, he could retreat westwards to Kordofan and Darfur. The last alternative was not unreasonable, for it would deprive Kitchener of the support of the steamers. If the Khalifa were to withdraw to the west, the Sirdar would have the enormous problems of organizing camels and porters. There would be the danger of a second Hicks disaster, but on a larger scale.

On the other hand, a retreat to the west would mean the sacrifice of Omdurman and all that implied in terms of morale. The Khalifa, like any head of state, had a sense of pride that deterred him from allowing his capital to fall into the hands of the enemy. The capital was the symbol of his state. If Omdurman were abandoned, so would be the Mahdi's tomb, the magnet that attracted thousands of warriors to defend the Call and all it stood for.

There were also operational difficulties. Abandoning Omdurman would mean the loss of the arsenals and factories. He too would have to organize supplies. The difficulties that Kitchener would face would, in part, also be faced by the Khalifa. The retreat would be tough going, and it would not be easy to feed the huge army in the west especially after the *amir* Mahmud had dragooned the last sympathetic hand and drained the last grain of *dhurra*.

It is believed that Ya'qub favoured the idea of retreat to the west. He persuaded al Zaki 'Uthman, as one familiar with the enemy's methods of warfare, to propose it to the Khalifa in the last week of April.

Al Zaki put forward his proposal, explaining that the Khalifa lacked the means to defeat the enemy in Omdurman, which, after all, 'is not our original home even when we defend it. Let us rather withdraw to the west to el Obeid. If they overtake us there let us go to Shakka and make a final stand there and so die in our own lands and among our own people.'

The Khalifa, however, saw himself not as the leader of a Baqqara tribe and the people of the west only, but, as the successor of the Mahdi, of the whole country. His reaction was violent. 'Are you not ashamed of yourself, man? 'Abd Allah wad Sa'd with a few hundred men stood in the path of Mahmud's huge army and refused to surrender a single village. And you want me, with all the armies of the Mahdiya at my disposal, to be a coward and to flee, leaving Omdurman and the whole country in the hands of the infidel? I shall fight until I am triumphant or until they destroy my army altogether. If that happens then I shall sit on my *furwa* at the Mahdi's tomb and commend my soul to God.' He ordered al Zaki to be imprisoned.[1] All present were silent and no one ventured to mention the matter again.

In his foreign policy the Khalifa was more flexible, moving away from the idea of isolation and hostility to all who rejected the Mahdiya. But in contrast to other African rulers, such as Menelik, King of the Ethiopians, the Khalifa never tried to exploit the conflicting imperialist ambitions of the European states.

When Menelik wrote to the Khalifa announcing his victory over the Italians at Adowa and renewing his offer of peace and a treaty of cooperation against the Europeans, the Khalifa consented, though his terms were harsh. Menelik should refrain from commercial relations with Europeans. 'There is nothing between them and us except war'. This was too much for Menelik, whose strength depended on French arms. The Khalifa's roving ambassador, Muhammad 'Uthman Khalid, brought back a refusal. Dipolmatic relations, however, continued and ambassadors were exchanged. The last Ethiopian delegation visited Omdurman as late as April, 1898.

The Khalifa prepared a crowded programme for the visit. He intended to dazzle his guests with the glory of his state. For this the religious laws of the Mahdiya and its rigid social rules were relaxed. Wine and *'araqi* were offered to the guests and the arsenal arranged a great display of fireworks.

In the closed session held by the Khalifa and the Ethiopian delegation, the latter offered him the benefits of French military technology which he could use for the protection of the state. The Khalifa would be independent, albeit under French protection. He thanked them and kept the knowledge to himself.

During the early part of 1898 a large part of the Khalifa's army was scattered. Apart from the garrisons of the north, he had three armies available. There was the army of the *amir* Ahmad Fadil in the east of the Sudan, based at al Qadarif, with 8,000 soldiers. In the south at al Rajjaf was the 4,000-strong army of 'Arabi Daf' Allah. Then there was the garrison of al Khatim Musa in Kordofan with its headquarters at el Obeid.

The Khalifa was deterred from summoning all his forces to Omdurman, for in the east the Italians were threatening to push back into the Sudan after the intervention of the British. News, furthermore, was coming regularly from 'Arabi Daf' Allah that 'other red-faced infidels' (Belgians) were advancing into Bahr al Ghazal. Then again, in Darfur the tribes were returning to their natural rebellious state. In Kordofan the Kababish were already in touch with the enemy and the Hamar in al Nahud were making trouble.

Thus the Khalifa had no alternative but to leave many of his soldiers at their posts.

When he decided to order Ahmad Fadil to guard the eastern bank of the Nile he did not know of the advance of the 'Friendly Arabs', men from the Ja'li and Sha'iqi tribes under the command of Major Stuart-Wortley. But he was alive to the danger of leaving this right flank exposed.

He ordered Ahmad Fadil to come first to Omdurman with his entire army. Ahmad Fadil gathered his forces at al Qadarif. His plan was to move to Omdurman in stages, to facilitate the provisioning of a force of 8,000. He also wanted to avoid abandoning the frontier and so kept a large body of men at al Qadarif.

The Khalifa also called upon the services of an outstanding general of an earlier generation, al Nur Anqara, now ill in bed at al Qadarif.[2] The Khalifa asked Ahmad Fadil to get him to stay in al Qadarif as he was the best man to command that troubled area in Ahmad Fadil's absence.

The Khalifa did not attempt to summon the army of 'Arabi Daf' Allah, partly because it was scarcely able to deal with the aggression from the south-west, partly because it was so far from Omdurman. He turned his attention to other districts to the west and the Jazira. After repeated news of tribal rebellions he decided not to summon complete units but to be content with volunteers.

From the west he ordered the *amir* al Khatim Musa to send any man capable of bearing arms to Omdurman and only to retain a force necessary to keep the peace in the vast area of Darfur and Kordofan, but Mahmud wad Ahmad had already exhausted most of the available manpower. Furthermore the force of al Khatim Musa was scarcely enough to check the stirrings of revolt in the provinces, not least in the Kababish area.

Although the Khalifa regarded the Jazira as the area that provided corn and crops rather than recruits, always trying to leave sufficient men there to till the land, he was forced in the end to call upon every arm that had hitherto wielded the scythe to take up the sword.

Normally the Khalifa did not bother about the provision of horses but relied on people's preference for fighting on horseback. This time it was not enough. He ordered Ya'qub to buy or commandeer all he could.

In this general mobilization the Khalifa did not forget

Osman Digna who had left the battle of 'Atbara with his army intact. Osman gathered his men and brought them to Omdurman. When they reached the bank opposite the capital, the Khalifa prepared a fitting reception. He sent one of the steamers to bring him across to Omdurman. The Khalifa sat on horseback until Osman Digna disembarked, followed by his men. Then he dismounted and embraced Osman. They both went off to the Friday prayers where Osman stood immediately behind the Khalifa.

On that day the Khalifa did not deliver the sermon as was his wont. Instead Osman Digna mounted the pulpit and delivered a rousing speech describing the circumstances of the defeat at 'Atbara. 'Do not be sad', he said, 'because the *amir* Mahmud has fallen a prisoner into the hands of the infidel. It is true that he is the Khalifa's cousin. But al Zubayr was twenty thousand times better than Mahmud and he also fell prisoner. It is not always possible to be victorious, but we may have to accept defeat and turn it into victory.' His sermon lasted from the midday prayer until sunset. Some collapsed because of the heat of the sun, but Osman Digna spoke on without interruption.

The Red Standard, under which were gathered the people of the north and the Jazira, had been disbanded after the revolt and imprisonment of the Khalifa Muhammad Sharif. The Khalifa, however, felt that such critical times necessitated its revival, and made the announcement at an official celebration, attended by the Khalifa 'Ali wad Hilu, the council of his judges and the senior *amirs*. The Khalifa said that he wanted the Red Standard revived under Muhammad Sharif. The council gave its consent, and the Khalifa took the Red Standard from an *angarayb* and handed it to Muhammad Sharif. He in turn handed it to Ahmad 'Abd al Karim who had been chosen as acting commander. The standard was hoisted on its pole and former members began to flock round it once again.[3]

What was the final number that entered the battle in the ranks of the Khalifa? Those who saw the army on 1 September reckoned the force to be about 30,000. Witnesses included war correspondents and commanders of detachments, and it appears in a number of sources and reports. But after the battle the official figures issued by Kitchener and Wingate had swollen to 52,000. All historians since then have accepted this figure.[4]

General Hunter, commander of the Egyptian division, in the report that he submitted a few days after the battle – and which was not published among the intelligence reports – mentions quite specifically that 'the enemy, estimated at 30,000, was seen by the Sirdar to be advancing on us from a distance of five miles'. The *Daily Telegraph* correspondent, Bennet Burleigh, says in his estimate of the Khalifa's forces, 'Counting as carefully as I could, I estimated the enemy who were to be seen, at least numbering 30,000 and perhaps 35,000.'

Could it be that after the ferocious battle in the north, when the proportion of casualties reached 80% of the whole force, and when the British press accused Kitchener of unjustifiable savagery, that the number of the Khalifa's warriors was inflated after the battle so that the proportion of casualties would be 50% instead of 70–75%? Could it be that the magnitude of the victory was enhanced by exaggerating the strength of the defeated enemy?

Wingate and his Intelligence Department were too astute to make any such distortion without offering solid evidence, and this they found among Ya'qub's papers. But his inventories were far from up to date. They consisted of a roll-call of the Omdurman garrison dating back to before the campaign in the north. Indeed they were possibly several years old. They were certainly not an accurate reflection of the force that took the field in September, 1898.

The *mulazimin* were alleged by Wingate to be 14,000 strong. This figure was accepted by Churchill and by other historians, though Broadwood reckoned they numbered only 10,000,[5] a figure supported by the historian Muhammad 'Abd al Rahim. Wingate's case is strengthened by the figures of al Tayyib al Husayn, who handed information over to the invaders days before the battle. He gives a breakdown of the *mulazimin* which adds up to 15,000. Some of these, however, took hardly any part in the actual fighting – among them the 2,000 fighters of Shaykh al Din's private guard.

The assault of the first phase – Ibrahim al Khalil and 'Uthman Azraq – was estimated by Wingate to include 15,000 men. However, Churchill, an eye-witness, estimated 'Uthman Azraq's force at 8,000 and two other sources – al Tayyib al Husayn and G. W. Steevens – put the Kara garrison as low as 2,400 men.

The Green Standard was given by Wingate as 5,000 strong. Churchill and later historians accepted this figure, although al Tayyib al Husayn puts it at 2,800, a figure supported by other eye-witnesses.

The Black Standard has, following Wingate, traditionally been put at 14,000. But Gatacre and al Tayyib al Husayn give 12,000. Both those who saw the army from the top of Surkab and those who fought them put it at the lower figure.

Finally the smallest unit – that of Osman Digna. The Intelligence Report claims that the force was 3,700 strong. But Churchill, who was in the Lancers' charge and would certainly have been in no mood to lessen their tally, thought they numbered no more than 700.

There is insufficient evidence for us to state categorically what the size of the Khalifa's army was on 2 September, 1898. However, one can assert that the hitherto accepted figure of 52,000 is open to question. This figure has hitherto been unchallenged but there is sufficient evidence dating from the day of the battle itself to suggest that the army may have been smaller. In spite of the universal conscription imposed by the Khalifa, many factors hindered the call-up. The experience of Mahmud's army had demoralized many who sought retirement rather than an apparently futile struggle against overwhelming odds. The ravages of previous wars – in the north, in Ethiopia and in the west – had limited the ability of the Khalifa to raise numbers that might have been available ten years earlier.

In the months before the battle there were two schools of thought about the strategy to adopt in the forthcoming struggle. One school recommended a move to the north to face the enemy at Sabaluqa. Their spokesmen were Shaykh al Din, Ibrahim al Khalil and the Khalifa Muhammad Sharif. The second school of thought, representing the views of the western tribes and the Council of Notables under the leadership of Ya'qub were resolved to enter the battle at Omdurman.

The Khalifa worried over the dilemma during these days. His companions report that he often seemed to gaze into the distance, preoccupied and grave. He sought advice from a council which was called together in the first week of May. Among those who attended were the Khalifa 'Ali wad Hilu, the Khalifa Muhammad Sharif, the *amir* Ya'qub, 'Uthman Shaykh al Din, Osman Digna, Ibrahim al Khalil, Ahmad 'Abd al Karim (deputy of the Yellow Standard), 'Abd Allah Abu Siwar (Commander of the Green Standard), Ya'qub Abu Zaynab, 'Uthman Azraq and Muhammad Bishara. The Khalifa laid before them the latest information he had received from the reconnaissance scouts, namely that the enemy had spent the last few months consolidating their position at 'Atbara, ready to move when the Nile rose. The Khalifa Muhammad Sharif started the discussion: 'The Mahdi told me in a vision that if the Turks came past Wadi Sayyidna they would conquer us. It is incumbent therefore upon us to move and to encounter them. We have no alternative but to leave a part of the army behind in Omdurman. I suggest we place one of the strong *rub's* of Shaykh al Din under my command and advance north with it to occupy Sabaluqa.'

The Khalifa Sharif's attitude aroused the Khalifa's anger. 'When we want your opinion, we shall ask for it. You speak to us in riddles. Such talk is useless. Religion belongs to God. He lets men choose. He gives victory and He does not abandon his men.'

Ibrahim al Khalil and Osman Digna were quick to understand the situation. Ibrahim put forward a comprehensive plan for dealing with the situation. His plan was to move north and engage the enemy at Sabaluqa by building forts either side of the Nile, to transport the fifty cannons there, part of the army remaining there to guard it. The bed of the Nile should be piled up with obstacles, rows of large stones on top of each other.

Such a plan, he argued, would guarantee protection against the gunboats. The narrow channel would force the gunboats into close range and the obstacles would prevent or at least hinder their passage. This would make them an easy target for the Khalifa's infantry who would wade into the shallow water to deal with them. Kitchener would have either to separate from the gunboats and outflank the heights of Sabaluqa or stop where he was with his paralyzed gunboats.

Ibrahim al Khalil had never in his life seen these parts, and yet he put forward such a plan, relying on a vicarious familiarity with the nature of the area. He took his ideas from Osman Digna, who had spent some time there. It is worth mentioning that the opinions of Osman Digna and Ibrahim al Khalil often coincided or were complementary. It was most probable that they had coordinated their plans before they entered the council. Ibrahim's plan was a purely defensive one. It revolved around the idea of drawing Kitchener's army away from the gunboats. He would be leaving the initiative to the enemy. This probably weakened his own position somewhat. All present at the council were aware that, since the first days of the Mahdiya, victory had been theirs so long as they took the initiative.

Then Osman Digna spoke in support of Ibrahim al Khalil. As usual he spoke at great length on the nature of the terrain and on the nature of war with the English. He differed from Ibrahim, however, in preferring to attack rather than to adopt a defensive stance. He thought that, after the sites were fortified and the river obstructed, the whole of the Khalifa's army should attack Kitchener at a time to be determined by reconnaissance. The general view of the council was agreement on the principle of fighting at Sabaluqa. Discussion continued on all aspects of the question. The meeting went on and on until Ab Jukka, the Khalifa's bodyguard, reminded them of the Mahdi's prophecy that a huge army of infidels would be utterly destroyed in the hills of Karari.

Here Ibrahim al Khalil got fed up and turned to his neighbour, 'If the matter rests with Ab Jukka, we might just as well go home.' The meeting then concluded, after resolving to fight at Sabaluqa.

The Khalifa now set about implementing the council's decision. He ordered Ya'qub to collect the necessary food to provision the army. His memories of the Battle of 'Atbara persuaded him to accept Osman Digna's argument for advancing to attack the enemy when they were in the vicinity of Sabaluqa, rather than just to occupy it before them. He ordered a senior *amir*, Yunus al Dikaym, to take up positions on the al Dabba road. Even now he still reckoned that the enemy would advance on two roads, as had the Relief Expedition.

The Khalifa, however, did not order the immediate and complete occupation of Sabaluqa at this stage, Instead he decided to occupy it with only a small part of his army. He wanted to be sure that the greater part of his army was ready to pounce on the enemy, whatever they did. He realized that whoever occupied Sabaluqa would control the river, but first he had to take a number of preparatory measures. He would have to occupy the area of the cataracts to prevent the enemy taking them. Then he would have to transport all his artillery to Sabaluqa. And thirdly, his army had to be ready to spring upon the enemy once they knew whether they would advance through the straits or describe a wide circle to the west, away from the river. To carry out this last stage of the operation the Khalifa had to rely on sound and accurate intelligence reports.

The Sabaluqa mountains stand as an isolated outcrop. They are volcanic rocks that sometimes rise to more than 400 feet and press up to the west side of the Nile, stretching more than seven miles to the north and over nine miles west. The river rushes through a gorge, its flow checked by a group of islands.

The *amir* Ya'qub gave Yusuf Mansur responsibility for the fortifications for the artillery.[6] He was well known for his technical ability. Ya'qub explained to him the necessity of constructing defences which enabled the cannons and rifles to reach the gunboats. He also assigned to him 200 *mulazimin* to carry out the building operations. Yusuf showed Ya'qub plans for the forts: the radius of each was to be forty yards, the walls ten feet thick, and would be able to hold three cannons and a section of riflemen.[7] Ya'qub approved the plans, and Yusuf went north to carry out the building. While he was gathering the necessary equipment, a force of infantry occupied Sabaluqa where they awaited the arrival of the commander of the northern area.

The Khalifa assigned to the *amir* 'Abd al Baqi 'Abd al Wakil the command of the whole district north of Omdurman. He placed under his command 300 horsemen armed with rifles. Their main task was to send daily reports about the enemy.

They received clear instructions to avoid clashing with the enemy, and to withdraw south whenever they advanced.

'Abd al Baqi divided his forces into three parts, the greater part to be kept with him to deal with all eventualities. A second part was formed of a hundred horsemen who went ahead to observe the enemy and to gather news about them, either by raiding or by taking prisoners. 'Abd al Baqi would review the information himself and interrogate prisoners. He would then write a daily report which would be sent to Omdurman. The third part was concerned solely with communicating with the capital. This consisted of about twenty horsemen based at postal stations where the exhausted horses would be exchanged for fresh ones, and the reports and perhaps prisoners would be passed on to the Khalifa and Ya'qub in Omdurman.

'Abd al Baqi waited for a while at Sabaluqa before going on to his own headquarters at Wadi Bishara, but straightway patrols were sent north to reconnoitre. When these scouts returned he relayed the information to Omdurman. On 6 June, for example, he wrote to the Khalifa:

'I submit to your noble ears what has been heard of the enemies of God. They rallied and came to al Hawsh and Shandi and we had to learn more of the truth of this. So when we came here we sent our brother Hamad Ruqay'at and gave him one hundred horse with some worthy comrades . . . They crossed to the east bank and proceeded with God's grace on Tuesday, and on Wednesday at midday they launched a raid on al Hawsh but found nothing there. Then they launched a raid on Shandi but found only a steamer point. The horsemen attacked the steamer point and found a cousin of the accursed 'Abd Allah wad Sa'd and one other Ja'li assistant. They were building forts. At the attack on the village of Shandi they killed them. The enemies of God returned to the steamer and went into midstream. Our people came on horseback to Shandi looking all round them but found nothing. They entered the village and rested till the afternoon. Then they got up and when they returned and reached al Hawsh they found somebody called 'Ali wad Sarira who had left Omdurman making for the enemy. They arrested him and today brought him here ... It is clear to our Lord that the enemies of God have not moved on the east bank as far as Shandi except for the steamer point, which is near al Matamma, but the movements of the steamers show their cunning and deception and that every day they have come by islands as far as Umm Jarki, Salamatu and Hajr al 'Asl. They burn the grass and clear the islands of houses. It has been heard that they move their armies on to these islands secretly.'

But the apparent speed of the enemy did not last long. Two weeks later 'Abd al Baqi's intelligence sources reported that the Sirdar himself was advancing from Berber with four steamboats to explore the land with a view to bringing up all his fleet. The speed, 'Abd al Baqi said, 'was nothing but a ruse and a deception'.

Building operations at Sabaluqa continued and 'Abd al Baqi reported on 28 June, 'The work on the forts is in progress. They include an observation post from which it is possible to see the infidel boats, once in the narrows.'

Ya'qub now sent the commander of the artillery, the *amir* Sayyid Jum'a, with two batteries, to arrange the siting of the cannons and to inspect and report on the forts.

But suddenly, after all this vast work of construction, after Sayyid Jum'a's inspection, after his return to bring the rest of the artillery in the first week of June, the Khalifa ordered the evacuation of the Sabaluqa positions and the return of the advance column.

In Omdurman there had recently been increased activity on the part of Wingate's intelligence agents. As Babikr Badri says, every day people would talk about somebody who had been detained with papers or with instalments of money on him paid to him by Wingate.

Wingate knew of the Khalifa's plan to transport his artillery to Sabaluqa and to defend the gorge. His agents were urged to try and discredit the scheme in whatever way they could. Even in the Khalifa's last council of judges, there were some judges who were in Wingate's pay. They knew of the Khalifa's plan, and even before their advice was sought formally they poured scorn on the policy in private conversations with *amirs* of the army.

The Khalifa was troubled by the advice of his council. He sent out agents to ask people in Omdurman about anybody who had heard the prophecy of the destruction of the enemy at Karari from the mouth of the Mahdi himself.

But it was for practical reasons that the Khalifa abandoned Sabaluqa. He anticipated enormous logistic difficulties in the transporting and provisioning of such a huge army. He had already seen the difficulties faced by Mahmud. His anxieties were reinforced after he received a petition from the Sabaluqa garrison who, in spite of their small numbers, were suffering from problems of food supply. How much greater would the difficulties be with a huge army? How could he drag the cannons along and bring provisions and ammunition with his limited supply of animals?

Furthermore, he was loth to leave the capital for the north. The furthest north the Khalifa ever went in his life was Hujra wad al Basir, or to Karari on three occasions to receive his generals. Thus if he went north he would be fighting on land he did not know and had never seen. His instinctive preference was to fight on familiar ground. If he had decided to move north he would have entrusted the overall command to one of his generals. But he wished to lead his army in this battle himself, and the Omdurman district was thus the most suitable for taking his last stand.

The Khalifa was haunted by the memory of the Battle of 'Atbara. He felt unable to rely on any of the people of the north. If they were not open enemies like 'Abd Allah wad Sa'd, then they were covertly hostile and he could not entrust them with any of the secrets of his army. Thus he decided to concentrate his efforts on a battle in the Omdurman district, and straightway set about preparing its defences.

The Khalifa ordered the construction of forts for the artillery in Omdurman. His idea was to direct the greater part of his artillery fire to silencing and sinking the Nile steamers. One of the *rub's* of the *mulazimin* was detailed to undertake this task. The *rub'* consisted of 2,000 men armed with rifles to defend the batteries on the Nile. The Khalifa first thought he would place them all on the west bank. It would be easy to protect them with his army, and he feared losing them if some were on the east bank far from the main army. But he listened to the sound advice of the Egyptian artillerymen who knew about the effective range of the cannons, which in this case did not exceed 700 yards. To cover the whole river they had to be placed on both banks. Ibrahim al Khalil gave his backing to the idea and the Khalifa approved.

Cannons were placed in forts built on the east and west banks of the Island of Tuti and at al Muqran. A third of the cannons were to go to the battlefield itself to back up the army if they were on the offensive or to bombard the advancing forces of the enemy from afar if they were defending.

There were eight forts in Omdurman. The chief artilleryman of each was Egyptian, the fort commander usually a western Sudanese. In Khartoum there were two forts: at the Old Palace and at al Muqran. Both were commanded by a Habbani, al Rashid Karuma. On Tuti Island there were two forts: one on the north, the other on the south of the island. On the east bank were also two forts, at Shambat and at Sababi. Both were commanded by Ta'aisha. The Khalifa lost his last real chance of dealing with the destructive power of Kitchener's steamers when he abandoned his position at Sabaluqa. But another chance of dealing with them occurred when one day a prisoner called al Hajj Munawwar al Maghrabi came to him and said he could destroy the gunboats with mines that exploded as soon as the steamers touched them. The Khalifa ordered Ya'qub to give him every facility and to see what he could do, though he had to remain in chains all the time.

The elaborate experiment to demonstrate the effectiveness of the explosive was so successful that it caused the accidental destruction of more than half the steamer that was towing the charge and the death of all on board, about twenty people including the inventor himself. Later, pieces of his body were found still in chains. The Khalifa was interested in the catastrophe only in that it proved the effectiveness of the charge, and he ordered the speedy manufacture of more mines on the same principle.

What were things like in the Khalifa's capital in the last weeks before the battle? During the day life continued much the same in the *suqs* and restaurants of the city, now swollen with people who had come in as reinforcements from outside. As usual every citizen gathered to pray five times daily in the mosque, and as usual the Khalifa led the prayers. There were one or two differences, however. He now only occasionally addressed them. After prayers he would hasten back to his house to attend discussions on the war situation.

In the last few mornings before the battle there were signs of the impending struggle. Life almost came to a standstill. All the citizens used to assemble on the parade ground. Each standard took a roll-call of its fighting men. Then after midday they would all disperse.

The *mulazimin* were in their huge training camp. Drill began at dawn and continued till dusk. They did not join with the rest of the standards on the parade ground.

This is how things appeared outwardly in the city. But deep down it was a little different, especially in the afternoon. The city seethed with rumours that spread like wildfire. All were eager to hear them, and equally to pass them on. Babikr Badri recalls how he invited some guests to his house. He was absent for less than a minute calling his servant. When he returned they asked him, 'What news?' Whimsically he invented some tale about the enemy's advance. Two days later the same tale was reported back to him.

NOTES

1   Later Shaykh al Din had him pardoned and released.

2   The Khalifa repeatedly deplored al Nur's personal conduct. It was well known that al Nur drank and smoked openly. There is a famous tale about the Khalifa and al Nur Anqara. One day the Khalifa consulted two people and felt from what they said that one was not being straightforward, and the other was speaking the truth in spite of any harm that might befall him. He turned to them and said, '*You* fear me but do not fear God. *You* fear God but do not fear me. Al Nur Anqara does not fear me – does he fear God?'

3   Sources that I have consulted show that the restoration took place at the same time as the marriage of al Radiya, daughter of the Khalifa, to the Mahdi's son, al Bushra. This was an attempt at a final settlement of the dispute.

4   What first roused my doubts was the poem 'The Battle of Omdurman' which was published immediately after the battle and was based on the

descriptions of war correspondents who had cabled through their reports. In it is the stanza:

> 'With fierce and frenzied cry,
> From many a camp and ken,
> The proud Khalifa came
> With thrice ten thousand men'.

5   Churchill's estimate tallies completely with local sources when he describes the clashes he saw himself, such as the attack of Ibrahim al Khalil and 'Uthman Azraq or the Lancer engagement. But as for the attack of the *mulazimin* or of the Black Standard, he was wide of the mark. It seems he used Wingate's figures so that his total would come to 52,000.

6   Shaykh Ibrahim al Hajjaz, one of the elders of the district, was a boy when Yusuf Mansur arrived. He has told me that Yusuf was a red-faced man with a thick beard. The small boys of the area used to help him. He recalls that Yusuf began to construct a huge chain to join both banks as part of a plan to place obstacles in the Nile.

7   Traces of the forts still remain at Sabaluqa.

CHAPTER ELEVEN

The Enemy

THE Sirdar spent the months after the Battle of 'Atbara rallying his forces and waiting for reinforcements promised by the British Government. He sent steamers south as far as possible – Nasri Island – with the objective both of reconnaissance and of collecting firewood. The four Sudanese battalions cut down trees and piled the timber up on the banks from 'Atbara to al Matamma.

On 14 July the railway reached 'Atbara. Then reinforcements and tons of supplies began to pour in. A second British brigade arrived, then the 21st Lancers, a squadron of Egyptian cavalry and two squadrons of artillery armed with British cannons.

Colonel Wingate spent his time strengthening his network of spies and organizing the 4,000 or more warriors from northern tribes under the command of Major Stuart-Wortley, with the help of Shaykh Farah, 'Abd al 'Azim Bey Husayn Khalifa and Maysara al Zubayr Pasha.

In late July the Sirdar set up forward positions at Shandi and at al Matamma. He also established an advanced administration post on the Island of Nasri, the last point that could be reached by the steamers, only twelve miles from the Sabaluqa gorge. Provisions were stored in barges that would suffice for three months for the English division, and for two months for the Egyptian.

'Abd al Baqi was soon sending daily reports on the enemy to the Khalifa, and sometimes two or even three in one day. He delegated duties well and had an able and energetic officer in al

Madd al Ghali, who scarcely knew the meaning of tiredness. 'Abd al Baqi watched the enemy's movements on both banks of the Nile, and also the formation of the 'friendly Arabs'.

At the same time the Khalifa was keeping a check on 'Abd al Baqi'. Information reached him from various sources that the enemy had arrived at al Matamma. He also sent Bashir al 'Abadi to 'Abd al Baqi asking why such important intelligence had not been reported. 'Abd al Baqi replied in his polished and forceful style that such was not the case at the time. The Khalifa was assured that 'Abd al Baqi was not relaxing his vigilance for an instant.

The Sidar's concentration, when complete, contained 24,000 soldiers, of whom 8,200 were British and the rest Egyptian and Sudanese. The composition of the force was as follows:

Commanding the force: General Sir Herbert Kitchener.
Chief of the Staff: Major-General Leslie Rundle.

Infantry
British Division: Commanding, Major-General W. F. Gatacre.
   1st Brigade: Brigadier-General A. G. Wauchope, with four battalions.
   2nd Brigade: Brigadier-General N. G. Lyttelton, with four battalions.
Egyptian Division: Commanding, Major-General A. Hunter.
   1st Brigade: Colonel H. MacDonald, with one Egyptian and three Sudanese battalions.
   2nd Brigade: Colonel Maxwell, with one Egyptian and three Sudanese battalions.
   3rd Brigade: Colonel Lewis, with four Egyptian battalions.
   4th Brigade: Colonel Collinson, with four Egyptian and three mixed Egyptian and Sudanese battalions.

Mounted Forces
The 21st Lancers with four squadrons.
A camel corps with eight companies.
Battalions of Egyptian Cavalry with nine squadrons.

Artillery
Officer Commanding: Lieutenant-Colonel C. J. Long.
Two batteries of British machine guns, each with ten Maxims.

One battery of British artillery with eight 40-pounder cannons.
One battery of British artillery with six 5-inch Howitzers.
Four batteries of Egyptian machine-guns, each with six Maxims.
A detachment of the Royal Engineers.

Nile Flotilla
Commanding: Commander Colin Keppel.
Three armoured steamers of type 1896: *Fateh, Naser, Zafir.*
Three armoured steamers of type 1898: *Sudan, Melik, Sheikh.*
Four gunboats: *Hafir, Abu Klea, Tamal, Metemma.*
Five transport steamers: *Dal, Akasha, Tahra, Okma, Kaibar.*

On 14 July, the Sirdar, assured of sufficient provisions on
Nasri, ordered the advance. The British division went ahead in
the steamers. The Egyptians went on foot, one brigade after the
other, accompanied by the Egyptian and British cavalry.

The Sirdar learned with relief that his enemy had abandoned
their base at Sabaluqa. The brigades marched in stages to al
Matamma by al Maghawir and al Tarajma on their way to the
new assembly point at Wad Hamid, south of the Island of
Nasri. All supplies were transferred to Nasri and the new camp
at Wad Hamid filled up and expanded day by day as each
brigade arrived.

'Abd al Baqi, ever vigilant, withdrew from his position in
Wadi Bishara. Advance units of the enemy almost swept away
his headquarters, and he was obliged to move to the west of the
river. He was thus still able to observe the enemy at fairly close
quarters.

In early August 'Abd al Baqi succeeded in infiltrating the
ranks of the enemy and was able to gather intelligence from a
regular soldier in the Sirdar's army. From him he gained a
much clearer picture of events. His reports on the enemy take
on a greater precision.

The Nile, tinged purple from the silt of the flood as it sped
north, blended with the khaki of the soldiers. There were armoured steamers, transport boats, hundreds of barges and
forests of wooden masts. All were filled with khaki: thousands
of soldiers on board the ships and barges. Their cries and their
shouts assailed banks that had been silent for centuries. Thus

was the English division borne on steamers in one stage from
'Atbara to the camp at Wad Hamid. To the din were added
clouds of dust that were thrown up on the west bank by scores
of horsemen, as the Egyptian division continued its advance by
long exhausting stages, preceded by the cavalry and accompanied by the war correspondents and the camels. The land
march stopped only at al Matamma, where the men saw traces
of the recent massacre, and also of the trenches built by
Wolseley's Gordon Relief Expedition thirteen years earlier.

At Wad Hamid, the last of the bases, the camp stretched for
more than two miles along the Nile, which provided protection
for the eastern flank. To the south-west the limits of the camp
were marked by a thick *zariba* which extended until it joined up
with the *khur* on its northern side. In the southern half were the
tents of the British division. The northern half was full of the
grass huts that sheltered the Egyptian division. The great white
tent of the Sirdar stood slightly raised. Before it fluttered the
Egyptian flag. The Sirdar's orders were for all the forces to be
assembled by 16 August.

After the Wad Hamid camp was set up, 'Abd al Baqi
transferred his base south of al Rawyan, putting the mountains
of Sabaluqa between him and the enemy. But his horsemen
continued to give a clear picture of the situation with the
precise number of combat steamers and a description of the
camp.

Soldiers of the Khalifa who had been taken prisoner in
former battles and enlisted in the Sirdar's army began to desert
to 'Abd al Baqi in order to join up with former comrades in
arms. The skill in assessing the intelligence improved to the extent that the intentions and timing of the enemy's movements
were known.

'Abd al Baqi had been amazed at the readiness with which
the Khalifa gave up Sabaluqa. He was unable to accept the
reason for the Khalifa's orders to leave the enemy alone during
the march towards Omdurman and begged the Khalifa to
allow him to harass the enemy. When precise orders from the
Khalifa reached him forbidding him to obstruct the enemy he
acquiesced unwillingly, though making one last attempt to
persuade him of the effect of forays against the enemy: 'We

learn with sadness, my Lord', he wrote, 'of your noble order directing us to be alert and watchful day and night to discover news of the infidels. When they move in on us we are not to harass them, but we yield to our Lord to the end complying with the noble order he has placed before us. We are blessed by reading it for it is to our interest and for the increase of our religion'.

Stagnation followed. The Sirdar paused for all his units to be assembled. 'Abd al Baqi passed the time observing the enemy and receiving valuable new sources – fugitives – and sending them on to Omdurman.

On 25 August the enemy resumed the advance. The Sirdar ordered the Egyptian division to make a wide flanking movement to the west to avoid the mountains. As a vanguard, the force advanced to reassemble once again at al Rawyan on the Nile. Nothing now lay between them and Omdurman except the hills of Karari. After the cataracts of Sabaluqa there was no obstacle to navigation on the Nile. All this time a precise report on every movement was forwarded to Omdurman.

The Sirdar's procedure in his march from Wad Hamid to al Rawyan was to send his mounted troops ahead for a few miles. 'Abd al Baqi, under pressure from these horsemen, was obliged to retreat to al Sururab. Here he advised the Khalifa to delay his departure from Omdurman if he wished to meet the enemy at Karari. He estimated that the enemy would reach there within a few days.

'Abd al Baqi established his new base with his usual speed. It was his practice to select a base on the bank of the Nile where he was able to observe the passing of the enemy's steamers and yet remain concealed by high, thick trees on the banks of *khurs* sloping into the Nile. His base buzzed with the activity of horsemen as they set off to reconnoitre, striking west to avoid direct confrontation with the enemy, or as they returned to present their reports and snatch a meal. Inkwells and reed pens were already prepared in the tent of 'Abd al Baqi, who used to hand them out in person. In his camps, one tent served as his residence and office. Here he would interrogate captives and fugitives. Here he would piece together information from the horsemen on their return. Here he would plan his lightning

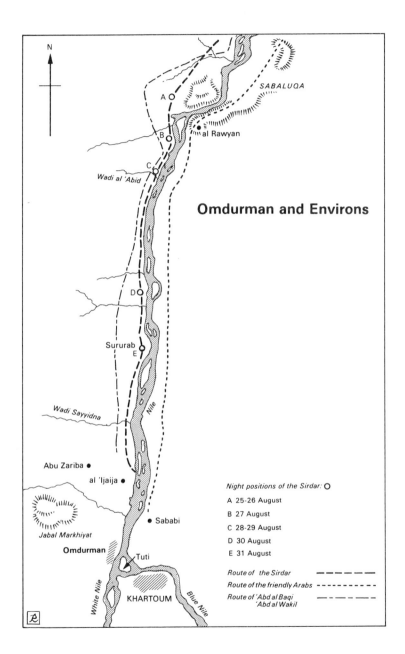

Omdurman and Environs

SABALUQA

A O

B O
al Rawyan

C O
Wadi al 'Abid

D O

Sururab
E O

Wadi Sayyidna

Nile

Abu Zariba ●
al 'Ijaija ●

Jabal Markhiyat

● Sababi

Omdurman Tuti

White Nile KHARTOUM Blue Nile

Night positions of the Sirdar: O

A 25-26 August
B 27 August
C 28-29 August
D 30 August
E 31 August

Route of the Sirdar — — — —
Route of the friendly Arabs – – – – – – –
Route of 'Abd al Baqi — — — —
'Abd al Wakil

129

raids, until they were forbidden by the Khalifa. Round about would be scattered mats for the horsemen and *angaraybs* for the *muqaddams*. 'Abd al Baqi ran his small force of 300 horsemen and fifty rifles with a high standard of discipline. Only once was his camp discovered before it was abandoned.

The Sirdar's army advanced on 25 August in two long parallel columns. The vanguard was composed of two brigades – Wauchope's British brigade on the left clinging to the river and Lewis's Egyptian brigade on the right out in the desert far from the river. Behind them the rest of the brigade took up their positions in a concentrated formation. On their left the Sirdar's flotilla advanced slowly, sailing at the same pace as the infantry and keeping watch on the left flank.

This huge human cube was concealed in a storm of dust kicked up by the Sirdar's mounted forces which set out at dawn into the desert. When his infantry had reached its furthermost point west of Sabaluqa the Sirdar ordered the van to stop and the forces camped in the open, spending the two nights of 25 and 26 August in a vast camp behind a thick *zariba*.

Meanwhile the Sirdar's flotilla was pressing forward, slowly and with difficulty, through the narrow gorge among the cataracts of Sabaluqa. The fleet was alone, for the Sirdar had withdrawn the covering land force, knowing that the Khalifa had already withdrawn his garrison. They imagined the danger they would have been exposed to, as they passed the five forts built and then abandoned by the Khalifa.

The Sirdar stopped the advance at al Rawyan where he returned to the river once more to join the fleet. He constructed the usual *zariba* and spent the day there. At 1600 on 28 August he ordered the next stage of the advance, to Wadi al 'Abid. The army was in a widespread semi-battle formation this time, for the open nature of the terrain allowed him to spread out into the desert on a front of more than two miles. He stopped his forces after only six miles of marching, for gathering clouds warned him of the prospect of rain.

The 21st Lancers advanced and occupied Jabal al Shaykh al Tayyib, which had been used by the Khalifa's advance forces as an observation post and was now abandoned. The Lancers spent time making long-range reconnaissances. Sometimes an individual from one of the Khalifa's parties approached them. They would dash to catch him up, but the swift horseman would elude them and disappear into the distance.

Here and there they came upon small mud villages but they did not turn aside. On Wingate's instructions the cavalry surrounded one such village near the river. The inhabitants were taken from their houses and interrogated. Suddenly a warrior appeared wearing a patched *jubba*. He was taken prisoner and sent to the intelligence department.

The man who caused such consternation in the camp by his audacity in appearing in the garb of the *ansar* was in fact one of Wingate's spies.[1] He told Kitchener that the Khalifa had decided to attack his enemy near Karari with an army numbering around 40,000 men. The agent explained the details of the force, its composition and its positions. After that Wingate held a meeting with Kitchener that lasted far into the night.

The mounted forces returned to the *zariba* at about 2100. The *zariba* closed behind them. Fires were forbidden and the camp was plunged into silence, unbroken except for distant shots and muffled fire from the Khalifa's observation posts in the distant hills.

The reports of 'Abd al Baqi now increased to three a day. We learn from them that he was unable, in the increased tension, to restrain the wilfulness of his horsemen, or to prevent them from making contact with the enemy. He gave an account of the lone charge made by one of his horsemen called al Tahir who 'on his horse made for the enemy's position which was at Wadi al 'Abid and hid until the middle of the night. He lay concealed and got near them. Then he attacked a group in the *zariba* under cover of darkness, stabbing one of them.[2] They shouted and there was an uproar. God came to his assistance and he was not badly hurt. Today he reached us with his news and with blood on his spear. He left the enemy in the same place.' 'Abd al Baqi tried to excuse himself in his report of 27 August to the Khalifa. 'This was a creditable and effective deed which people of zeal and honest enthusiasm commit. Rest assured that this was the isolated act of an individual, committed in submission to his Lord, my Lord, on whom be peace.'

The sun rose on the morning of 31 August and life began to stir slowly in the great camp only twenty miles from Omdurman. Thousands rubbed the sleep from their eyes. The gates of the *zariba* opened and all the mounted forces set off into the wide open space. The Sirdar mounted his horse. Above him fluttered the Egyptian flag and about him were his general staff. All waited for one of the horsemen to return with news of the Khalifa's army.

As usual the Nile steamers were ahead of everybody else, even of the horsemen and cameleers. They had the first clash of arms with the advanced troops of the Khalifa under the leadership of Yunus, who had joined up with 'Abd al Baqi and his men as they prepared to withdraw and join the main army in the rear. The steamers opened fire on the contingents of Yunus and 'Abd al Baqi, which had fanned out in three thick groups facing north, the right flank two miles from the hills. Broadwood's camel corps, in the course of its advance reconnaissance in the desert, exchanged some shots with the left flank of 'Abd al Baqi's force. Soon a semaphore signal gave the Sirdar's headquarters the latest news of the army.

The Sirdar's forces covered no more than eight miles that day. At midday he ordered a halt in the village of al Sururab and forbade further advance, for he wanted sufficient time to consolidate his position for the night. Soon the plain was covered with hundreds of white tents that grew over the ground like small bushes.

From this distance reconnaissance units of the Lancers were able to see Omdurman and the junction of the two Niles through a telescope. But the sky was heavy with clouds and they were not able to distinguish the features clearly. The vast stretch of land that divided them from Omdurman was empty except for the Khalifa's horsemen, who were like black spots dotted here and there. A column of smoke pierced the horizon indicating that the observation posts of the Khalifa were at work. A few minutes later another column arose, this time from Jabal Abu Zariba, the highest hill in those parts. The little spurts of flame appeared in a more or less regular line to the south towards Omdurman.

The Sirdar set up a thick *zariba* this time, the thickness being appropriate to the short distance separating him from his enemy. For the second time this week he was to spend a troubled night. Since noon the clouds had gathered, presaging a night of rain. Soon the skies opened and the downpour soaked the tents. Thunder deafened the ears of the invading army.

The Sirdar sat inside his tent fighting to master the anxious thoughts in his mind. What was preventing the Khalifa, only a few miles away, from attacking him now? The dark night and the din of the thunder were enough to conceal the noise of an advancing army.

It was true that he had taken every precaution. He had constructed his usual *zariba* and had closed off all entrances at sunset. He had despatched numerous scouting parties so that there would be ample warning in the event of an enemy assault. Old friends of Slatin had set off in the dead of night to hide and listen. But vision was restricted and hearing was dulled. It was true that he had ordered all ranks to sleep fully dressed in their battle order and with their weapons within reach. But was this enough? Would it not all be useless in the face of a sudden assault? The Sirdar's machine guns and heavy artillery would mow down friend and foe alike.

The night passed in peace. When the pale light of dawn began to filter through the tents, Wingate and Kitchener breathed sighs of relief. The Khalifa's army was bound to be waiting for them at Karari, now but a few thousand yards away.

Anxiety also dominated the mind of 'Abd al Baqi as is clear in his final report of 31 August in which he said that the enemy were at the gates. After writing it, he speedily joined forces with Yunus in Jabal Karari and from there went off to Omdurman to meet the Khalifa.

NOTES

1   This was al Tayyib al Husayn. He was indeed an invaluable spy for Wingate. He had been secretary of the *bayt al-mal* in Dongola. He had been imprisoned but was released on the personal intervention of the Khalifa. He was an able and highly placed man. Wingate appreciated the value of his report. Anybody who browses through its pages marvels at the precision and detail of the information. Al Tayyib described the

situation accurately, explaining all the Khalifa's preparations. He also presented Wingate with a long list of the Khalifa's units and a census of all the fighters, a list of firearms and horses – both inside and outside Omdurman. Finally he explained to Wingate the Khalifa's battle plan for dealing with the invasion. Wingate made a sketch of this, relying on al Tayyib's information, whose knowledge of the plan shows that he was close to the Khalifa's inner councils. Al Tayyib was taken prisoner by Winston Churchill himself; by sparing his life he did Wingate a great service.

2   Churchill describes this operation: 'But a single dervish horseman managed to evade these, and just as the light faded, rode up to the Warwickshire Regiment and flung his broad-bladed spear in token of defiance. So great was the astonishment which this unexpected apparition created that the bold man actually made good his escape uninjured.'

CHAPTER TWELVE
The Advance

AT dawn on Wednesday, 31 August the rhythm of the drums and the sound of the *ummbaya* announced the advance of the armies of the Mahdiya to the battlefield. The various divisions gathered in the great mosque and in the space to the east of the *qubba*. At 0600 the soldiers began to march, four abreast, in their *rub's* to the parade ground. Before each *rub'* rode an *amir* with his sword unsheathed. As they marched they cried, 'There is no God but God . . . Fight the infidels for the cause of God.'

The commanders of the *rub's* were instructed to go to the parade ground and wait there until the Khalifa arrived. From the west gate of the great mosque on the road to the parade ground masses of armed men poured forth all day. By 1630 the standards were all ready, waiting for the Khalifa to arrive.

The Khalifa left the *mihrab* of the *qubba* in the afternoon. He mounted his white camel and made his way to the parade ground. He began his usual round of inspection and was greeted by his men with a shout of 'God prosper you', to which he replied with a wave of his sword. The old warrior was returning to the battlefield after an absence of more than thirteen years. The effects of the long years of toil and anxiety were clear to all. He had got stouter and his movements were heavier. His beard had turned white. The old serenity and geniality were now mixed with sternness and sadness.

The Khalifa 'Ali wad Hilu was on the extreme right. Behind him flew the Green Standard. His ranks were thronged with people of the White Nile tribes – mainly Dighaim and Kanana. They stretched out for more than half a mile. On his left waved the huge Dark Green Standard over 'Uthman Shaykh al Din who today was flushed with pride, for he was commanding the largest and best armed force on the field. Moreover, his ranks were made up of the flower of the armies of the Mahdiya, the blacks of the *jihadiya*, the *mulazimin*, and the sons of tribal leaders. On Shaykh al Din's left stood the Khalifa Sharif with the Red standard fluttering over its Ja'li and Dongolawi sentinels. Finally on the farthest left were the men of Osman Digna. Behind them all flew the Black Standard, an army by itself. Its *amir*, Ya'qub, as soon as he saw the Khalifa's procession, came forward to greet him. He rode on the Khalifa's right during the review of the army.

The Khalifa then addressed them, urging them to the utmost bravery on the decisive day. Just before sunset he ended his speech. The *amirs* were ordered to spend the night with their men on the parade ground, ready to march in the morning. The Khalifa passed the night there himself in a beautifully decorated tent that had been used by King John during his invasion of al Qallabat ten years earlier. The embroidered crosses had been removed and Qur'anic verses substituted.

Dozens of senior *amirs* were scattered around according to their rank. The rest of the army camped in a huge irregular semi-circle, the arc of which faced north. The tents did not accommodate the whole army, and thousands of warriors huddled together on the parade ground for protection against the cool breezes that heralded the downpour that drenched Omdurman at 2100 that evening.

Here and there fires were made by the soldiers to cook their dinner. All had brought provisions with them except the *mulazimin* and the men of the Black Standard to whom *dhurra* had been distributed.

'Abd al Baqi arrived straight from Karari, whence the last of the observation posts had been withdrawn. He found the Khalifa alone and submitted his final report on the enemy. After he had left Ya'qub called on his brother, staying there until late in the night. Then the advisory council was instructed to come in and the Khalifa presented them with the latest information on the enemy's whereabouts.

The Sirdar, knowing that the Khalifa's army was inside Omdurman, was aware that his greatest danger would occur if the Khalifa made his last stand in the narrow streets of the capital, where the limited field of fire would provide the best opportunity for hand-to-hand fighting. The advantage would go to the side with the greater numbers and blinder bravery.

Kitchener knew that he could flatten Omdurman with his artillery, but he also knew that a battle is seldom won solely by artillery fire. He hoped that the information presented to him by Wingate's spy the previous night was correct, and that the enemy would await him by the hills of Karari where the open country provided an ideal site for mass slaughter.

The last intelligence report stated: 'As it was in our interest to fight the Khalifa in the open, special agents were sent by the Intelligence Department to Emirs who were known to be well disposed to the Government, to persuade them to convince the Khalifa that his only chance of victory lay in his taking the initiative and attacking the Government army. They pointed out that whenever the Government troops had attacked, as at Firket, Dongola, Abu Hamed and Atbara, they had been successful; they reminded him also of an old prophecy of the Mahdi that an advancing force would be attacked and defeated near to Kerreri.'

But the Khalifa needed no persuasion. He had already decided to advance to Karari. When he met his council for final discussions most members were quick to support his plan.

The armies of the Mahdiya were never composed of people who sat at home and waited for the enemy to arrive. Both their nature and their weapons forced them to take the offensive; even their defence was defence through offence. They were armies whose glories and experience were derived from action. Even the apparently static battles such as the siege of Khartoum, or their ambushes, used always to end up with an assault. An army of this type, with up to 40,000 men, needed a wide terrain to enable it to deploy in offensive action.

The Khalifa decided to embark on a great offensive battle on the lines of Shaykan. He explained this to his commanders, who concurred. His plan as presented in Wingate's intelligence diary two days before the battle shows that he decided to divide his forces into two. The rifle section was made up of Shaykh al

Din's *mulazimin*, taking the role played by the *jihadiya* of Abu 'Anja at Shaykan. The assault section was composed of the greater part of the Black Standard, the role played before by Wad al Nujumi. The two sections would attack from different directions. The *mulazimin* would advance north towards the enemy until they had them within effective range of their rifles and then open fire. The assault section, made up of foot soldiers and horsemen, would form a right angle with the riflemen and swoop down suddenly on the enemy from the west, under cover of their fire.

The nature of the terrain, however, differed radically from that of Shaykan. The grass and trees of Kordofan gave cover for Abu 'Anja's *jihadiya* as they assisted the assault from very close range. Hicks' army, moreover, differed a great deal from Kitchener's in weapons, equipment and composition. It would be difficult for the Khalifa's army to get into a comparable position. He worked out the time it would take to get to grips with the enemy if the *mulazimin* opened fire at night. The Black Standard and the horsemen should swoop down on the enemy before dawn from a totally different direction. At Shaykan, the *jihadiya* on the flanks kept firing from behind the screen of grass and trees until the assault units with their spears were able to dash in on the enemy and destroy them. The execution of the plan meant that the Khalifa would have to time his march from Omdurman with precision. He made up his mind not to engage with the enemy before the last third of Thursday night. This meant that he would have to stop the march about five miles from the enemy.

The tactics he decided to employ on going into battle dictated the line-up in the advance. The Khalifa relied on the fire power of the *mulazimin* to guarantee his assault troops, the Black Standard, sufficient protection.

Why did the Khalifa not follow this plan and draw the enemy on into Omdurman? Why was there no effective large scale harassment apart from a few of 'Abd al Baqi's men? Was it because the nature of the terrain between 'Atbara and Omdurman did not permit it? Or did the nature of the enemy's advance allow time for them to create a defensive screen with long-distance reconnaissance? Was the Khalifa unable to countenance the splitting-up of his army? Did he resolve to fight one final battle, and fear dissipating its strength lest there be another resounding defeat? Did he fear the effect of any such defeat on the morale of the rest of the army?

He was facing an intelligent general whose army did not advance in one group as Hicks had done; mounted scouts were scouring the country to the west and south before the general advance. Thus there was an early warning system, enabling the enemy to be immediately on the alert if any danger occurred at night when they were at rest. The open terrain between 'Atbara and Omdurman prevented any force bigger than that of 'Abd al Baqi's from making lightning skirmishes, as Abu 'Anja had done with Hicks. On top of all this the Khalifa, after continuous setbacks, was sensitive about the competence of his commanders. In his heart of hearts he trusted nobody but himself to lead his army into battle.

On the morning of Thursday, 1 September, the whole army offered up prayers at dawn, led by the Khalifa. Cries of 'Allahu Akbar' drowned the noise of distant gunfire coming from the bank of the river where an artillery duel had started between the forts and the Sirdar's gunboats. The Khalifa did not stop to preach as was his custom after prayers, for there was nothing more to be said. After prayers, senior *amirs* of the standards gathered round him to receive their final orders before the march. Then each returned to his own force. At 1105 the Khalifa's horse stepped forward, to the beat of the drum, cries of *'la Illaha ila Allah'* and the shrieking of women – the first step of the Khalifa's army on the advance to Karari.

During the night Osman Digna had drawn the Khalifa's attention to the danger of leaving the right flank exposed, and of the road to Omdurman being without cover; so his forces were placed to cover the retreat and to prevent any attempt on the part of the enemy to bypass the main army and occupy Omdurman. Thus Osman Digna and his men were placed nearest the river and the city.

The high command of the army consisted of the Khalifa's staff and his private guard, numbering 2,000 men armed with rifles. They took up their position directly behind the *mulazimin*. A reserve force followed them under the command of

Ya'qub, composed of soldiers of the Black Standard, representing some forty tribes from Western Sudan mostly, armed with spears and swords. Ya'qub's task was to reinforce any weakness that appeared in the forward assault force. The task of 'Ali wad Hilu was to safeguard the left flank and to prevent Kitchener from encircling them. The Khalifa seemed to be particularly alive to this danger for the reports of 'Abd al Baqi had stressed that the mounted force which reconnoitred in the west was their main mounted force. Kitchener had concentrated most of his mounted troops – seventeen squadrons of camels and horsemen under Broadwood – on the right wing far from the river.

The formation of the advance was deployed to meet all contingencies. But there was one fatal flaw. There was hardly any space, not even a few yards, between one individual and the next, which could minimize the effect of the enemy's fire. Everybody's shoulder was rubbing against that of his neighbour. These masses of men were sitting targets for heavy fire from the enemy. However, had the army been spread out, it would have extended over a front of many miles and been difficult to control. The Khalifa even now relied on the nimbleness of 'Ali al Julla and his other messengers as the only means of communication. This problem of control was to lead to disastrous consequences.

Nineteen cannons were assigned to the battlefield. The rest were in the forts around the capital. The primary duty of the Khalifa's artillery was to tackle the enemy artillery in the gunboats. The artillery in the field advanced to the right of the Khalifa's headquarters. It comprised thirteen mountain cannons, one Krupp, three *Mitrailleuses*, one Remington and one French cannon. The guns were drawn by horses and camels. Behind them other camels carried ammunition in thick bags made of tent cloth.

The gates of Kitchener's *zariba* at al Sururab opened at 0500 on the morning of 1 September and his mounted forces emerged. As usual the Lancers spread out to the left, while most of the others, the Egyptian cavalry and camelry on the right, struck out into the desert. Before long they formed into a crescent shape guarding the van and the right flank of the army.

The mounted forces had covered more than eight miles before the infantry was on the move. Meanwhile the river fleet also set forth. Their task was to destroy the fortifications of Omdurman and to silence the artillery in the forts on the river bank. But this involved the construction of a solid base for the heavy Howitzer cannons. The most suitable site was on the east bank, so Major Stuart-Wortley and his 'Friendly Arabs' were ordered to co-operate with the flotilla in occupying the eastern bank to make it safe for the cannons to bombard the city.

As soon as the Lancers climbed the left peak of Jabal Karari they saw the *qubba* of the Mahdi on the distant horizon. Omdurman stretched out to the south and west. Jabal Surkab (Surgham) concealed part of the land west of Omdurman. Broadwood's cavalry, however, debouched to the west of the Lancers and had an uninterrupted view. They saw the Khalifa's tents spread out like mushrooms, horsemen taking turns to let their horses drink from the pools of water left by the rains of the previous night and the first moves of the Khalifa's army to get into position only two miles away.

The *amir* 'Isa Zakariya, in charge of the east bank had known for two days that things were mounting to a crisis. He now learned that a large force was advancing towards him. His own position was serious. Originally the *amir* Ahmad Fadil had been appointed to defend the east bank. But instead of Ahmad Fadil's army, 8,000 warriors mostly armed with rifles, 'Isa found himself with no more than 1,020 men with 100 rifles and two cannons. He had been sent at first to inspect the forts and to submit to the command of Ahmad Fadil on the latter's arrival. After waiting in vain for Ahmad Fadil, 'Isa crossed the river to consult Ya'qub. He explained that he now had the fourfold task of facing a land force of more than 3,000 soldiers, of dealing with the armed flotilla, of commanding the two forts on Tuti Island, and of having to sever the enemy's lines of communication with the tribes of the Butana and of the Blue Nile.

Ya'qub reassured him that the enemy's force on the east bank was not that big and was mostly armed only with swords. The main enemy was advancing on the west bank. Ya'qub undertook to send assistance as soon as possible when the main enemy had been dealt with. But Ahmad Fadil was expected to arrive before then.

The *amir* 'Isa went back and set up his defences to deal with his various difficulties. He had two possible courses of action. He could make a stand in the forts, bringing all his men together. This had the danger of placing him between two lines of assault, the enemy on the land and the gunboats on the river. Like others, he had heard from survivors of the Battle of 'Atbara about the fearful firepower of the steamers and about the machine-gun fire that swept clean the land and all on it. Men compared the rattle of the Maxim gun to a jug with a narrow mouth when water is poured out of it. Alternatively, to avoid the gunboats, he could withdraw and defend his present position from the village of al Sababi, which consisted of only a few houses; but he then ran the risk of letting the enemy pass him by, cutting his communications with the forts.

In the event 'Isa reached a compromise, deciding to defend the village with part of his force and to reinforce the river forts with the rest. He sent twenty soldiers to Wad Fayit, commander of the fort at Shambat. Twenty more were put under command of Jawda, commander of the fort at al Sababi; most of the remainder were deployed in the village of al Sababi. Finally, thirty horsemen went to the area south of the village among the trees. The commanders of the forts were instructed to withdraw and join him, if they faced an attack.

Six armoured steamers had been moving forward since dawn to provide fire support for Major Stuart-Wortley. After a short conference between him and Commander Keppel, the ensuing action was planned. Major Stuart-Wortley returned to his men and explained his plan to them, based on information obtained from the interrogation of captured prisoners.

There would be three axes aiming at three objectives. The first axis, under the command of Shaykh Ibrahim wad Farah with 830 men, would move along the Nile and attack the forts from the rear, with the aid of fire from the flotilla. A second force with 600 men would make a direct assault on the village of al Sababi. The third force, under the command of Maysara al Zubayr Pasha, was to advance away from the river and outflank the *amir* 'Isa, thereby cutting off his line of retreat.

The action began at 0740. The steamers were the target for 'Isa's cannons, but before the Shambat fort was able to fire a single shell, the gunboats opened fire and with six shells destroyed 'Isa's artillery. Meanwhile intermittent machine-gun fire swept the positions of the riflemen near the fort. During the clash with the Shambat fort, the al Sababi fort opened fire. It was able to fire eight shells in the first seven minutes, all of which fell into the river missing the gunboat, which then changed direction, confronted the al Sababi fort and destroyed it with five shells. The aim was good, the target close and the crew well trained.

Shaykh Ibrahim's men advanced along the Nile, surrounded the village of Shambat and found it deserted. He turned west towards the fort, a mile from the village. Its commander, Wad Fayit, and those still with him – only eight men, for the rest had been either wounded in the bombardment or had joined 'Isa at al Sababi – handed the fort over to Shaykh Ibrahim. His men then advanced towards al Sababi.

The commander, Ghali Jawda, rallied his men after the destruction of the fort, and took cover among its ruins. They opened fire on the advancing troops and a fierce battle took place until Ghali Jawda decided to withdraw and join 'Isa in accordance with his instructions. He and his men tried to slip unobserved through the trees, but Shaykh Ibrahim noticed them, caught them up and annihilated them.

'Isa placed his men in five houses in the village, one hundred men in each house. Two hundred more were under his direct command in the biggest house. Some climbed on to the roof-tops, others took up positions inside and made openings in the walls for the riflemen. The horsemen had their lances ready and waited behind the houses.

At 0900 the van of the central section under the command of Major Stuart-Wortley was seen advancing. 'Isa's men were ordered to hold their fire until the enemy were near. When they were 400 yards away, he made a signal from a window. The horsemen charged and broke Major Stuart-Wortley's ranks, wounding three men. The others withdrew in disorder. The horsemen then spread out to pursue the retreating enemy.

But Shaykh Ibrahim suddenly appeared from the Nile, bringing his men quickly to the rescue. The leader of the horsemen saw that his position between two fires – Shaykh Ibrahim's reinforcements and Stuart-Wortley's men who were now rallying – was dangerous. He gathered his men together and withdrew to the village to rejoin 'Isa.

Finally the three enemy forces advanced on the village – Ibrahim wad Farah from the west, Stuart-Wortley from the north and Maysara al Zubayr from the east. From a distance of 150 yards 'Isa opened fire on the advancing enemy and held their advance for over forty minutes. Then Shaykh Ibrahim's men wheeled round the village, climbed on to the roofs and fired into the rooms. This led to a great slaughter of the defenders whose fire was silenced. Major Stuart-Wortley then succeeded in storming the houses. An unequal battle with swords followed but 'Isa lost more than 200 soldiers and was himself taken prisoner. He was taken to one of the steamers under guard and thence to the Intelligence Department for interrogation but one of the guards pulled out a knife and wounded him fatally.[1] Major Stuart-Wortley was furious at this loss of a valuable source of information and shot his killer. Thus ended the operations on the eastern bank.

Sayyid Jum'a's responsibilities were heavy, for, in addition to his duties as commander of most of the Khalifa's artillery on the western bank, he was also in charge of a front more than six miles long. Two thousand riflemen were under his command.

When the first steamer appeared, the first fort, Shambat west, opened fire. Four shells fell fifty yards short of the gunboat; the riflemen opened fire, but most of the bullets fell far from the target, which answered with rapid artillery fire. This caused no great damage but continued rapidly with the aim of enabling the next steamer to go south under cover and destroy its assigned targets.

According to Commander Keppel's instructions, the priority of targets were: first, the destruction of the Mahdi's tomb; secondly, the destruction of the walls of Omdurman; thirdly, the silencing of the forts.

These priorities to a certain extent reflected the advice of the Intelligence Department, for it was the Assistant Director, Colonel Slatin, who insisted on the destruction of the Mahdi's tomb. In his ten years in Omdurman he had seen thousands of people make pilgrimages to it. He had drawn a pencilled plan of the whole city, pointing out all the vital targets to destroy after the *qubba*: the treasury, the armoury, the barracks of the *mulazimin*, the Khalifa's house and so on. With this information in mind the Sirdar's staff had devised a complete plan for bombarding the city as a first step to storming it. Thus a battery of Howitzers was provided with special ammunition being used for the first time, specially designed for the destruction of fortifications and buildings.

As soon as the first fort opened fire on the advancing steamers, Sayyid Jum'a ordered all the artillery on the banks to open fire. He observed that most gunboats were trying to push through to the south towards Khartoum. Two of them, however, were stationary and were concentrating on the forts. Soon, smoke from the artillery covered both banks of the Nile for four miles. Most of Keppel's fleet was hit by shrapnel from the Khalifa's guns but no great damage was caused except by one shell which pierced the armour plate of *Fateh* with a direct hit.

The gunboat carrying the Howitzer battery succeeded in getting south under cover of the fire of the first steamers. As the Howitzers were being installed on the eastern bank near Tuti, the artillery battle reached its peak. In vain did Sayyid Jum'a seek to get his shells to reach the steamers, which were exploiting the width of the river to keep out of range of the Khalifa's cannons – which at the best of times was never more than a thousand yards.

But the steamers' cannons did not make any appreciable impact. The quick-firing fifteen pounders, in spite of their precision, only partly destroyed the forts. They were only able to silence them completely after the Howitzer battery was installed. The Khalifa's artillery was in charge all along the bank until three o'clock in the afternoon.

After securing the eastern bank, Commander Keppel proceeded to occupy Tuti. He then placed a Howitzer battery on the northern point of the island; but they found themselves within range of the Khalifa's guns, so he was obliged to move them to the east bank, from where they could still reach the *qubba*. But it was impossible to bombard the *qubba* and the walls while there was still a hail of fire from the forts. The Howitzers had a substantial range, so the battery commander changed the priorities and began to pound the forts one by one. Large stocks of ammunition had been deposited inside the forts and now Sayyid Jum'a and his gunners were exposed to the danger of the ammunition blowing up. There was a series of explosions and in four of the forts pieces of stone, human limbs and parts of the cannons flew up into the air. As the sun sank in the west, the fire of the Khalifa's artillery ceased.

Small boys in Omdurman climbed on to the roofs of their houses that morning. Their teacher had dismissed them early so they could take shelter in their homes. But it was more interesting to watch the battle. They were able to see the struggle for the eastern bank between the *amir* 'Isa and the infidels quite clearly.

Meanwhile the mosque began to fill up with women and children who had fled from their houses near the river bank when they came under fire. Later they were joined by some of the artillerymen after their guns had been destroyed.

The dome of the *qubba* was over one hundred feet high. It was supported by a vast square base which housed the tomb of the Mahdi. The walls were three feet thick. At 1510 a 50-pound shell whistled across the Nile. There was a terrible explosion, then silence. But soon screams could be heard from people trying to leave the mosque. A second shell exploded in their midst. In less than a second six score people were turned into a mangled mass of blood and bones.

Now the shells were striking the *qubba* itself. In ten minutes seven shells had made a gaping hole in the cupola. Kitchener's army, as well as the Khalifa himself, was able to see the damage from a distance of more than seven miles.

The Khalifa's army advanced in order until it crossed Khur

Shambat. At 1405 the Khalifa ordered a halt. The army stopped and with one voice cried out *'Allahu Akbar'* and discharged their rifles into the sky.

Shortly after the stop the Khalifa ordered the *amirs* of the standards to come to him. He sat on horseback among them and described by gestures the position and direction of each standard. They received their orders from him and departed to put their soldiers in a state of alert, keeping the same battle formation.

The Khalifa took up his headquarters inside Khur Shambat itself. Osman Digna waited with his men in the depression of the *khur*, out of sight, with the Red Standard in front. The Khalifa Sharif chose a shady tree before which he planted his standard. 'Uthman Shaykh al Din, on the other hand, took up his position south-west of Jabal Surkab, left of the Khalifa in a long line, the end of which was not concealed by the hills from Kitchener's *zariba*. But to avoid being conspicuous he changed from a square formation to a scattered formation with his force in four rows, a hundred yards between each row.

'Ali wad Hilu faced due east, towards the *zariba*, but the folds and undulations of the ground concealed his standard from the Sirdar. His right flank was 500 yards from the western end of Jabal Surkab and his formation stretched north on a front more than a mile long.

The Khalifa ordered his army to stop six miles from the enemy because the time was not right for an assault. Had he wanted a day battle it was still possible, for there were still four hours of daylight left and circumstances were very suitable. The enemy was on the move and would not be dug in behind a high fortified *zariba* in deep trenches. If the Khalifa's intention had been to wait until the following morning there would not have been the series of councils through the night, nor would he have adopted that particular formation, more suitable for assault than for passing the night.

The men now settled down on the soaking wet ground. In spite of strict orders to each person to remain in his place, the warriors were unable to restrain their curiosity and groups began to climb up Jabal Surkab to observe the artillery duel. When the great hole appeared in the *qubba*, voices became gradually hushed. There came the muffled noise of distant explosions. Dust and smoke covered the *qubba* for minutes which seemed like hours. The dust settled and the *qubba* appeared once again. But its tapering cupola appeared to have had its top cut off. At this a heavy silence descended and, as Yusuf Mikha'il wrote, 'There was a natural and embarrassed silence in the ranks of the army.'

The Khalifa saw the sight from his headquarters and cried out, 'There is no power, no might except with God . . . They fear not God but have destroyed the *qubba*.' He soon recovered his composure and, when cries of confusion and dismay arose, he censured his men with the words, 'We built the *qubba* from mud . . . we will rebuild it with mud'.

NOTES
1   Shuqayr, following Major Stuart-Wortley's intelligence report, says that 'Isa was killed in battle. But I questioned Shaykh Ahmad al Nur, a survivor of the battle, and he confirms what I have written.

CHAPTER THIRTEEN

Night or Day

THE Khalifa's dilemma was not between night and day, but rather between the earlier part of the night and the later. On the Thursday afternoon he called an advisory meeting at his headquarters. Among those who attended were the Khalifa 'Ali wad Hilu, the Khalifa Muhammad Sharif, the *amir* Ya'qub, the *amir* Yunus al Dikaym, the *amir* Ahmad 'Abd al Karim, the *amir* Jabir al Tayyib, al Sayyid al Makki, al Tayyib al 'Arabi, 'Abd al Qadir wad Umm Maryum, and 'Abd 'Allah Abu Siwar.

The first to speak was the *amir* Jabir al Tayyib, one of the older Dongolawi *amirs*. 'According to what we hear, my Lord, these people are timid. The best battle plan is that we do not wait for dawn, but that we clash with them in the dark. If the Lord of our religion gives us victory then we will triumph.' The Khalifa expressed his agreement. Ahmad 'Abd al Karim and Ya'qub supported him. After that there was more or less un-animity on the principle of an early night attack with minor amendments. 'Fine', concluded the Khalifa, 'then you are all agreed on that?' They answered affirmatively. He then sent for Shaykh al Din and the *amirs* who were commanding formations.

Two evenings earlier Muhammad 'Abd 'Allah and a companion had sought leave of absence to visit their village of al 'Ijaija and bring their families back to Omdurman. The request was granted so long as they returned quickly. They were told to bring their families back on foot. They travelled slowly and spent Wednesday night at the village with their families. In the morning they pottered about and collected easily portable furniture and wood with which to build a *rakuba* to provide temporary accommodation for their families in Omdurman. As they were about to set out to return to Omdurman, there were suddenly some explosions in the village. All at once they found themselves surrounded by Lancers, who arrested them and took them to the Intelligence Department.

The Sirdar wanted to settle the issue before nightfall. He was very pleased when he saw the enemy advancing towards him and hoped that there would be a single engagement in broad daylight near the Nile and the gunboats. The course of events so far had been satisfactory, and Wingate's anxieties – that the Khalifa was planning a night attack – so far unfounded. This had led him to take a number of precautions during the previous nights. But now he saw the Khalifa's advance with his own eyes.

Wingate had a quick discussion with Kitchener and Slatin. If there was a night battle their superiority in fire-power, which had been amply demonstrated in the operations that morning against the Khalifa's artillery and infantry on the Nile, would be seriously reduced. Vision for the gunners and soldiers would be cut to 400 yards. The Sirdar had the steamers' searchlights at his disposal, and he could also order the detachment of Royal Engineers to light flares. But this would be of small value in the face of 40,000 warriors famous for their courage. The darkness would give them cover to advance from behind the mountain to within a few hundred yards of the *zariba*, the defences of which were not yet completely finished. Kitchener decided to amass his army in a circular formation to produce the largest amount of fire in all directions.

Now it was up to the Intelligence Department. Slatin planned a great deception. It was necessary to get in touch with the Khalifa by any means possible. The Lancers in the van were ordered to obtain a prisoner at any price.

In the Intelligence Department headquarters a European dressed in the uniform of a colonel approached the al 'Ijaija villager Muhammad 'Abd 'Allah and his companions and addressed them in perfect Arabic. They recognized him at once as the Khalifa's old attendant, who always used to march by the Khalifa's horse. Slatin asked them where the Khalifa was. They replied that he was behind the mountain with his army. He asked them to go to the Khalifa and tell him not to leave the field of battle and flee. The Sirdar would advance on him the following day before dawn with all his army. If he advanced then the Sirdar would be ready to meet him. Muhammad 'Abd 'Allah and his companions left to go back to the Khalifa's camp. They had an audience with Ya'qub who asked them some questions and then took them to the Khalifa. They repeated what Slatin had said, and were questioned about the enemy's preparations. They reported his exact position and described how the dust had been stirred up by the Egyptians digging trenches. They were ordered to return and bring back more information. The two men went back to the Sirdar's camp, but were bound and sent to one of the steamers under guard.[1]

Before sunset Ibrahim al Khalil, after checking the dispositions of his *rub's*, climbed to the summit of Jabal Surkab and watched Kitchener's *zariba* in the last moments of activity that preceded nightfall. The sentries were in pairs in front of the *zariba*. Trenches were being dug. The English division was gathering piles of thorn bushes. When night fell Ibrahim al Khalil went down to the east accompanied by two soldiers of the *jihadiya*. He went back to his soldiers in the Khur Shambat and was told that the Khalifa was asking for him.

The Khalifa's last council was attended by the *amirs* Ya'qub, Osman Digna, Ahmad 'Abd al Karim, 'Abdallah Abu Siwar, Shaykh al Din, Ibrahim al Khalil, Yunus al Dikaym and 'Uthman Azraq. Others present were 'Uthman Dikaym and Muhammad wad Bishara.

It is not known how the Khalifa opened the council, or how far they were influenced by the information of the men suborned by Slatin. It seems more likely that he laid the information before them and waited for discussion to crystallize than that he disclosed his own inclination to abandon the night offensive. The council would not otherwise have taken up so much time.

The first to speak was Ibrahim al Khalil. He called for an immediate offensive. Shaykh al Din opposed him from the beginning and a row flared up between them, feeding on former animosities. Ibrahim al Khalil said, 'I have had the chance of seeing the defences of these infidels. If you give me the *rub's* of Shaykh al Din I will deliver to you the corpses of the invaders in the morning.' He meant by this that if they started with the fire of the *mulazimin* under his command at about midnight, then the rest of the army would be able to storm the Sirdar's *zariba*. Ibrahim al Khalil did not confine himself to the problem of 'night or day', but put forward a comprehensive plan. Shaykh al Din was furious at Ibrahim's suggestion that he take over the *mulazimin* with himself as a subordinate. Ibrahim harped on the overwhelming superiority of the enemy's firepower; a day assault could not possibly succeed. He also referred to the fire of the flotilla, which all had seen in action.

The Khalifa then turned to the others. Osman Digna proceeded to make a long speech, ending up by supporting a night attack. 'By God, these English. I have known them for fifteen years and I think we should attack them by night. You cannot beat the English without deceit.' Hitherto the Khalifa had not set eyes on a single English soldier – apart from the body of Hicks and the head of Gordon. He used not to make much distinction between one European and another. All were 'Turks'. Most of those present, including the Khalifa, were impressed by Osman Digna's speech, which was based on experience.

'Uthman Azraq then spoke in support of a night attack. Then the Khalifa turned to Shaykh al Din sitting on his right. He made a long speech that resembled a rousing sermon. He began, 'I will not give away my *rub's*', and then made a number of points. 'Who will control these Arabs during a night attack?' He was referring to the people of the west in the Black Standard. Ibrahim replied emphatically, 'I will.' Shaykh al Din ignored him and argued that the effect of firearms in such visibility would be slight. He was of course referring to the firearms of the *mulazimin*, for he wanted his own units to play a major role in the rout of the enemy. Darkness would not help. 'Let us attack in the morning after dawn prayers. Let us not be like mice or foxes slinking into their holes by day and peeping out at night.'

Shaykh al Din overestimated his firing capacity. He wanted a morning fight for the same reasons as Kitchener. Good visibility was needed for effective use of firearms. The debate continued until it became a verbal slanging match between Ibrahim al Khalil and Shaykh al Din. This had a demoralizing effect on the others, which communicated itself to all ranks. Then for a long time the Khalifa remained silent. Finally he said, 'The best course is what God chooses. We fight in the morning after prayers.'

The meeting broke up. Ibrahim stood up and brushed down his *jallabiya*, for they had been sitting on the ground. He said to the others as they left, 'The best course is what God chooses. But there will be no victory.'[2]

The Khalifa's strategic sense, it must be admitted, was neither very sound nor practical. The effect of his own military background on his capacity as a field commander differed a lot from the effect on his capacity as a grand strategist. Negative factors outweighed the positive. During his long period of rule, in which he was never a commander in the field, he lost any sense of the development of modern weapons and tactics. His last experience had been with the slow-firing rifles and the cumbersome cannons of Hicks, nearly all of which had a limited range of fire. He had never been able to assess the effect of Maxim machine-guns or anything like the Nile flotilla with the best gunners of the British Navy, who were themselves the best in Europe. He had seen no shrapnel, with its splinters that showered down on soldiers. He did not know case shot, with its capacity for destruction at short range. Finally, he was not to know that a direct assault in broad daylight without strong cover was almost impossible after the introduction of the Lee-Metford rifle, with its ability to produce a vast weight of aimed fire. Furthermore, the modern Egyptian army was quite different from the soldiers of Hicks. Here was a new generation not only untainted by a sense of banishment, but assisted by one of the strongest armies in the world.

On the other hand the Khalifa was aware of his own ability to control his forces, and so insisted on directing the assault himself. He knew that his personal presence would encourage his men. Darkness might rob him of this advantage. He delegated much responsibility to his commanders but had little confidence in their capacity to carry out his orders in the way he wanted. 'Uthman Shaykh al Din was no Abu 'Anja, to whom he had entrusted an army twice the size of the present one. And 'Uthman Azraq was no Wad al Nujumi.

Nor were the soldiers any better than their commanders. The *jihadiya* of Shaykh al Din, in spite of their training and discipline, were quite different from the experienced *jihadiya* of Abu 'Anja. Most of the rank and file of the Black Standard were men from western tribes. Their courage and loyalty were beyond question, but there was doubt about their self-discipline in battle as a regular army. Mahmud wad Ahmad had often complained of their lack of submission to any law or discipline. He had insisted that any battle should be under his direct control.

The Khalifa now wanted the issue settled with the invaders once and for all. The last thing he sought was the chance for them to withdraw, reorganize themselves and harass him anew. His objective was total destruction, not a temporary success or an empty *zariba*, which in his view was what a night offensive would at the most achieve.

Furthermore, the darkness was not enough protection to enable him to get near the *zariba*. Lights were blazing in front of it and he would be attacking an enemy that was able to see him quite plainly, but whom he was unable to see.

He realized that he had lost the artillery battle of the morning, and that his cannons would not be able to stand up to the guns of the infidel. He began to reassess his forces in the light of the result of the morning's battle, although he had not yet learned all the details.

Most of the Mahdiya's early victories had used guerrilla tactics, avoiding a direct confrontation with the enemy, except in favourable circumstances. They had refrained from a second assault on el Obeid, preferring to besiege it for four months. They had refused a direct confrontation with Hicks until they had drawn him for hundreds of miles to a convenient battle ground. They had resisted the temptation to make an assault on Khartoum, choosing rather to besiege it for a whole year. Such were the principles of guerrilla warfare: attacking when the enemy was weak and avoiding him at his time of strength. But the time for guerrilla tactics had passed. The army of the Mahdiya had become a regular army. But had the commanders and the Khalifa himself become ordinary generals who by their nature avoided night offensives in preference for traditional battles?

Kitchener was relying on his fire-power first and last. The steamers' searchlights and the flares would not enable their fire to have much effect for more than 300 yards. The distant shelling from artillery to which the Khalifa's first assaults were exposed the following morning would not have been so effective in the darkness of night. No artillery would be able to adjust its firing to have such impact, no steamboat would be able to intervene with its fire so decisively and so speedily as it did the following morning. If the Khalifa's army had been able to clash at close quarters with the enemy the result would have perhaps been different, as was demonstrated when the only unit of the army that managed to do this had their opportunity with the Lancers in Khur Abu Sunt.

As for the possible retreat which the Khalifa worried about, there were enormous practical difficulties involved for Kitchener, who had doubtless thought about it. Not all the steamers were suitable for transport, and they would certainly not have been able to carry all his army, his artillery and his animals. Moreover, there would not have been sufficient time to organize an orderly withdrawal in the event of a night attack.

NOTES

1   There are four accounts of this incident which sometimes contradict each other. First there is the account of the people of al 'Ijaija themselves. This I have related above. It is generally corroborated by the account of 'Abd 'Allah, the Khalifa's servant, who was interrogated by H. W. Jackson six months afterwards. Then there is Wingate's account and finally the account of Slatin himself, recorded by H. C. Jackson in *Osman Digna*.

2   I have relied on the evidence from Shaykh Amin Ahmad Sharfi, who

heard it from his maternal uncle, Ahmad 'Abd al Karim, one of the *amirs* of the Red Standard who took part in the council, and on the evidence of Sayyid Musa Ya'qub, son of the *amir* Ya'qub, who heard it from the *amir* Yunus al Dikaym and the *amir* Isma'il Ahmad, who were both participants. The accounts tally, even in the statements I have quoted above. There are also many oral traditions about what went on. They are all unanimous on the violent dispute between Shaykh al Din and Ibrahim al Khalil.

CHAPTER FOURTEEN
The Last Night

DURING the night of 1 September the men of two mighty
armies chatted in groups together while they waited for their
commanders. The warriors of the Khalifa were scattered in
small groups in Khur Shambat and on the plain by Jabal
Surkab. They were preparing their evening meal. Fires were
being lit here and there for brewing tea and coffee. On the
slopes of Khur Shambat servants and slaves of the wealthy were
busy with provisions already cooked which they brought from
Omdurman.

The soldiers of the Black Standard behind Jabal Surkab were
scattered over a wide area. They spent the evening discussing
the rumours that were flying around the camp. Talk was on
topics of the moment. Some said that there would be a night
attack. Others spoke of the dispute between Ibrahim al Khalil
and Shaykh al Din. Nearly everybody agreed that it would be
best to engage the enemy far from the Nile. It would be ad-
visable to keep well away from those contraptions that swam in
the river hurling their lava and bullets. Total silence settled on
the Khalifa's ranks after evening prayers. Each commander
had been ordered to impose silence; even the beasts had to be
muzzled if they made a noise.

A number of the Khalifa's scouting parties were scattered in
the plain between Jabal Surkab, Karari and the Nile, the no-
man's land between the two armies. One of the groups dodged
the searchlights of the steamers and made its way unmolested
right up to the *zariba*. They remained there for a while and then
turned back to report to the Khalifa. The enemy did not

engage with any of these scouting parties for, apart from the sentries, the Sirdar had ordered all infantry and cavalry forces to remain inside the *zariba*.

After the final council, some of the senior *amirs* returned and gathered round the Khalifa's *angarayb*, sitting on the ground. Among the last to arrive was Ya'qub. The Khalifa's dinner was brought in and placed on the ground. He invited the *amirs* to eat with him and sent for Osman Digna, who was among his men in Khur Shambat. They ate only a little. Even Osman Digna, with his enormous appetite, did not eat much. Finally the Khalifa stretched out his hand and took a few morsels, staring grimly into the darkness. Then he reclined on his *angarayb*, propping his chin first on one hand, then on the other, chatting from time to time with 'Uthman Azraq, who did not leave him all night. He asked many questions about his enemy, this tribe that had invaded his land. 'Uthman Azraq's answers helped to fashion the plan that finally took shape in his mind.

Two matters in particular troubled the Khalifa. The first was the destruction of the *qubba*. It was not because of the labour that had been expended. All the building materials had been transported from the ruins of Khartoum. The best architect who could be found in the capital had been commissioned to design it. In the depths of his soul he did not care about *qubbas* and tombs, for when major *amirs* of the Ta'aisha had asked him to build a *qubba* over the tomb of his father at Abu Rukba, he laughed and said that if the choice was his he would not bother. But he knew the customs of the people of the Nile valley, that they were used to perpetuating the memory of their learned and holy men with fine tombs. It was the symbol of the destruction of the *qubba* that upset him. He had relied on the Mahdi's name and instructions for thirteen years, and he was aware of the effect of the ruined *qubba* on the morale of his army.

The other problem troubling him was the searchlights that lit up the plain of Karari. This prevented him from sleeping, for he wondered whether the enemy might launch a night offensive. When the lights approached his position, 'Uthman Azraq kicked the Khalifa's white tent over so that it collapsed to the ground; in light like that the white tent was an un-mistakeable target.

After midnight the Khalifa summoned the senior *amirs* of the three standards, Ya'qub, 'Abd 'Allah Abu Siwar and Ahmad 'Abd al Karim. They decided who should be their successors if they should fall.

Later a scout returned from his reconnaissance and explain-ed to the Khalifa roughly the enemy's position, and the dis-tribution of his forces. It had not been possible to gather precise information because of the searchlights and because of the sentries with whom Ya'qub had forbidden them to clash. The report showed the Khalifa that the English were camped by the river but that the Egyptians were moving towards the mountains of Karari.

It was after midnight when Wingate left the Sirdar's tent, abandoning him to his thoughts and fears. Kitchener had taken the initiative for over two years. He had been confident whenever he had entered a battle. One initial artillery bom-bardment would break the enemy's back, the cannons and the gunboats would crumble the defences, mow the enemy down and sweep the ground clear. The infantry and cavalry would get to grips with what was left. Fortune and his clever in-telligence officer had always enabled him to get what he wanted. Now he wanted the same kind of battle as Firka, al Hafir and 'Atbara. The Sirdar had taken the greatest care. He had considered every factor from the extension of the railway line to the availability of sufficient war material. But this novel situation which he found himself facing could turn his calculations completely upside down.

The Intelligence Department was swollen with scores of war correspondents, representing more than ten newspapers and magazines. The German Chief-of-Staff had asked London if they might send somebody to observe the lessons the cam-paign might illustrate. The British War Office agreed and the German, Baron Adolf von Tiedemann, kept muttering to Kitchener his favourite expression, in which there was a trace of mockery, 'The first of September – your great day and our great day . . . *Sudan* and *Sedan*!'

CHAPTER FIFTEEN

The Plan

IN broad outline the Khalifa's plan was an assault in two phases, each phase consisting of two axes. The first phase was to be undertaken partly by the 4,000 men of the Kara led by Ibrahim al Khalil. They were placed on the southern slope of the extension of Jabal Surkab. The second axis of the first phase was made up of the 8,000 men under 'Uthman Azraq. These were detached from the *mulazimin* and contained other reinforcements. They were to the south-west of Jabal Surkab. The second phase involved Shaykh al Din. His force, made up of the *mulazimin* minus those with 'Uthman Azraq, were to cross the plain between Karari and Surkab far from the *zariba* and then make a broad flank movement to storm Jabal Abu Zariba. They were then to wait for the moment to launch the second phase. The Karari hills, as they were occupied by the enemy, would be an objective in the first phase and a forming-up line for the second. The Green Standard, 4,000 men, under the command of 'Abd 'Allah Abu Siwar, moved into a position north-west of Shaykh al Din. Finally the Black Standard, 12,000 men under Ya'qub, occupied the area west of Jabal Surkab.

Osman Digna's men occupied Khur Abu Sunt. Their role was to guard the road to Omdurman, preventing the enemy from moving forward and cutting off the Khalifa's army.

Two cannons on Jabal Surkab were attached to 'Uthman Azraq to back up his assault.

The first phase was to start after dawn prayers. 'Uthman Azraq and his *mulazimin* were to advance to the north-east to

Jabal Surkab, turn east to face the Nile and make a frontal attack on the middle of the *zariba*. Ibrahim al Khalil and the Kara were to advance to the north-east and then turn and make a flank assault on the *zariba*. It was necessary to launch the two assaults simultaneously and under cover of the artillery attached to 'Uthman Azraq. However, the firepower of this assault was about one third of the Khalifa's total strength in the battle, and was small in proportion to the numbers it had to cover.

Meanwhile the *mulazimin*, under Shaykh al Din, were to advance, while the enemy was dealing with the assault of the first phase, to occupy the hills of Karari and then wait.[1] The Green Standard was to move behind the *mulazimin* and occupy a line north of Jabal Abu Zariba and to stay with the *mulazimin*. The role of the Black Standard, the reserve for the first stage, should the first stage be successful, was to advance and finish off the enemy.

The assault of the first phase had one of two purposes. Either it would succeed in inflicting heavy losses on the enemy and leave the reserve force to deal the knockout blow, or it would cause only partial losses to an enemy who would repel them, when their main task would be to act as bait to draw the Sirdar out of his *zariba*. The second phase was left to the Green Standard, the Black Standard, the *mulazimin* and most of the firepower that was kept in reserve far from the field of operations.

Success depended on timing and the enemy's response. If the horsemen and infantry of the Sirdar's army were to advance towards Omdurman, they would be at their most vulnerable – exposed outside their defences, their gunboats unable to offer assistance. This was to be the moment for the second phase. There would be an assault from the south-west undertaken by the Black Standard, led by Ya'qub and his 12,000 men behind Jabal Surkab. They would attack the flank of Kitchener's forces as they were facing south. Under cover of fire from the *mulazimin*, they would get to grips with the enemy. The northern axis of *mulazimin* would be supported by a shock assault launched by the 4,000 men and 400 horses of the Green Standard, led by the *amir* 'Abd 'Allah Abu Siwar, from their positions on Jabal Abu Zariba. They too were to be covered by fire from 10,000 *mulazimin*. It was essential that these two assaults took place at the same instant.

Meanwhile Osman Digna was to protect the line of retreat to Omdurman. In the event of failure on the field he wanted to keep open the option of a battle in the streets of the city.

The Khalifa's plan was flexible. The main flaw was his complete ignorance of the enemy – in contrast to the enemy's knowledge of his own forces and dispositions. The plan showed a careful balance in the distribution of firepower and manpower. It was hoped that an element of surprise would be achieved and take the enemy off balance. The plan was, as it were, an ambush on a huge scale.

This challenges the notion that the Khalifa threw tens of thousands to certain death in one of the biggest massacres in history. The idea of a huge planned ambush explains the freezing of the Black Standard for three hours. It also explains Shaykh al Din seeking to avoid the *zariba* and its fire in his advance north to Karari.

In fact both phases were like enormous pincers closing in on the enemy from different directions. It was an intelligent exploitation of human resources, for the plan guaranteed an engagement and dispersed the efforts of the enemy over several fronts. It was much better than the first simple plan for a night offensive in which he poured all his men from one side and all his fire from another.

It may seem that the Khalifa, by insisting on the complete separation of the firepower of the *mulazimin* from the assault forces, strained the two arms of the pincers. This may be true of the first phase, but when we see the whole plan we note that the terrain of Karari itself was tailor-made for such a plan – relying on two land masses, the hills of Karari and Jabal Surkab, as cover for the warriors.

One must not assess the plan with too much hindsight, but from the resources and information available to the Khalifa on the day. Even so, we are bound to admit that Karari was not the brightest day for the Khalifa as a field commander.

Did the Khalifa realize that the enemy would be weakest when he left his defences on the way to Omdurman? If so why did he not wait for that moment and save himself the trouble of a costly assault when they were strong? Did he wish to deceive the enemy by concealing another large part of his army among the hills in an attempt to persuade them that what they could see comprised his entire army? Or was he afraid of leaving the initiative to the enemy? The answers lie, once more, in the Khalifa's fatal miscalculation of the enemy's firepower.

The Khalifa's forming-up lines were a long way from the objectives. Shaykh al Din had to go ten miles to reach his objective, Ibrahim al Khalil and 'Uthman Azraq seven.

The Khalifa was unwise to distribute his horsemen among the various fronts. If he had collected them together, or at least assigned a large part of them to either of the phases, it would have been much more useful. The speed of the horsemen would have guaranteed that their assault reached Kitchener's *zariba* in spite of strong concentrated fire, for the slope of the ground towards the Nile and the undulations here and there would help to reduce losses.

In all battles of the Mahdiya, however, horsemen were hardly ever used as a single unit. Most of the horses that entered the battle – about 2,000 – were the private property of *amirs*, *muqaddams* and the wealthy. To gather them into one group would have meant depriving the army of leadership at all levels.

Finally, timing. The dawn attack meant that the enemy had the rising sun behind them. The sun lit up the advancing soldiers, dazzling them and reducing their ability to discern their objective.

In short, nonetheless, the underlying flaw in the Khalifa's plan was his insufficiently detailed knowledge of the enemy. He received no further report on the enemy's dispositions throughout the night. The searchlights probably prevented the reconnaissance patrols from getting near the *zariba*; they also prevented Wingate for the first time from getting precise information of the Khalifa's intentions.

An hour before dawn the Khalifa took up his position in front of his army on a slight elevation, behind the standard of the Black Standard which was planted beside him. Behind him stood the *khalifas*, then Shaykh al Din and then the senior *amirs*.

His armies stretched out from him in two great wings.

The mountains returned the call of thousands as they prayed with their leader. The ranks surged in unison as they knelt and bowed and stood up again. Among them were more than ten thousand men who were praying for the last time.

The Khalifa ended the prayers and recited the *Fatiha*, to be echoed by 40,000 soldiers. He then took out his sword and brandished it three times in the direction of the river and the enemy, calling out *'Allahu Akbar'*.

The leaders of the Standards then gathered round him to receive their final instructions – ,'Abd 'Allah Abu Siwar, Osman Digna, Shaykh al Din, Ibrahim al Khalil, 'Uthman Azraq and Ya'qub. The Khalifa, mounted on his horse in their midst, explained his plan, indicating with his hand the positions among the hills. He then dismissed them, wished them well and dismounted from his horse.

At 0340 the banks of the river echoed to the sound of reveille inside the Sirdar's *zariba*. All within pulled themselves together, shaking themselves to get rid of the effects of an uncomfortable night on the damp ground. The Sirdar had ordered all ranks to sleep fully dressed, with their arms at hand. The soldiers assembled to take their breakfast, and each took as much as he could. A long day was before them, full of fighting. None knew when he would next eat.

The Sirdar had passed a tense night. He was still anxious for he could not see how any commander could think of launching an attack in daylight on this wide plain in the face of such sophisticated weapons of destruction. He ordered his cavalry to advance to discover the enemy's intentions. If the enemy remained in their places he would take the initiative and attack. He wanted a quick battle and then an advance on Omdurman, in order to avoid a close engagement with the enemy inside the city.

The gates of the *zariba* opened at five and the Lancers slipped out to the left. The rest of his mounted forces – the cavalry and camelry of Broadwood and the Egyptian mounted artillery – had already moved to the north-west to take up positions on the hills of Karari at 0300. Broadwood placed his cavalry facing south-west and arranged his artillery to their left. The Lancers advanced with two platoons in front and two behind. They scaled Jabal Surkab and sent a report back to the Sirdar about the position and intentions of the enemy. Groups of Lancers reached the summit of Jabal Surkab and beheld a great human throng whose cries were re-echoed by the valleys. The horsemen hurried down the hill to inform the platoon commander, 'The enemy is advancing towards the *zariba*.' The platoon commander reported to the regimental commander. He in turn quickly reported to the Sirdar. Soon the news spread – 'The enemy is on the move'.

The banner of the Black Standard flew high over the Khalifa's head. It was the most prominent among hundreds of flags and proclaimed his position among his bodyguard. The army moved forward and passed on either side of the Khalifa to take up their appointed positions.

The Khalifa and his guard proceeded to occupy the position he had already chosen, south-west of Jabal Surkab.

As the great army marched into battle the hills reverberated with the echo of their anthems and their intonings of 'There is no God but God'. The drums beat in time to the quick march of the army. To this was added the high whistle of the *ummbaya*, to be heard for the last time in action.

At 0520, two miles from Jabal Surkab, the Khalifa's army began to split up. The left and centre, the Green Standard and Shaykh al Din's force, peeled off towards Karari. They crossed the wide plain four miles from Kitchener's *zariba*. The forward ranks of 'Uthman Azraq marched round the north of Jabal Surkab and then faced due east. The army of al Kara, led by Ibrahim al Khalil, turned to the east and concealed itself behind the extended ridge of the hill and placed the left flank on the enemy *zariba*. Battle was about to be joined.

NOTES
1   Winston Churchill's presentation of the Khalifa's plan was fairly accurate. He either deduced the situation from the course of the battle, or learned from local sources about the Khalifa's reactions when his plan went awry. Churchill saw the Khalifa's dispositions himself at the begin-

ning of the battle. He also visited Cairo in 1899 to gather information for *The River War*, when Wingate and the Intelligence Department provided him with what they had obtained from the interrogation of senior *amirs* who had been taken captive.

CHAPTER SIXTEEN

The First Phase

At dawn all the Sirdar's forces were drawn up facing west. He had massed his infantry and artillery round the *zariba* in the form of an arc, the length of which was about one mile and the chord 1,300 yards.

From left to right, that is from south to north and following the line of the *zariba*, the disposition of the forces was as follows: furthest to the south on broken ground were three companies of infantry from the British division. They blocked the gap between the *zariba* and the Nile. To their right were three batteries of artillery. One battery, the 32nd, had six-pounders, and two had Maxim Nordenfeldt twelve-pounders and six Maxim cannons. Ammunition lay within reach of each team. Lieutenant-Colonel Long commanded all the artillery. Between the brigades of Lyttelton and Wauchope were placed two Maxim machine-guns. Then two more cannons and two Krupp batteries – six-inch cannons, drawn by mules – were placed between the British and the Egyptian brigades. A battery of Maxims was between the brigades of the Egyptian division, commanded by Maxwell and MacDonald. A battery of Maxim Nordenfeldts was placed among MacDonald's brigade.

The front rank was formed of men two deep, and stood directly behind the thorn bushes of the *zariba*. The second line was thirty yards further back. This enabled riflemen to take turns, for ammunition to be brought forward and for the wounded to be evacuated to the back.

Between the arc of the *zariba* and the Nile were placed the

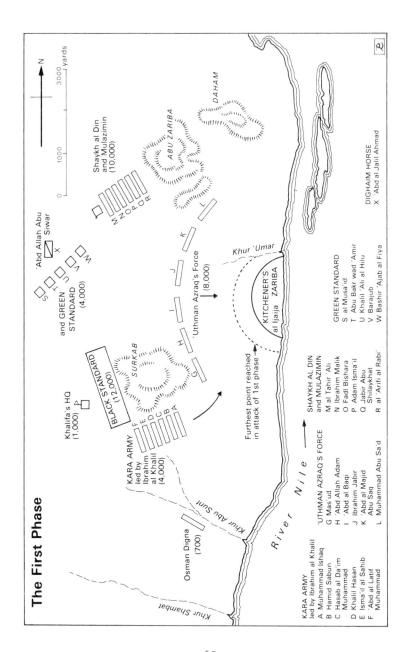

The First Phase

KARA ARMY
led by Ibrahim al Khalil
A Muhammad Ishaq
B Hamid Sabun
C Hasab al Da'im
  Muhammad
D Khalil Hasan
E Isma'il al Sahib
F 'Abd al Latif
  Muhammad

'UTHMAN AZRAQ'S FORCE
G Mas'ud
H 'Abd Allah Adam
I 'Abd al Baqi
J Ibrahim Jabir
K 'Abd al Majid
  Abu Saq
L Muhammad Abu Sa'd

SHAYKH AL DIN
and MULAZIMIN
M al Tahir 'Ali
N Ibrahim Malik
O Fadl Bishara
P Adam Isma'il
Q Jabir Abu
  Shilaykhat
R al 'Arifi al Rabi'

GREEN STANDARD
S al Musa'id
T Abu Bakr wad 'Amir
U Khalil 'Ali al Hilu
V Barajub
W Bashir 'Ajab al Fiya

DIGHAIM HORSE
X 'Abd al Jalil Ahmad

supplies, a field hospital, tons of ammunition and about 3,000 camels in the care of Collinson's Egyptian brigade. The strongest steamers of the flotilla, *Melik, Sultan* and *Zafir*, were anchored, while the other gunboats patrolled the Nile. The Sirdar placed all his long-range firing power, particularly the Maxim guns, in the front line, to produce the largest volume of fire in the first phase of the battle. The weight of the fire-power was concentrated on the left of the *zariba* to face the impact of the expected attack. Here were three batteries of Royal Artillery and the fire of the British division with their long-range modern rifles.

In the face of this terrible concentration of fire, more than one hundred cannons, thirty machine guns, and the rifle fire of two and a half brigades, Ibrahim al Khalil and 'Uthman Azraq launched their attack in broad daylight and on open ground over 3,000 yards.

The Howitzer batteries began the battle at 0520. They bombarded Omdurman and now opened fire on the vanguard of Osman Digna's forces as they were taking up their positions in Khur Abu Sunt.

The army of the Kara, led by Ibrahim al Khalil, advanced alongside Jabal Surkab and then to the eastern ridge that concealed them from the enemy. Ibrahim was in the front row on horseback, followed by a servant holding a second horse. He always went into battle in this way, and always named them 'Aim' and 'End'. At this moment he was riding Aim. The ranks of his *rub'* advanced in a human mass on a front of 800 yards and ten men deep. The rows were parallel and the men in step. Ibrahim exercised complete control over his soldiers. There were over 500 banners indicating the positions of the officers and commanders of the various units.[1] Most banners were concentrated around the centre of the front where Ibrahim was, with his standard-bearer behind him and his deputy to his right.

The front line reached the slope of the eastern ridge of Jabal Surkab. Ibrahim stopped on the slope and turned to rearrange his men into an assault formation. Without a word he nodded as each commander took up his position. Muhammad Ishaq al Ta'aisha was the commander of the biggest *rub'*. He lined up in front. Behind was the *rub'* of Hamid Sabun. Then the *amir* Hasab al Da'im. Finally the ranks of al Kara, crowded together in a thick mass 1,000 yards wide and eight men deep. Then Ibrahim al Khalil turned to advance towards the enemy.

'Uthman Azraq was along the northern end of Jabal Surkab. He first faced north-east, then changed direction to face east towards the *zariba*. 'Uthman's ranks stretched out in a crescent shape. The two wings of the crescent stretched out from a dense concentration at the angle itself, where men stretched back for 300 yards in eleven rows, to the wings where the men were only three or four deep. His front covered two miles of the plain. Thus his formation was roughly parallel to that of the *zariba*. The right extremity mingled with the forces of Ibrahim al Khalil as they were ascending the ridge, and so the whole of the assault line was two and half miles long.

The left wing was less dense. 'Uthman Azraq did not arrange his assault units in *rub's* one behind the other, as had Ibrahim, but all were stretched out in one line: the *rub'* of Mas'ud on the far right, then 'Abd 'Allah Adam, then 'Abd al Baqi. In the middle was the *rub'* of Ibrahim Jabir, representing the hard core of the assault. Muhammad Abu Sa'd held the left flank, to the left of 'Abd al Majid Abu Saq. The advance was less organized than Ibrahim's, for there were gaps between one man and the next.

When the right wing carried out a movement groups of Lancers opened fire on them. The *amir* of the standard which was on the farthest right moved forward at the head of twenty horsemen to clear the Lancers off Jabal Surkab, but 'Uthman Azraq sent a horseman to order them to desist, for the main enemy was less than two miles away in front on them.

'Uthman's mounted troops were scattered here and there among the lines. His artillery was under the command of Muhammad 'Abd al Rahman and 'Ali al Misri. The guns were drawn by camels and horses. They advanced at a slower pace than the rest, struggling along slowly in the middle. When they turned to face the *zariba* 'Uthman stopped the advance to allow the cannons to come forward and take up their position in front.

At 0635, when 3,000 yards from the enemy, the cannons

were fixed and steady. 'Uthman Azraq raised his hand. Two shells were fired but they failed to reach their target. One fell 500 yards, the other 100 yards, short of the *zariba*. Nevertheless the cannons continued to fire, though not one shell reached the target. After these first shells, the Sirdar ordered all his cannons on the left to return fire on the ranks of 'Uthman Azraq, who were now an ideal target – only 3,000 yards away and over a front of two and a half miles.

The first line of the Kara army reached the summit of the ridge of Jabal Surkab at 0640, and then went down the other side. Ibrahim himself had reached the level plain when his last men topped the ridge. Now they were able to see the *zariba*, 2,800 yards away. As soon as they set eyes on their enemy, they cried *'Allahu Akbar'* with one voice. Their pace quickened and they opened fire. Puffs of white smoke from their rifles appeared in Ibrahim's ranks. They fired their weapons without stopping or taking aim. There was no attempt to take cover, nor to concentrate their fire. Some of their bullets went over the heads of the British division. Others fell short of the *zariba*.

Now, when they were only 2,800 yards away, the battery of thirty-two cannons, the two Maxim batteries and the artillery on the gunboats *Melik* and *Fateh* opened fire on them. Twenty shells fell among their ranks in the first minute. The effect was lethal. The earth shook and the violence of the explosion disrupted the regularity of the advancing men.

The smoke and dust from these first shells settled. The effects were at once revealed. Wide gaps appeared among the ranks, and the pattern of the advance was upset. Each shell brought down roughly ten people, but the feelings of dismay lasted only a short while. The advance was renewed with extra vigour. The voices of the *amirs* and warriors were heard above the din of explosions: 'Fill up the gaps. Fill up the gaps.' Only a few seconds passed before they closed ranks again and began to fire at the *zariba*. They prepared to reload the rifles and fire again, but the shells exploded in their ranks once more, now with greater intensity. The explosions covered the whole front and penetrated to the back. Some shells burst in the air above their heads and a shower of red hot metal came down.

The fiercest fire came from the artillery of the British division on the left side of the *zariba*. Ibrahim al Khalil was in the front line, restraining his horse to keep it at the same pace as his infantry. Thus the force remained tightly knit, in spite of the wide gaps that were beginning to appear in its ranks. When the horse had covered a quarter of the distance between the ridge and the *zariba* it collapsed suddenly under its rider. For a moment confusion reigned. But Ibrahim al Khalil rose from the ground unhurt. A large splinter had wounded the horse's neck and brought it to the ground. Aim had fallen, so Ibrahim now mounted End. After an interruption of but a few seconds, the advance was renewed. They were now 800 yards from Jabal Surkab, but their numbers were dwindling with the hail of fire. As they approached the enemy, their rifle shots began to kill a few soldiers. But there was little opportunity for them to reload or to take aim.

Detachments of Lancers were, up to this moment, occupying Jabal Surkab. At 0705 a message came from the Sirdar to return at once to the *zariba* to avoid the machine-gun fire.

One thousand yards from the enemy Ibrahim al Khalil was learning of the devastating effect of the enemy artillery. The plain was filled with thousands of corpses. Yet they had had the enemy in sight for only half an hour. Aware of his acute disadvantage in the face of this massive firepower, Ibrahim decided, at a distance of 800 yards from the *zariba*, to veer to the right and enter one of the *khurs* where he might pause, take stock, realign his forces and continue the attack. There he would be only 1,200 yards from the *zariba*. He motioned to his men to follow him to the right. Then at this moment, 0705, he was hit in his chest and head. He fell from his horse. End also fell, for he too had been hit. The Maxim machine-guns had opened fire, and one of their first victims was the commander of the Kara army. It was remarkable that he had survived so long, for throughout the long artillery bombardment he had been in the front line. Four horsemen dismounted and bore Ibrahim back amid a shower of bullets. The ferocity of the fire was such that the army's pace was checked, preventing it from turning to the right to shelter in the *khur*. But even so the scattered survivors continued to advance. Shells exploded on all sides. Many men fell; few rose again. When they had the chance they fired their guns, but it was an unequal contest. Moreover, the twelve machine guns of the three steamers were all now firing at a range of about 1,000 yards. Shaykh Babikr Badri, who was a few miles away, described the regular volleys as being fired 'at intervals and the enemy fired on them with a sound like "runnnn"'.

The command now fell on the shoulders of Muhammad Ishaq who tried to rally the reduced force. He indicated the new direction with his hand, but was immediately and fatally struck by a whole volley of bullets. In the open space there was no cover for a warrior to concentrate his aim and direct his fire, apart from a few scattered bushes, and even when these were reached the machine-gun fire was directed at them, and men and trees were torn up without discrimination.

During the heavy fire not one soldier flinched or turned back except to carry a wounded comrade. This significantly reduced the fighting number in the battle, for a large part of the force was diverted to succour the wounded. It was the tradition for the wounded to be borne by those who were on his immediate right and left. As each standard was made up of a family or tribe, succour to the wounded was founded on tribal loyalty.

By 0720 there was no longer a front line or a rear line, but a number of groups gathered together in two large conglomerations. One group organized itself into a single line, most of them bearing swords and spears. They advanced in a desperate assault on the *zariba*. When they were 500 yards away they were utterly wiped out and not a man survived. The second group wheeled round to the left to join up with the ranks of 'Uthman Azraq north of Jabal Surkab. Their battle at this point had reached its most violent climax.

The Khalifa in the midst of his attendants went north-west towards Jabal Surkab. South-west of the hill he stopped and set up his headquarters on a low stony plain, with Jabal Surkab between him, the Nile and the enemy. The Khalifa's private guard sat round his headquarters in rows. *Angaraybs* were put down but the Khalifa did not sit on one. Instead he spread out his *furwa* and sat on that, surrounded by Khalifas, advisors, senior *amirs* and his private guard. Among those with him at his headquarters were the Khalifa 'Ali wad Hilu,[2] the Khalifa

Muhammad Sharif, al Sayyid al Makki, Muhammad 'Umar Banna, 'Abd al Qadir wad Umm Maryum, al Mudaththir al Hajjaz – the Khalifa's seal bearer, al Tayyib Hashim, Muhammad al Badawi, Ab Jukka – the Khalifa's personal attendant, the messenger 'Ali al Julla and Yunus al Dikaym.

The Khalifa stood up. Meanwhile Ya'qub continued to advance with the Black Standard. The Khalifa handed the banner to a horseman who raced ahead and handed it to Ya'qub. Ya'qub then turned to his forces, who were not properly organized, and called on the *amirs* of the *rub's* to call their men into order. They stretched out on a 2,000 yard front facing north-east, but Jabal Surkab concealed them from the rest of the battle.

Two cannons were placed in front of the Khalifa. After a while the sound of distant intermittent gunfire could be heard following the start of Ibrahim al Khalil's assault. 'Ali al Julla was sent to climb Jabal Surkab and report on the situation and the development of the first assault. Did Ibrahim need reinforcements? 'Ali al Julla returned and gave a detailed and optimistic report of the assault. The Khalifa commented, 'That's settled the score with his cousin,' meaning that Ibrahim's cousin, Mahmud wad Ahmad, still in captivity, was now avenged. The *amir* Khayr al Sayyid was then ordered to occupy the summit of Surkab. Khayr climbed the hill with one hundred soldiers. He stationed them on the summit and returned to the Khalifa's headquarters.

Shaykh al Din and 'Abd 'Allah Abu Siwar had detached themselves from the main body of the army two miles away when the soldiers for the first phase had peeled off. Shaykh al Din was in front and 'Abd 'Allah behind. Shaykh al Din headed north-east where the peaks of Abu Zariba blocked their path. He formed his force into a thick rectangle more than 1,200 yards long, made up of *rub's* of *mulazimin*, densely packed. The *rub'* of al 'Arifi al Rabi' was in front, all of them armed with rifles. His four sections formed the front line, and the *rub'* of Shaykh al Din overlapped it a little on the left. Behind it was the *rub'* of Jabir Abu Shilaykhat, then those of Ahmad Isma'il, Fadl Bishara and Ibrahim Malik, with the *rub'* of Tahir 'Ali at the back. The formation was for assault and the pace was rapid in spite of the slopes of Abu Zariba.

Two hundred yards behind Shaykh al Din's formation another force was drawn up, about 2,000 strong, in the form of a huge square. This was Shaykh al Din's guard, led by Rabih al Habashi, who was on his horse in the middle. Shaykh al Din was a long way from the front ranks, hidden away among thousands of men. In that position he was unable to control the fast-moving situation. Effective command of the force devolved on the *amir* al 'Arifi al Rabi'.

The Green Standard, led by 'Abd 'Allah Abu Siwar, proceeded in its normal parade formation. 'Abd Allah was in front and behind him were the *rub's* of the standards in rows, each *rub'* made up of one hundred warriors from White Nile tribes. Behind 'Abd 'Allah marched his own *rub'*, then the *rub'* of Abd 'Allah Barajub, then Muhammad al Musa'id, then Bashir 'Ajab al Fiya. The horsemen of the Dighaim trotted alongside on the left to guard its flank.

At first the Green Standard marched as one group with the *mulazimin*. But the gap between them grew as the latter wheeled slightly to the east to cover and then to attack Abu Zariba, at that time occupied by Broadwood's mounted troops and horse drawn artillery.

The first shells were now discharged by 'Uthman Azraq. However, the copper casting was extremely thin. This weakened the effect of the shrapnel and most of the shells fell hundreds of yards short of the *zariba*. 'Uthman ordered his artillery to the right to Jabal Surkab, to take up positions on the summit and assist the assault from there.

The two wings spread as they advanced towards the enemy and the crescent shape began to change slightly. The flanks had been told to spread out so that the whole *zariba* might be covered. 'Uthman Azraq positioned his riflemen haphazardly among the assault troops, and thus failed to take advantage of effective concentration of fire. He raised his rifle and fired a shot as a sign to his riflemen to open fire and for the spearmen to attack. Puffs of smoke appeared from rifles here and there on the wide front, but they had no appreciable impact on the *zariba*.

Kitchener had placed a complete battery of Maxims – six

cannons – exactly in the middle of the *zariba* and also a group of 15-pounder cannons. At 0655, when 'Uthman Azraq's men were 2,800 yards away, the Sirdar opened fire, not from the cannons alone, but also the machine-guns and all the 12,000 infantrymen whose position enabled them to take aim. The first wave of firing had little effect on the massed troops. The distance was relatively great and the plain between Surkab and Karari was covered with bushes and grass that had sprung up after the rain. Away from the river these lessened, giving way to the pebble-strewn plain.

The fire of the Egyptian brigades on the right of the *zariba* had absolutely no effect on the assault. Their Martini-Henry rifles had less range than the Metford rifles of the British division, who were preoccupied at that moment with checking the charge of Ibrahim al Khalil.

'Uthman Azraq slowed his men down, but the enemy artillery soon found the right range. His front lines stopped to fire. Bullets found their way into the *zariba*, especially among the British division where men were standing up. The Egyptian brigade was not a clear target, for only their heads could be seen above the trenches. Although 'Uthman's fire was haphazard – the distance varied between 1,600 and 2,000 yards – some bullets found their target inside the *zariba* and soldiers of the British division began to fall; the number of casualties, dead and wounded, topped forty.

The Sirdar stopped his horse behind Wauchope's brigade. When he saw a lot of activity on the part of his stretcher-bearers he ordered the centre of the *zariba* to be reinforced with artillery from the left, as the impact of the assault of Ibrahim was waning. At 0700 two cannons were brought forward. Four other Maxim cannons were withdrawn from the Karari hills where they had been reinforcing Broadwood's mounted troops.

The second salvo was more effective. It exploded among the front ranks and gaps appeared as thousands fell. Whole standards were seen to disappear. As the second salvo died away a third followed. The ranks instinctively closed into the centre. They thus became even more vulnerable. Hitherto many of the enemy's bullets had missed their mark because of the gaps. But as the whole assault force packed into one massed body, a massacre began. The whole fire of the enemy was concentrated on a human target now less than 1,200 yards from the *zariba*.

In vain did 'Uthman Azraq reform his force and scatter his men again. The only effect of his shouting and gesticulations was to spur them forward. He noticed that the fire that was massacring his men came from the right. In order to avoid this he decided to change his direction to the left, where stood the Egyptian brigades with their relatively short-range guns and where the cannon fire was much less intense. Although the enemy was less than a mile away it was clear that if they crossed this distance at the same pace most of his force would be destroyed. He therefore decided to launch a quick attack with his horsemen. They would charge the *zariba* and tear it down so that the infantry could follow and engage the enemy in hand-to-hand combat.

'Uthman Azraq detached fifty horsemen and one hundred foot soldiers. He unsheathed his sword and dashed forward. His standard bearer followed and then the rest of his standard.

His assault was in the face of the Maxim battery at the middle of the *zariba*. The battery gave them everything it had. The horsemen began to fall around 'Uthman Azraq as he charged forward, but the distance steadily decreased. Then a bullet struck him in the thigh, but his horse still bore him forward as the bullets rained down on him. He fell from his horse 400 yards from the *zariba*, the bullets found him even as he lay on the ground. The standard bearer and five other dismounted horsemen continued their charge towards the *zariba* but the fire mowed them down one by one.

'Uthman Azraq had ordered a second group to break into the *zariba* under the command of Ibrahim Jabir. The latter was able to cut his way through in spite of the fire, but when he saw the weight of fire bearing down on him he decided that his aim, at this stage at least, should be to find a strong position from which he could direct his own fire towards the enemy and thereby give cover for the assault troops to reach the *zariba*. There was no suitable elevation, but there were depressions, so he ran with 300 riflemen behind him to a sandy depression 500 yards in front of Wauchope's brigade. The depression protected them somewhat from the artillery fire. They lay down and began to fire at the British brigade who were standing up. In the first ten minutes they brought down five of the enemy, then five more, then twenty, then fifty. The artillery relaxed their fire to deal with the larger mass that had succeeded, in spite of the slaughter of half its numbers, and in spite of the storm of hot metal that was pouring into their faces, in getting within 200 yards of the *zariba*. Twenty cannons and the machine-guns continued to pound away at the advancing mass at a rate of sixty shells a minute. The great din of the artillery and the cloud of dust it sent up paralyzed mind and feet. Their pace was checked and this gave greater opportunity to the machine-guns and to the thousands of riflemen.

By 0740 the fury of the attack was largely broken. The various advances, without standards or centurions to keep them together, split up into small groups here and there. These disintegrated into smaller groups of three or four. Now the enemy artillery began to sweep the plain clean. In the end the whole plain was covered with dead and wounded. The only survivors were those carrying the wounded to the rear and the standard of Ibrahim Jabir which was still in its hiding place, directing steady fire at the enemy.

The extension of the battle for at least half an hour was the result of the efforts of this group. In spite of the fact that the distance was too great for effective fire and in spite of the fact that they had little opportunity to take careful aim, and that they lacked sufficient ammunition, these few men managed to stand firm for a whole hour while the battle raged around their heads. Indeed, Wauchope was seriously thinking of requesting the assistance of some cavalry to clear them out of their position. Most of the losses of the British brigade in the first phase were caused by the fire of Ibrahim Jabir's standard.

At 0755 the fire of the 15-pounder battery on the left of the *zariba* was trained on the sandy depression to silence the riflemen of Ibrahim Jabir. Shells fell round the standard; then one fell right in the midst. The cannons had found the range and more shells fell inside the depression. Ibrahim Jabir found that his fastness had become a death trap. He ordered his men to advance on the *zariba*, but the fire of the machine-guns and the artillery picked them off, until they were almost all wiped out. Ibrahim Jabir was wounded in the stomach and two men carried him back.

Thus ended the first phase. Losses amounted to about 7,000 – 2,800 dead and 4,200 wounded.[3] Among the dead were the *amir* Ibrahim al Khalil and 'Uthman Azraq. The enemy lost five officers and 155 men, dead and wounded.

The attack of the first phase was against a well-entrenched enemy fortified within its defences. The two attacks of 'Uthman Azraq and Ibrahim al Khalil were launched from no tactical base. All that was seen was several thousand warriors apparently hurling themselves at death.

Mistakes crept in at an early stage. There was inadequate preliminary reconnaissance. Ibrahim al Khalil made no attempt at cover. It would appear that hardly anything was known of the enemy's position, but, in fact, Ibrahim al Khalil was one of the few who had made a reconnaissance on the Thursday afternoon. His time and opportunities were limited, but was he unaware of Khur Abu Sunt on the right, and the scores of twists and turns in the land that led to the Sirdar's *zariba*? Or did he expect that the attack would be at night and that the cover of darkness would be a greater guarantee than the terrain?

The task of reconnaissance itself was not alien to the armies of the Mahdiya. Both long-range reconnaissance and personal inspections of the land by the commander go back to Shaykan.

Most commentators on the Battle of Omdurman have said that the assaults of Ibrahim al Khalil and 'Uthman Azraq were made over open ground; this was not entirely true. The plain in front of and to the right of Kitchener's *zariba* was full of twists and turns in the land. We have seen how the standard of Ibrahim Jabir took advantage of a depression not more than 150 yards long which enabled them to stand fast for more than an hour.

Was Ibrahim al Khalil rash? He had been the staunchest advocate of a night offensive and was most concerned about the importance of cover to guard against the superior firepower of the enemy. But one tends to think that Ibrahim al Khalil attacked in order to die and not to win a victory. He had been furious at Shaykh al Din's scorn. His head was bowed as he led the attack, and he was silent up to his death.

If one follows the path of the assault of Ibrahim al Khalil in early September, one will see that the terrain between the hills of Karari and the Nile is not entirely a flat plain, but is covered with small bushes to a distance of 2,000 yards from the Nile. Then there is a large area of bare ground covered by pebbles as far as the river. The real collapse of the attack took place between 1,200 and 500 yards from the Nile.

After the introduction of the Lee-Metford rifle, any frontal attack in broad daylight was doomed to failure. When we add to the rifles the terrible new fire of the machine-guns the chance of a direct attack achieving any success is further reduced. Commanders needed twenty years and a world war to absorb this lesson.

In the space between Surkab and Karari there is a network of watercourses and *khurs* indicated by trees and an extra greenness and thickness of vegetation as one approaches the river. The watercourses finally meet in one large deep *khur* full of trees – Khur 'Umar. This slopes directly down to cut the Sirdar's *zariba* at its weakest point, at the positions held by the Egyptian brigades. It was as if Nature herself was pointing out the ideal path for attacking the *zariba*. The failure to take advantage of this cannot be blamed wholly on Ibrahim al Khalil or 'Uthman Azraq; the allocation of troops for the various phases was the role of the higher command, and their concept of the first assault was as 'bait' to draw the Sirdar out.

'Uthman Azraq's military fame rested on the practice of the indirect approach. He had favoured a night assault, and his complete neglect of the ideal way of getting near the enemy – such as by the Khur 'Umar – is strange.

Churchill observed that the early wars of the Mahdiya – 1884, 1885 and 1889 – anticipated the outstanding courage of September, 1898. But there the similarity ends. Forethought and adherence to sound tactical principles seem to have been abandoned.

For most of the last two centuries the main objective of an infantry attack had been to get the assault forces as near to the enemy as possible. The soldiers armed with swords and spears should be preceded by riflemen who open fire as the others advance. The riflemen were exposed to heavy loss from the defenders, but their continuous fire and their relentless advance should hinder the enemy in his aim. Eventually the assault force should be able to get to grips with the enemy.

In the years 1884–1885 the Mahdists owed their success to the fact that the commanders and the armies behind them understood these theories. Wad al Nujumi had applied them with success at Shaykan when Abu 'Anja's *jihadiya* led the firing section and Wad al Nujumi himself the assault section. Abu 'Anja carried them out with skill in his attack on Omdurman. Al Nur Anqara followed them out at Abu Tilayh against the Gordon Relief Expedition. Even in 1888 Abu 'Anja was able to apply the principles successfully in Ethiopia against forces that were superior in numbers and firepower. The Sirdar practised the same tactics against the Mahdists when he attacked Mahmud's *zariba* at 'Atbara.

The military commanders of the Mahdiya went through no military academy. Instead they had talent and imagination, stimulated by experience. During the early years the commanders always bore these principles in mind. As the army increased in size, the standard of leadership rose to take on the greater responsibility. The commanders developed these principles by using cannon fire to increase the volume of cover by organizing the artillery into batteries and by manufacturing ammunition locally.

But these fine principles seem to have been abandoned in 1898. The firing force was not kept distinct. It did not act as one group. The Khalifa had planned a separation between his firing power and his assault forces in his original plan, for he was of the older school. But the assaults of Ibrahim al Khalil and 'Uthman Azraq were conducted quite differently. When 'Uthman's assault was neutralized and his forces immobilized, the objective of the riflemen was thwarted. The objective was not to kill or wound the enemy but to provide cover for the assault force. But the spearmen had been wiped out.

The nub of the problem was generalship. All the outstanding commanders of the Mahdiya were absent from the field on 2 September. Wad al Nujumi had been killed on a suicidal mission. Abu 'Anja was dead, as was Al Zaki. Al Nur Anqara was far away in al Qadarif. The commanders of 2 September were quite different. Ibrahim al Khalil, for all his intelligence and maturity on strategic matters, had not had the experience of facing Hicks or Graham or Gordon.

At 0650 Shaykh al Din was on his way to the hills of Karari. With their broad front it was clear that the *mulazimin* would be able to cover the whole of Jabal Abu Zariba. The *amir* al 'Arifi al Rabi', with a strong, well-armed *rub'*, organized the first wave of the assault. To his right was the *rub'* of 'Uthman Adam. Behind him were all the *rub's* of the *mulazimin*. A thousand yards divided the bloc of *mulazimin* and the Green Standard. The assault of Ibrahim al Khalil and 'Uthman Azraq had been intended to divert the enemy artillery from 'Uthman Shaykh al Din and 'Abd Allah Abu Siwar. The *mulazimin* were thus able to occupy the areas required without any interruption from enemy fire. After 1,000 yards they reformed, and their front line reduced speed a little to enable the *rub'* of 'Uthman Adam to overtake on the left and then to wheel round to the right of the enemy and prevent them from withdrawing to the north.

The hills of Karari are made up of two natural knolls that in places reach a height of 300 feet. These are Jabal Abu Zariba and Jabal Daham. Between them is a ridge over 1,000 yards long. Jabal Karari, after which the area is named, is only a small isolated hillock near the bank of the Nile. The bigger of the two masses, Jabal Abu Zariba, is made up of three peaks, forming an axis from north-west to south-east. The whole area is covered with dark sharp rocks that hinder the movements of camels and horses.

When Kitchener sent all his Egyptian mounted forces to occupy Jabal Karari before dawn, his prime objective was to prevent the enemy from turning and surrounding the Egyptian brigades on the right of the *zariba*, particularly after they had been weakened by the transfer of four Maxims to the British division. Broadwood, the commander of the mounted forces, distributed his strength in the following way. Eight camel companies occupied the northern and central hills. The horse-drawn artillery occupied the southern hill and faced south-west. They lined up in rows and had a firm foothold. The nine cavalry squadrons were placed in the depression between the central and southern hill, while all the horses and camels without riders were gathered on the rear slopes of Abu Zariba. Whereas Broadwood was expecting a small secondary flank attack, he found himself facing a major assault by 10,000 men, most of them armed with rifles, and behind them 5,000 more.[4] The situation became critical, for the Sirdar had taken away his main firepower – four Maxim cannons – and had ordered them to be sent to the *zariba* to help check the direct assault.

The gap between the Green Standard and the *mulazimin* expanded as they headed for divergent objectives, the Green Standard going to the north of the mountains, and the *mulazimin* heading for the peaks of Abu Zariba. Broadwood saw the great mass of men advancing towards him and became apprehensive. He realized that he did not have the power to deal with them. The *rub'* of 'Uthman Adam managed to scale the northern peak and overtook the *mulazimin*. Broadwood then ordered his dismounted camelmen and horsemen to withdraw at once, to return to their beasts and retire to Jabal Daham. He also ordered the horse-drawn battery to withdraw south of Jabal Daham.

The Sirdar saw the situation quite clearly from the *zariba*. He was aware of the threat to his mounted force and sent Broadwood a signal ordering him to return at once into the *zariba* to take cover with the infantry. Broadwood, however, refused to carry out the order, choosing to withdraw to the north and to draw with him the whole of Shaykh al Din's force. Broadwood's defiant action has received much praise. His initiative had a decisive and far-reaching effect on the course of the whole battle and not just on the safety of the camel and horse squadrons. But even had he wished to obey he would have been unable to do so. For, with the *rub'* of al 'Arifi al Rabi' already on the southern peak of Abu Zariba, any attempt to withdraw, avoiding the bulk of the *mulazimin* infantry, would have been impossible. His decision at first was not so much to withdraw to the north as to withdraw to Jabal Daham and to occupy it with his horse artillery who would then be able to cover a withdrawal to the *zariba*.

When the camelmen and horsemen reached their tethered beasts, 'Uthman Adam was already occupying the northern peak. The riflemen stopped shooting at the retreating enemy, and those with swords and spears rushed forward. The force caught up with the scattered camelmen among the sharp rocks. There was a clash with the last of the camelmen's ranks and the latter were swiftly eliminated. Within minutes more than fifty of the enemy fell and more than seventy camels were lost. The engagement with the rearguard of the camelmen provided a brief respite during which the others got free and retreated in haste to the north-east towards Jabal Daham. The batteries of horse-drawn artillery also had time to open fire on the advancing *rub'* from their new position of Jabal Daham.

The rest of the *mulazimin* reached the three peaks and scaled them. They stopped for a while until they caught sight of their prey trying to escape. They then dashed out towards the ridge and made for the last of Broadwood's retreating force. Soon they were mingling with the men of 'Uthman Adam as they pushed eastwards. The two forces made up a broad front once more.

This engagement could not be seen from the *zariba* but most of the artillery of the Egyptian division directed their fire towards the thousands who were pursuing Broadwood. They joined the cannons of the horse artillery, and the Krupp 9-pounder joined them from Jabal Daham. The fire intensified, but did not daunt the pace of the pursuing thousands.

Broadwood realized that by taking up position on Jabal Daham he was only postponing disaster. The fire of the horse artillery was directed at the ranks of the *mulazimin* at close range, but had no apparent effect on them. Nor was the distant but denser fire from the *zariba* able to check their pace. The camels with their slow strides gave cause for concern, as did the other animals as they struggled among the sharp rocks. The horses succeeded in manoeuvring and withdrawing quickly. Broadwood noticed one of the steamers, *Malek*, observing the situation from afar. It had not so far been able to intervene, for the battle had been confined to the hills. But the steamer began to move north so it could intervene at the appropriate moment. Broadwood then decided to send the camelmen back to the *zariba* under cover of gunboat fire.

The camels would go eastwards towards the Nile and then turn south to the *zariba*, instead of crossing to the *zariba* as the crow flies. The longer route gave the horsemen a chance to cut off the *mulazimin* line of assault. It would then be possible for the steamer to extend a helping hand.

After being joined by the *rub'* of 'Uthman Adam, al 'Arifi al Rabi' gathered his force together. They all advanced under his command, which now consisted of four complete standards with about 1,000 warriors each. Al 'Arifi realized that the aim of the camel corps was to cross the rocky area and reach the Nile, and then to seek refuge in the *zariba*. Until then they were exposed. Then were 1,200 yards away. The horsemen 800 yards to their left were also vulnerable. The camel corps were 1,500 yards from the *zariba* once they had reached the low ground; then they had to turn south, parallel to the Nile. If he followed them this way the chase would yield nothing, for his pace was the same as theirs. Therefore al 'Arifi decided to go straight to the *zariba* and cut off their escape route by the Nile.

He tugged at his horse's reins and turned it to the east. With his rifle he signalled to his men to follow. Behind him was the whole force of the *mulazimin*. Within seconds thousands changed direction. They went off with their usual speed not straight for the camel corps but diagonally, aiming at a point halfway to the *zariba*. Al 'Arifi abandoned all the horsemen to his left, for he had now decided that his true prey was the camel corps.

Broadwood saw that this manoeuvre would expose his men to a clash that threatened to wipe them out. Their new direction and pace ensured their reaching the camels. Only one recourse remained for the camel corps and that was for the cavalry to undertake a charge at the thick mass of *mulazimin*, delay them and thereby gain a few minutes to permit the camel companies to reach the safety of the *zariba*. Broadwood ordered all his cavalry to get into line on the slopes of Jabal Daham and prepare for a charge.

At this moment the position of the camel corps seemed desperate. Here were the *mulazimin* on a front 600 yards broad, thousands of men charging forward at the vulnerable corps. A clash on their flank seemed inevitable. There were but 400 yards to go. Broadwood's camels faced apparent imminent destruction.

Suddenly the situation changed. By altering direction and crossing to the open ground the *mulazimin* had become exposed to the fire of the gunboat, *Malek*, the strongest in the flotilla. Hitherto it had had no effect on the course of the battle, but now it opened up full blast and gave all it could. The effect was instantaneous and devastating. There was one quick-firing 12-pounder, two Nordenfeldt cannons, one Howitzer, four Maxim cannons and twenty-five riflemen. Soon the gunboat *Zafir* joined in to complete the job. A wall of hot iron, of dust and of pieces of rock appeared to spring up and cut the *mulazimin* off from their prey. Hundreds fell in seconds. The first two rows were wiped off the face of the earth.[5] At the moment of complete exposure the fire of the brigades of Lewis and MacDonald from the *zariba* to the south, and the fire from the gunboats directly in front of them and the horse artillery behind them, all joined in.

The bombardment stopped for a few moments, sufficient for the camel company to slip away from the dangerous collision point. The *mulazimin* paused to reorganize. Meanwhile al 'Arifi's horse was injured. His force tried to rally, but was unable to advance and keen to retreat.

Frustrated and furious, they returned once more north to Jabal Daham to give vent to their anger by clashing with the rest of Broadwood's force still drawn up in assault formation.

The *mulazimin* soon crossed the distance separating them from the enemy. The artillery battery, which had turned its cannons to face the south, was their nearest target. Bombardment continued on the *mulazimin's* flanks. The first of the *mulazimin* saw the enemy attempting to withdraw. As the cannon teams assembled their cannons and ammunition, the *mulazimin* poured their fire at them. Some horses and men were injured; the others were then ordered to abandon the cannons. At that moment some horsemen charged ahead to storm the artillery positions. But the two cannons had already been abandoned. Broadwood now ordered a general retreat. He had no alternative. The road to the *zariba* was blocked. To the west was the

Green Standard. To the south the first phase had reached its climax. Thus he had no choice but to retire to the north. It was fortuitous that he also drew off the *mulazimin*.

They passed the two cannons and went after the horsemen in retreat northwards over the rocks and stones. At first it was an equal pursuit, but soon the horsemen of the *mulazimin* were gaining on their enemy. Then the infantry joined in the pursuit, and they too reduced the gap between them and the enemy, thanks to the rocky terrain that hindered the horses' movements. On the northern slopes the horsemen began to engage with the rear elements of Broadway's cavalry. The latter, under the command of Major Mahon, swerved round and launched a flank attack from the right. It was a successful manoeuvre, for they were closely packed, whereas the *mulazimin* were scattered. Major Mahon's assault succeeded in checking the horsemen's pace. Finally the pattern of the pursuit emerged: one group of horsemen and behind them a group of infantrymen going as fast as their legs could carry them. Meanwhile on the river, advancing at the same speed, were two gunboats firing shells at the flanks of the vanguard whenever they had the chance.

Broadwood was soon able to get his squadrons away from the rocky Karari area and on to the open ground. The *mulazimin* continued the pursuit with most of their force. They lost not more than 1,000 warriors in the engagement with the gunboats. The cavalry slowed down from exhaustion, and the distance between the pursuers and the pursued diminished but then widened again.

Where was Shaykh al Din all this time? All who saw him maintain that he was far from the scene of action. He was content quite simply with following the bulk of the *mulazimin* within the bosom of his own private guard.[6]

What was the purpose of this futile chase? Was it thought that foot soldiers might catch up men on horseback? Perhaps catching them up was not an objective at first, although the slackening of the pace of the cavalry from time to time suggested that they could overtake them. Or was the aim just to chase them off the battlefield? If that was so, then they also managed to remove 10,000 fighting men, the Khalifa's strongest units, just at the moment when they were most needed.

At 0800, when the Sirdar was ordering his forces to leave the *zariba* and advance towards Omdurman, at the moment planned for the launching of the second phase in which Shaykh al Din was to be assigned a major role, his forces were sitting on the ground after a quick half-hour gallop, four miles from the battlefield.

At 0750 the Khalifa began to notice wounded men and their bearers trickling back in their hundreds, then in their thousands. They separated into small groups on each side of Jabal Surkab. Some went north and thence into the desert. Others made their way south to Omdurman. These were the survivors of the first attack of Ibrahim al Khalil and 'Uthman Azraq.

On the battlefield itself the ground was strewn with thousands of bodies in battle order just as they had advanced.

The Khalifa's reconnaissance units on the summit of Surkab observed two things: first, the last of Shaykh al Din's forces, now almost out of sight behind the hills of Karari on their way north in useless pursuit of Broadwood's cavalry, and secondly, a stir of movement within the *zariba*. The British Division opened their ranks to let the 21st Lancers through.

The Khalifa turned to 'Ali al Julla and said, 'Go, tell my son 'Uthman to return to the infidels on the mountain.' The crucial moment had arrived, the time for launching the second assault. 'Ali al Julla was at this moment on foot, for his horse's leg had been broken in the first phase of the battle. He left to cross the broad plain. Before he was lost from view the Khalifa sent one of his *mulazimin* to give Shaykh al Din the same message in the event of any mishap befalling 'Ali al Julla. He then ordered Ya'qub to send a *rub'* to strengthen Osman Digna in the Khur Abu Sunt, for it seemed that he would be the first to face the Lancers. The Khalifa ordered riflemen from his private guard to join this *rub'* from the Black Standard. He then went south of Jabal Surkab and into Khur Abu Sunt near to Osman Digna. He was to witness the anticipated collision between the Lancers and Osman Digna, with his forces from the Hadendowa tribe and his reinforcements from the Black Standard.

1   Churchill and other historians call Ibrahim's division the 'White Flag'. As part of the *mulazimin* the colour of their main standard was dark green. The many lesser standards were white, with Qur'anic verses embroidered on the cloth.

2   *Pace* other historians, the Khalifa 'Ali wad Hilu never took part in the attack of the Green Standard. As the second man in the State he did not leave the Khalifa's quarters. The error derives from the fact that the Green Standard was his, and because it took part in the assault it has been assumed that he led it. The Shaykh 'Abd 'Allah Muhammad Nur told me quite categorically on 29 June, 1971, that he was in attendance on the Khalifa 'Ali wad Hilu and never left the headquarters throughout the period of the battle. In fact, *khalifas* had not taken part in battles since Qadir. The leader of the Green Standard in the attack of the first phase was 'Abd Allah Abu Siwar.

3   This estimate is based on the number of corpses counted by Captain Burgess in February, 1899, five months after the battle. He counted 2,300 bodies in the course of this first phase. If we add another quarter – his estimate – as the number probably buried on the battlefield or in Omdurman, we get 2,800 or 2,900 as the number of slain. If we assume the proportion of dead to wounded as two to three, then the total wounded is 4,200 to 4,500.

4   Here we note a great difference in the estimates of the size of the Khalifa's army. Historians have relied on Wingate's information and all say that the strength of the *mulazimin* that stormed the hills of Karari was 15,000. But Broadwood, who clashed with them, estimated them at 10,000. In his report to General Hunter, commander of the Egyptian Division, he said, 'The force attacking us, which was now at right angles with the force attacking the *zariba*, was some 10,000 strong and came on with great rapidity.'

5   'Ali wad al Zayn described this to me on 23 May, 1971. He is one of the few, apart from the *amir* al 'Arifi al Rabi', who survived these minutes. With a quaking voice he told me that a relation of his was at the left end of the broad front and he was at the right end. Four complete standards separated them. When the machine-guns began to fire on them from the gunboat he turned and found that all four standards had vanished. He saw his cousin's standard far off. Later he too fell. When I visited Shaykh 'Ali he was blind and hard of hearing. His daughter, herself an elderly lady, passed on his broken speech to me. She said her father never ceased to wonder why he had been spared, the only survivor of his friends and tribe who had been wiped out in seconds.

6   There are several stories about Shaykh al Din's attitude. 'Ali al Julla told his grandson, Babu Nimr, that when he reached Shaykh al Din, he found him far from his men, 'riding behind them'.

CHAPTER SEVENTEEN
Clash of Arms

O SMAN DIGNA set off at the head of his men towards Surkab. At first he followed Ibrahim al Khalil's soldiers, but then left him, heading due east, taking a road concealed by the bushes of Khur Abu Sunt. Osman Digna himself was on foot but the *amirs* were scattered among the men on horseback. Neither the legendary hero nor his men were at their best on this day. He missed his best lieutenants – Muhammad Musa Digna, his nephew and chief of staff, and Muhammad al Tahir al Majdhub, the ablest of his commanders. Of his earlier companions only Ibrahim Sa'id was with him still. The number of his men was not more than 700. They were the most devoted of his subordinates. Neither the years of fighting and continuous movement, nor even the rout at 'Atbara had succeeded in shaking their loyal allegiance to their leader. They did not have more than thirty rifles among them – all that was left of the thousands that had been plundered from the garrisons of Sawakin and Tokar and the battlefields of al Teb and Tamay. This shortage of rifles hampered Osman Digna in his task. The Khalifa had to be content with giving him the role of defending the line of retreat to Omdurman; no aggressive role was assigned him.

Osman Digna took up his position in a deep, wide part of Khur Abu Sunt, some little distance from the Nile. The *khur* extended in a depression towards the Nile and was still damp from the downpour of rain two nights before. The heat of the sun after the rain had resulted in there being a thin crust of dry mud, beneath which was a layer of sticky mud. The position taken up was about one mile from the Nile. The winding *khur* was sandy, the banks were fissured, with sand dunes here and there. The sheer banks made it a kind of trench six or seven feet deep.

Osman Digna did not arrange his men in lines over the wide expanse between Surkab and the Nile, for he was not a man to be content with a passive role. Instead he decided to exploit his role to the utmost. He quickly devised a plan which depended on one factor – drawing the enemy into a prepared ambush in a suitable terrain that would neutralize the enemy's advantages, and in which the superiority of the enemy's fire would be minimized.

The whole force of riflemen was placed on the northern bank outside the *khur*. They stood up so as to be seen from afar. The rest were ordered to sit on the ground. The bare-chested Hadendowa tribesmen soon covered the depression and the banks of the *khur*, their swords and their curved knives at their sides. For a while there was a low murmur, followed by complete silence. They had been trained for silent operations like this. Silence reigned until half past eight, when it was broken by the noise of reinforcements. The movement of the reinforcements from the Black Standard to Khur Abu Sunt followed the concealed route shown them by the Khalifa. They took advantage of the elevation of Surkab which hid their advance from the enemy, as represented by the advance patrols of the Lancers. They then used the bushes of the *khur* for cover until they reached Osman Digna, who was delighted at their arrival, for his position was none too strong. He soon reorganized his force, detaching the riflemen and joining them to his own riflemen on the bank. There were now 150 riflemen, each standing two or three yards from each other. As for those armed with spears and swords he tried to get them to sit on the ground with his own men. But the narrowness of the *khur* made it impossible for them all to take shelter, so he put them together in one tight group of 2,000 men. Their ranks were more than twelve deep and extended 400 yards to the east.

Thus Osman Digna crouched in silence waiting for his latest encounter with his old British enemies. Behind the *khur* to the south were a few thousand wounded men, a straggling group on its way to Omdurman.

When the Khalifa arrived just after the reinforcement party, Osman Digna was quick to greet him. The Khalifa told Osman about the movements he had seen of the enemy cavalry. He was so concerned with the conflict that was to take place that he left his secure command post in order to observe the battle at close quarters, for he was aware of the threat from the Nile to the road to Omdurman. This side had been protected by the cannons and rifles of the forts, but had become exposed after they were destroyed, thus giving the enemy mastery over the river bank for a long distance. From their position they could see the gunboats. What was to be done if the enemy was able to dash towards Omdurman under cover of the gunboat fire, getting there before the Khalifa? It is true that two-thirds of his army was still intact, and that the moment had not yet arrived to order them to attack the enemy. He did not see any signs to make him deduce that the enemy was leaving the *zariba*.

Kitchener's superior weapons had secured a quick victory in the first phase of the battle, almost without cost, but the situation was still in the balance. There were thousands of fighting men on their way back to Omdurman in front of him; if he delayed any longer in the *zariba* they would certainly reach Omdurman before him. However, it was not these remnants that gave him cause for concern; but where had they hidden those vast hordes he had seen the previous day? He had seen with his own eyes the rout of a large number of them. He had seen another intact group setting off to the north after Broadwood. This latter group had passed Karari behind the Egyptian horsemen and did not worry him too much for they were further from Omdurman than he was. Was this all there was of the Khalifa's army? He consulted Wingate, who confirmed his fears. The Black Standard, the biggest single Standard and one third of the whole army, had not been seen in the battle that morning. It must have set off with the remnants of the army and headed for Omdurman to take up a final stand in the streets of the city. It would not be easy for him to repeat the carnage of the plain of Karari with an enemy like this, for he had witnessed how these men died.

Kitchener was determined to reach Omdurman and to occupy it before the Khalifa, whatever risks were involved. The highest price he would have to pay would be a battle with the Khalifa's army inside Omdurman. He did not wish to engage in a fight in which his principal assets – the cannon and gunboat fire – would be neutralized. Therefore the cavalry should go ahead and engage the enemy, prevent them from reforming their ranks, cut off their line of retreat to Omdurman and deal with the missing force. General Gatacre rode over to Colonel Martin on the other side of the *zariba* and issued his intructions. After a few minutes the 21st Lancers gathered outside the *zariba* and at 0800 set off to the south.

The force advanced in four squadrons, two vanguard and two rearguard, and a column of infantry. At 0815 the regiment stopped on the northern slopes of Jabal Surkab where the great rocky outcrop obscured their view to the south and west and thus concealed the Khalifa's reserve force, the Black Standard. But they could see thousands of wounded on their way to Omdurman. The direct route from the *zariba* to Omdurman was parallel to the Nile. It was free of the enemy and there would be only nominal resistance. The route clung to the river and so cover would be afforded to the infantry brigades and they ought to be able to reach Omdurman before the rest of the Khalifa's army. A signaller flagged messages, and followed this up by sending a more detailed account of their position by heliograph.

Soon a message was being heliographed back from the *zariba* carrying the Sirdar's reply: 'Advance and clear the left flank [the Nile route] and make every effort to prevent the enemy re-entering Omdurman.' These orders were very precise and definite. However, the regiment's commander decided to reconnoitre before advancing.

Some of the Khalifa's soldiers were scattered around the summit of Surkab. They took up positions among the rocks. No sooner had the two reconnaissance parties set off from the regiment than one of them set off south towards Omdurman, slipping through the rocks and observing the right flank of the regiment. The other party turned to the left and for a while was hidden, but then appeared once again climbing the eastern extension of Jabal Surkab.

193

From the very beginning of the advance among the rocks the first reconnaissance party was exposed to fire from the Khalifa's riflemen. These men were part of the Khalifa's personal guard and had occupied the summit of Jabal Surkab as an observation post, sending reports to Ya'qub and the Khalifa. In spite of the danger, the reconnaissance party lingered awhile to have a good look at the view that stretched before them as far as the city of Omdurman. But they saw only the stragglers covering the plain. The mountain concealed the view to the south and west, so that they could not see the Black Standard. When fire began to be aimed at them, they turned back to report.

The other party turned left and climbed to the end of the eastern ridge of the mountain. When they reached the top they saw much the same sight, but in addition they noticed something else, which they examined for some minutes in order to plant the details firmly in their minds. Between the mountain and the fleeing soldiers that were between Kitchener's army and Omdurman they saw a group of men standing firm and facing north, quite separate from any other part of the Khalifa's army. This group stood on the bank of a watercourse which, judging from the trees on both sides, seemed small and dry. This force was, of course, the riflemen posted by Osman Digna on the north bank of the *khur*, who, seen from the mountain, seemed to be particularly conspicuous. Closer observation would have disclosed the advance of the reinforcements joining Osman Digna, and not even the corrugations of the land could have prevented them from seeing the whole force. In fact they were looking at the core of Osman Digna's men during the few moments of silence before they were joined by the reinforcements.

The leader of the party reported what he saw to the regimental commander, who questioned him about the men who were neither wounded nor in retreat. The idea began to form in Colonel Martin's mind of launching a cavalry charge at that group of men, piercing through them and then cutting their line of retreat. Colonel Martin was motivated by reasons of sentiment which had only the slightest connection with tactical realities. It would be the first test for the regiment in the field;

indeed they had never taken part in any operation outside Britain except for a period when they had had to guard Napoleon on St Helena. At last an opportunity was presented to launch a cavalry charge, the summit of the hopes of every cavalry officer at that time. As Churchill afterwards confessed, this feeling was uppermost in their minds. The enemy, the terrain, the circumstances, these were matters of secondary importance.

Thus Colonel Martin's wish to take part in the battle and to engage with the enemy was quite natural.[1] After all, a handful of ragged, barefoot savages would not daunt a regiment of British cavalry. And so Colonel Martin did not head for the Nile to open up a way for the infantry advance. Instead he decided to confront the enemy. Turning his regiment, which had assembled on the northern slopes of Jabal Surkab, he descended towards the river, but veering slightly to the south. He continued with his original formation until he was parallel with Khur Abu Sunt where the Ansar riflemen were standing. The latter opened fire on the regiment. Six hundred yards from the *khur* the regimental drum was beaten, a sign to form up in line and to prepare for a cavalry charge. While the regiment advanced at an even pace the horsemen in the rear began to move forward on the right making up a long line which extended for about 300 yards. Osman Digna's men stopped firing. They paused to look at the regiment as it advanced, stretched out before them. For one fleeting moment it looked as if they were about to surrender. But the Colonel at once banished this thought from his mind. He did not want the glorious charge for which he had long been waiting to be spoilt.

Four hundred yards from the enemy, at 0837 he motioned to the dummer behind him. A rapid drumroll signalled 'Charge'. The Lancers' charge began.

Osman Digna's force of riflemen was under the leadership of Ibrahim Sa'id. Most of them were from the reinforcements and they were standing ten yards outside the *khur*. Inside the *khur* the pressure of the reinforcements and the confined space made the ranks of the force armed with spears and swords extend for 400 yards. They were at their most dense on the left where the reinforcements had joined them. Here men stood shoulder to shoulder forming one solid mass. To the right the pressure lessened gradually.

More than 2,000 warriors concealed by the sudden six foot depression sat on the ground with their spears raised and ready. Above them stood a line of riflemen. Having organized his men, Osman then addressed them. He raised his voice so that the riflemen above with their backs turned towards him might hear. He reminded them that the first objective was to get the enemy off their horses and on to the ground. Then it would be possible to inflict greater losses. They were to kill the horses, however much they were themselves exposed to the fire of the enemy in their midst. Their numerical superiority ought to guarantee their victory. After he had wished them God-speed he withdrew a short distance to join the Khalifa and then climbed up the north bank of the *khur* to survey the enemy.

When the Lancers were 600 yards away, the signal was given to open fire. The fire was directed low and had its effect, for horsemen began to topple from their mounts one after another. The range was close and the target was clear. The

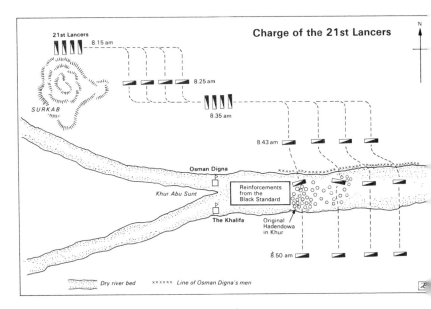

regiment slackened its pace to allow all the troops to fall into line in preparation for the charge. Osman Digna was worried in case the enemy was going to stop altogether, or alternatively to outflank him. He signalled to the riflemen to hold their fire. They stopped, even though the enemy horsemen were only 400 yards away. The line of the enemy was reformed and they galloped forward at full speed. There was now no alternative to a clash. Osman ordered the soldiers in the *khur* to get up and face the onslaught.

The cavalry spurred on their mounts and rushed at the enemy. A great yell broke from the long line of horsemen as they charged towards the *khur*.[2] A few horsemen were falling from their mounts, felled by enemy fire. But the enemy were only infantrymen and their numbers were slight. It would be possible to go through them, scatter them, cross the *khur* and charge on and complete their task. But suddenly the situation changed completely. Behind the line of soldiers that they had seen there emerged thousands more from the *khur* springing up like a fiendish plant. Instead of a simple depression that was almost level with the plain, there suddenly appeared before them a six-foot-deep trough covered with bushes and patches of sand, and behind that 2,000 fighting men. A dozen or so flags and *amirs* on horseback surged among the mass. The awful truth struck Colonel Martin as he galloped at full speed at the head of his regiment. But it was too late. He would not even be able to stop his own horse before he collided with the thousands lying in wait. There was no alternative but to spur the horses on and perhaps the impact of the onrush would force a way through.

Meanwhile the front line of Osman Digna's riflemen was forced forward by the pressure of the warriors behind, who leapt to face the enemy, oblivious of any danger to themselves. One man raised his spear. Another stood with sword drawn, ready to bring down the first man he met on horseback. Some lay on the ground holding up their spears and swords so that they might be a sharp and savage obstacle to anything that passed by.

The distance separating the two sides diminished. The awful clash occurred. There you had a line of horsemen 300 yards long rushing at full speed, lances raised high – facing them rows of foot-soldiers. A few yards from the *khur* the two sides met. Thirty horsemen fell to the ground on impact. Theirs was the worst fate of all. More than a hundred of Osman Digna's men fell. Seconds passed and the world seemed to have stopped on its axis. The regiment in their charge managed to sweep lines of riflemen in their path. Then, after an interval that seem an age, the horses landed in the body of the *khur*. There Osman Digna's men were waiting for them. The second clash lasted only a few seconds and the whole *khur* shook. The runaway horses now reached the far side of the *khur* and began to scramble up the southern bank. Lieutenant Grenfell's troop was furthest to the right and was confronted by the mass of reinforcements at its thickest point; so neither the men nor their horses were able to cross the *khur* or get through the mass of men. They were almost totally annihilated. The second troop, led by Lieutenant Churchill, charged and broke through the less dense ranks of the Hadendowa. The troops on the far left rushed ahead and broke through the *khur* but charged only thin air.

Swords slashed to and fro leaving behind streaks of blood on the beasts. One man plunged his spear into the side of a horse, another placed the muzzle of his rifle on a horse's neck, shooting it so that beast and rider fell to the ground only to meet the sharp edge of a sword. A group of warriors surrounded one of the horsemen and dragged him to the ground by his feet.

The battle took thirty seconds to reach its peak. There rose the din of steel striking steel, the short swords of the Hadendowa and the long lances of the cavalry. There was no longer any scope for the use of firearms. The Lancers could not use their pistols. Hardly an arm was raised to take aim. Nothing could be heard in those moments except for grunts as men sliced the air and the ping of an occasional bullet. Swords struck whatever was in their way – the harness of the horses, the thighs of their riders. Lancers' helmets fell all over the place. Two men could be seen struggling with their bare hands although their weapons were hanging at their sides. Weapons were not enough to sate the lust for combat; men fell to the ground clutching at their enemies' throats. Riderless horses wandered in search of their masters, whinnying and knocking over men from both sides.

In fact most of the force that had been squatting inside the *khur* did not even have the chance of joining in the battle. They were too tightly packed. The fight here was quite different from the course of events to the north. Here the struggle was between equal combatants – no gunboats to fire on them from afar, no Maxim guns to mow them down row after row, none of Kitchener's long-range cannon fire, but only man against man and blade against blade. The advantage was with the men who faced this stern challenge with a courage that knew no bounds. Both sides met the challenge successfully.

Eventually the horses, who had spurs pressed into their flanks till they dripped with blood, managed to push forward through the human obstacle. The survivors of the regiment reached the far side of the *khur*. They succeeded in shaking off their enemy and, after a short gallop, got some hundreds of yards out of reach.

The bloody conflict had lasted one hundred seconds. Valuable seconds were lost by each side as they were overwhelmed by the effects of the clash and confusion. Reactions on both sides were slow. The Lancers were slow in getting away from the trap into which they had fallen. Osman Digna's men were slow in recovering from the impact. In the frenzy the Lancers failed to notice the presence of a bearded man seated on a goatskin surveying the battle. The Khalifa 'Abd Allahi was only a few yards from the clash. He saw the whole battle from beginning to end, and moved only after the Lancers had passed on. He stared at this new enemy about whom he had heard so much but had not met before.

The Lancers stopped three hundred yards away and set about rallying their ranks, but in the same formation, ready for another charge. Osman Digna went once more among his men to reorganize their ranks. He too kept the same formation, but placed the surviving riflemen so they faced south. The others gathered behind them. The riflemen were ordered to open fire on the enemy once more, and the others prepared to bear the brunt of a second charge from the opposite direction.

Colonel Martin, however, had lost his taste for another bold experiment. He called his squadrons together, placed three in an assault formation and the fourth behind them. They wheeled to the right, skirting Osman Digna's men. Then they stopped, turned westward, faced the enemy and opened fire on Osman Digna's flank. It was easy for them, being on horseback, to complete their manoeuvre rapidly. But Osman Digna's reaction was just as quick. He reformed his men to reduce the exposure of his left flank. He pressed his men to leave the *khur* and face east, forming a front that cut the *khur* at a right angle. In fact both sides had moved round 90°. Firing continued for some minutes until Osman Digna gathered his men for an assault. No more than 600 yards separated the two sides. But the Khalifa, now on horseback, ordered him to hold back. For a short while the exchange of fire continued. Then the Lancers stopped, rallied once more and retired at a slow trot northwards to the *zariba*, bearing their dead and wounded with them.

The 21st Lancers suffered seventy casualties, dead and wounded, and 120 horses; for a cavalry regiment this was a serious and costly loss. Osman Digna, on the other hand, lost thirty men.[3]

Osman Digna was aware of his own vulnerability. A direct confrontation with the enemy could result in the annihilation of his men. From his position he could see thousands of casualties being taken to Omdurman. He had long been aware that the enemy differed in kind from his former enemies. Since the Battle of 'Atbara he was mindful of their clear superiority in modern weapons of destruction.

The only solution was to engage with the enemy as soon as possible and to avoid exposing his men to their long-range fire. For such exposure was to the enemy's advantage. With his slight force his only chance of getting even with the enemy was to prepare a tactical surprise.

Surprise depends on two factors. The first is putting the enemy in a completely unexpected situation in terms of arms or timing or position or concentration. The second factor is speed. After achieving surprise it is necessary to exploit it and to deliver the decisive blow before the enemy can recover. It is just like a quick stab; blood is seen before pain is felt.

Osman Digna's 700 men were largely unarmed and were unable to defend the broad front between Surkab and the Nile against the enemy. Nor were they able to delay them for any length of time. The wideness of the front and the smallness of his force had from the beginning deterred him from engaging in a traditional defensive fight. He was thus forced to choose terrain that suited the characteristics of his force. He chose Khur Abu Sunt where it was widest and was deep enough to conceal his men. All this aided an ambush. But an ambush normally takes place on a road or in a spot where the enemy is to pass. It is difficult to carry out an ambush against an enemy who is mounted and advancing on a wide front and has the freedom to choose one of several routes to his destination. Had the Lancers taken any other route, engagement would have been impossible. Osman Digna managed to entice the enemy to his chosen position. The information he received from the Khalifa that it was a cavalry force that was advancing defined the style of the brief conflict. For the situation was apparently made for a cavalry action. The Lancers' appetite for a charge was whetted by what they saw. Only a cavalry force travelling at speed would have fallen victim to this stratagem. Osman Digna was familiar with the tactics of the British and even of their cavalry. What happened was a repetition of what took place at Tamay against General Graham when Osman Digna with some of his men attacked Graham's cavalry, who then rushed out against him. Osman Digna was able to pierce the rear of the square with his foot soldiers armed only with spears and swords.

After making sure that he had laid a trap for the enemy, Osman Digna prepared for the first element of surprise – deception – by creating a situation which was not what it seemed. Instead of a single line of riflemen made up of only a few hundred soldiers in an exposed position, the enemy found themselves facing more than 2,000 men. Thus the element of surprise turned primarily on their capacity to hide the bulk of their actual numbers.

As for the second factor – speed – this must depend mainly on the prompt delivery of the fatal blow. The more time passes, the more the enemy gets used to the new situation and the blood begins to flow again after the limbs have been paralyzed by the shock. The quickly changing situation demands preparation and a careful disposition of forces, so that they will be able to inflict as many losses on the enemy as possible before they recover. In this plan of Osman Digna's there were some flaws that caused success to elude him to a certain extent. For when the Lancers plunged into the *khur* they landed among the thin lines of the Hadendowa, the early occupants, and not among the densely packed mass of reinforcements. Had it gone according to plan, the line of riflemen would have been immediately above the massed reinforcements, and the whole regiment, and not just Grenfell's troop, would have crashed headlong to their doom. Osman Digna was probably preoccupied with organizing the reinforcements and failed to notice the misalignment between the line of riflemen above, the bait, and the mass of men in the depression, the trap.

In this action Osman Digna was astute in planning and executing the engagement, masterly in exploiting the terrain to his own advantage and in concentrating on the destruction of the mounts before the men. He was quick in his response and wise in agreeing to refrain from an unequal pursuit.

Meanwhile to the north 'Ali al Julla slipped away to catch up 'Uthman Shaykh al Din, who was three or four miles ahead. In order to reach him by the shortest route he was obliged to branch off towards the Nile amid the bullets and shells directed at 'Uthman Azraq's survivors. He travelled the first two miles without mishap. But a mile from Jabal Karari his horse was wounded and he fell under it. He continued on foot with bullets buzzing around him, picking his way across the low plateau between Daham and Abu Zariba.

When he reached the range of hills he saw the dust that had been thrown up by Shaykh al Din's thousands as they tried to overtake Broadwood. 'Uthman was still more than two miles ahead.

'Ali al Julla sped on until he joined the rear of 'Uthman's army and talked with some of the *mulazimin*. They recognized

him and stopped one of the horsemen. He dismounted and
'Ali al Julla rode on at the gallop in order to reach 'Uthman.

As for 'Uthman himself, after he had left the hills in his futile
pursuit of Broadwood, he was in a dilemma. On the one hand
he thought it wrong that there was so much distance between
himself and the battlefield. He did not feel this all the time
because now and then, when Broadwood slackened his pace,
the two sides became closer and 'Uthman nearly caught up
with him. But then Broadwood would redouble his pace and
the gap would widen. On the other hand he yearned to take
part in the battle and he wanted some of the honour of
crushing part of the enemy's forces. He was thwarted by the escape of Broadwood's cameleers and frustrated by the fire of the
zariba. His fury had to be concentrated on the horsemen in
front.

'Ali al Julla finally reached 'Uthman Shaykh al Din and gave
him the Khalifa's orders. Shaykh al Din sent messengers ahead
to stop the pursuit. After quite a while the thousands stopped,
completely exhausted after their hour-long battle and hour-
long pursuit. 'Uthman ordered them to sit and rest. They then
set off to return to the main battle area.

1   Obviously Colonel Martin in his report was trying to justify his action.
     The proportion of losses in his regiment was the largest of all. He wrote
     that he was 'determined to turn their right flank' and denied facing them
     directly. On the other hand Churchill, who took part in the charge,
     mentioned that the colonel ordered 'Right wheel into line' to be
     sounded. The sixteen troops swung round towards the blue-black
     riflemen. Churchill's memory is vindicated by a comparison with a letter
     that Lieutenant Robert Smith, who also took part, wrote to his fiancée,
     describing the charge. 'See formed body of about 200 men six hundred
     yards to our left. Front troops left wheel. Immediately met by volleys
     fairly accurately aimed. Bullets seem to be whistling and splashing all
     round. My right hand drops. "Right wheel into line, Charge". Looking
     round see Khor 12 feet wide, 6 feet deep. IN FRONT. Every side a com-
     pact mass of white-robed men.' Martin's report continues: 'By this time
     we were within 200 yards of their right when a large body jumped up
     out of a small khor and commenced a very heavy fire.' Martin is arguing
     that he was exposed to heavy fire and this therefore justified the charge
     with its heavy losses.

2   The battle of Khur Abu Sunt was quite separate from the rest of the battle. There were, however, two men who saw Osman Digna's ambush right from the start. One was the historian Muhammad 'Abd al Rahim who was lying wounded in the *khur* and saw everything in the Lancers' advance. The other was Captain (later Admiral) Beatty, commander of one of the gunboats. He saw Osman Digna disposing his troops and realized as the Lancers advanced that a trap was being prepared for them.

The historian Muhammad 'Abd al Rahim had been wounded in the *mulazimin's* engagement in the hills of Karari and was resting in the *khur*, weak from loss of blood. On his way to the *khur* there had been rumours among the wounded that Osman Digna and the Hadendowa had fled from the battlefield. But he soon saw him busy with his troops, his great voice raised above the general din.

Captain Burgess found eleven skulls on the site. If the same ratio as before is applied then we estimate the casualties of Osman Digna to be thirty.

CHAPTER EIGHTEEN

The Second Phase

At half past eight the Sirdar closed his field glasses and noted that the enemy had been routed in the first phase. He ordered the advance to Omdurman to start. The city had to be occupied before the retreating enemy reached it. Bugles announced to the six brigades who were in the *zariba* that they were to assemble outside it and make their way to Omdurman. Ammunition was issued to all ranks, and all prepared to march. The Sirdar was taking a risk, for two-thirds of the enemy was still intact on the field, but he felt ready to deal with them. The British Division marched in the van, Lyttelton's brigade on the left, Wauchope's on the right. Maxwell's Egyptian brigade came up behind, then Lewis', then MacDonald's.

The plan had been for the brigades to stretch out to Jabal Surkab in battle order and advance to Omdurman on a broad front. But the Sirdar preferred the British brigades to take up a broader front and also to occupy the hill; so they commanded the whole field. The Egyptian Division brigades followed to the rear and the right of the British Division, away from the Nile. Thus the Sirdar's force advanced in the shape of an inverted L.

There was a large gap between the British Division and the other brigades. The third brigade, Maxwell's, quickly moved to bridge the gap. It had originally been planned that the next brigade would be MacDonald's, but Hunter, the commander of the Egyptian Division, made an adjustment so that MacDonald brought up the rear. Commanders with experience and ability were often left to guard the rear. Kitchener bore in mind the forces that had gone north in pursuit of Broadwood.

He felt that the real danger was the vulnerability of his rear to attack. He had to safeguard this, but there was also another consideration – the need for haste in reaching Omdurman with all his men. As for the enemy's missing division, the Black Standard, he thought that it had either withdrawn to Omdurman or had already taken part in the first phase. He was not aware of the threat that lurked not far away, concentrated on the other side of Jabal Surkab. He therefore placed MacDonald's brigade as far as possible from the supporting fire. He added to the brigade three artillery batteries with the most modern types of artillery – eighteen 15-pounder cannons and eight Maxim cannons. Horsedrawn carts also carried a huge quantity of ammunition including 900 shells. All this slowed them down somewhat. The Sirdar had seen the crushing effect of concentrating the fire of the cannons and the machine-guns, and was aware that the final word lay with such fire and not with rifles, bayonets or concentrations of infantry.

The two brigades of the British Division advanced directly towards the shoulder of Surkab. What did Surkab conceal? How did Omdurman look from up there? Were there more enemy soldiers? The Sirdar himself rode at the front between the two British brigades with the Egyptian flag flying over him and his Chiefs of Staff round him.

As soon as the brigades were organized in marching formation they were exposed to distant but heavy fire from the summit of Jabal Surkab where the Khalifa's reconnaissance units had taken up their positions. The fire was directed by the *amir* Khayr al Sayyid, who was also relaying intelligence rapidly back to the Khalifa's headquarters.

Neither the Sirdar nor his attendant brigades paid much attention to the fire of Khayr al Sayyid. They continued to march quickly towards the ridge that extended from the summit of Surkab. At 0935 they came to the small rocks that were scattered at the foot of the northern slope of the ridge. While the Maxim cannons were busy answering the fire coming from Surkab, and while the first part of the division was crossing the ridge, they met groups of wounded Lancers making their way to the rear. News of the Lancers' charge had not yet reached them. They were surprised, for they had imagined that others had shared their own fortune, bombardment only from a distance.

The Khalifa went over from Khur Abu Sunt to his former headquarters. His escort was small, for he had witnessed the Lancers' charge almost without his guard. The moment had now arrived for which two-thirds of his army had waited. The Khalifa had scarcely reached his headquarters when four men came towards him bearing a body. The arms hung limp as if the man was dead. The Khalifa asked, 'Whose body is this?' One man replied that it was the body of Ibrahim al Khalil. The Khalifa was silent for a short while. Then he raised his hands and recited the *Fatiha*. Those around him also murmured the *Fatiha*. He brought forward his *angarayb*, the *furwa* was placed on it and the body on that, to be borne away for burial at his house in Omdurman.

Soon information reached him from Khayr al Sayyid of the enemy's advance towards Omdurman. Firing could be heard at his headquarters. The enemy was on the move now in the broad open plain. They had no trenches to protect them, no gunboats to rely on. The knock-out blow had now to be launched by the Black Standard under the cover of fire from Shaykh al Din. But where was Shaykh al Din?

'Ali al Julla arrived as usual in good time. He dismounted. Both man and horse were sweating profusely and panting hard. 'Ali al Julla reported Shaykh al Din's position, and that he was returning to the battlefield.

The Khalifa spent a few moments in deep thought. Heavy silence reigned over the whole headquarters as all awaited his decision. It was a critical moment, for the enemy had almost crossed over Surkab. In a short time he would find himself on the defensive with the enemy on the march and his own fire-power four or five miles away. The Khalifa's plan had been flawed in a most unexpected way. The Black Standard, ready and capable of launching a sudden attack, now had nothing to rely on but sheer numbers and bare steel.

Ought he to hurl the Black Standard into an attack, albeit with little chance of success? Or should he wait for Shaykh al Din? Shaykh al Din was far away; nobody knew where the enemy would be when he arrived, or whether it would be possible to overtake the enemy before he reached Omdurman.

The Khalifa looked up at last. He spoke to 'Ali al Julla, confiding his instruction to him. 'Ali al Julla sped off once more to the *amir* Ya'qub and the Black Standard.

Shaykh al Din's men were again on the move after half an hour's rest. The men had been a little distraught after their quick sprint and after the continuous two-hour slaughter. One or two extra men were seated on some of the horses. The riflemen among them were exhausted after carrying their heavy weapons. As usual 'Uthman Shaykh al Din rode jauntily along among his guard of *mulazimin*. He did not advance due south, but turned to the south-west to join up with the Green Standard that had remained there inactive during all this time. 'Abd Allah Abu Siwar made no attempt to back up the pursuit of the horsemen. Nobody moved as they saw Kitchener's brigades gathering south of the hills of Karari. They remained concealed from view and sheltered from fire, carrying out the Khalifa's order to the letter. At 0930 Shaykh al Din was seen on the horizon.

As the Sirdar reached Surkab the whole force took up its assigned formation. Its great mass formed an acute angle with the Nile. The British brigades were nearest to the river. The three Egyptian brigades were advancing to the south-west parallel to the British brigades. Gaps appeared and became steadily bigger. Maxwell's task, as he and his brigade were marching just behind the British Division, was to move quickly to take his place to the right on Surkab, and to enable Lewis and MacDonald to form up on his right so that all could advance south to Omdurman on a broad front of five brigades. When the commander of the Egyptian Division placed MacDonald in the rear, the latter, who had been the first to leave the *zariba*, was obliged to move out westwards to let Lewis overtake him. So while the forward brigades were pushing quickly to the south, MacDonald faced west. The gap between him and the others became wider, and soon stretched to a whole mile.

Most of the Sirdar's brigades were now clear of the river on the broad plain between Karari and Surkab. MacDonald's was

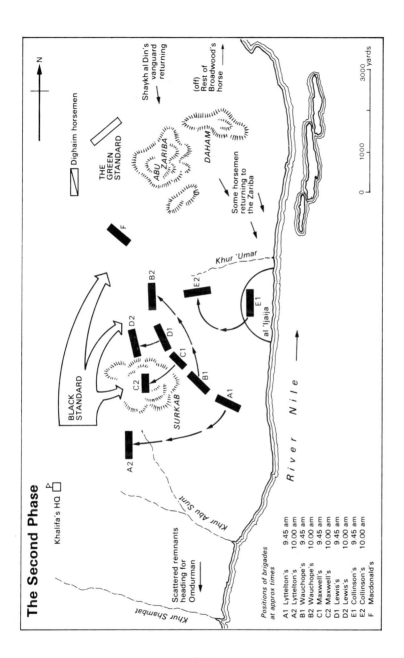

The Second Phase

Khalifa's HQ

N

Digham horsemen

THE GREEN STANDARD

Shaykh al Din's vanguard returning

ABU ZARIBA

DAHAM

(off) Rest of Broadwood's horse

Some horsemen returning to the Zariba

BLACK STANDARD

F

B2

D2

D1

C1

C2

SURKAB

B1

A1

A2

E2

E1

al 'Ijaija

Khur 'Umar

Khur Abu Sunt

River Nile

Scattered remnants heading for Omdurman

Khur Shambat

Positions of brigades at approx times

A1 Lyttelton's   9.45 am
A2 Lyttelton's   10.00 am
B1 Wauchope's   9.45 am
B2 Wauchope's   10.00 am
C1 Maxwell's   9.45 am
C2 Maxwell's   10.00 am
D1 Lewis's   9.45 am
D2 Lewis's   10.00 am
E1 Collinson's   9.45 am
E2 Collinson's   10.00 am
F Macdonald's

0   1000   3000   yards

209

the only brigade whose position enabled it to see anything of the expected attack, for the whole Black Standard was suddenly disclosed to their view.

At 0935 MacDonald caught his first glimpse of the Black Standard and ordered the battalions into order to face the assault. At the same time he ordered the nearest battery of artillery to open fire at once on the Black Standard.

A shell was fired from a distance of 1,500 yards. Then all the cannons joined in. The batteries engaged in a continuous bombardment and the battalions took up their new positions facing south-east. MacDonald placed all his artillery in the front line. There were eighteen cannons and eight machine guns. The brigade stretched over a front of more than 1,500 yards.

As the Sirdar approached the summit of the ridge, a reverberating thud suddenly drowned the ticktack of the small arms fired from the summit of Jabal Surkab. This was MacDonald's first shell fired at the Black Standard. The Sirdar looked back and saw that the whole of MacDonald's brigade had stopped and were changing their formation from column into line. He took the situation in at a glance and saw that the enemy had hemmed him in. He ignored the commanders of divisions and brigades and gave orders directly to the commanders of units. He scattered brigades as if they were pebbles. A difficult manoeuvre began.

The Sirdar's ultimate objective was to place all his five brigades and his artillery in one line facing west, instead of south, to allow his fire as much scope as it had had from the *zariba* and to close the gaps that had appeared between the brigades. He turned first to the British Division. Bypassing the Divisional Commander, he ordered Wauchope's brigade to change direction and occupy a position to the left of Mac-Donald, to block the gap between MacDonald and Lewis. The brigade moved to cover the distance accordingly, leaving its heavy equipment with Maxwell's brigade. Then the Sirdar made haste to Lewis, ordering him to go to the west to back up MacDonald and to direct his artillery – eight cannons and a Maxim battery – at the Black Standard. Finally the Sirdar ordered Lyttelton's and Maxwell's brigades to face west, to climb to the main summit of Jabal Surkab and to attack the right flank of the enemy hidden behind the hill.

The brigades soon executed the Sirdar's manoeuvre. Mac-Donald's brigade, with its wide front, was facing south-west. Some distance from it was Lewis' brigade facing due west. Wauchope was hurrying to block the gap between Lewis and MacDonald. Meanwhile Lyttelton and Maxwell with all their artillery reached the summit of Jabal Surkab. All the brigades were spread out in one long line. They seemed, to the fleet on the river, and at the same time to the Khalifa in his head-quarters, like a long human wall creeping westwards, more than 4,000 yards long, a line level with the plain, but with a sudden lurch upwards where the two brigades of Lyttelton and Maxwell were on the summit and slopes of Jabal Surkab.

At 0945 Kitchener's army, except for Wauchope's brigade still hurrying to fill the gap, faced and flanked the Black Standard as it was about to launch its major offensive behind the *amir* Ya'qub.

Ya'qub spent the time from 0900 reorganizing the ranks of his Standard. His basic force was augmented with remnants from the armies of the battles to his north and by rein-forcements that had only lately reached Omdurman. The Black Standard included different sections divided into fifty-one standards, the force of each varying between twenty-five and 1,500 men. Among their leaders were 'Uthman al Dikaym, Muhammad al Mahdi, the Mahdi's eldest son, Muhammad wad Bishara and Muhammad al Zaki 'Uthman, released from prison. During the last two hours the Black Standard had acted as a reserve force some distance from the battle, a refuge for the wounded and the bearers of the dead, the survivors of the attacks of the first phase and the Battle of Khur Abu Sunt. But among these great numbers there were not more than a thou-sand rifles of various kinds – elephant guns, revolvers and the throw-outs of the Khalifa's arsenal. All the good and relatively modern rifles, such as Remingtons, had been taken by Shaykh al Din and handed out to his *mulazimin*.

Ya'qub completed his reorganization and then summoned his *amirs* and explained their position to each. The force was drawn up in a line 4,000 yards long and behind it were twenty-three rows in no regular order. The men of the Black Standard were not like the trained *mulazimin*; most had come recently from the west of Sudan. Horsemen were at the sides and in front.

Before any instructions from the Khalifa arrived, Ya'qub saw MacDonald's brigade clearly in the final movements of its westward wheel. He could not see the other brigades, as Surkab stood between the two contenders.

Ya'qub stood steeling his nerve, with growing concern at the sight of the enemy passing before him. The long awaited moment was almost at hand. The noise of firing from the summit indicated how close the enemy was to Surkab. Then two enemy companies appeared on the summit. They stormed those who had occupied it and advanced relentlessly towards the Black Standard. At this point Muhammad al Mahdi cried out from his position on the right as he saw the enemy coming towards him, 'How long do we wait – till they grasp our hands?' He then spurred his horse on towards Surkab alone.[1] Soon a large part of the horsemen of the Black Standard led by 'Uthman al Dikaym and Muhammad wad Bishara set off behind Muhammad al Mahdi. The first men of Maxwell's brigade had almost reached the western side of Surkab and fired their rifles repeatedly. A Maxim cannon on the summit of Surkab began to fire, mowing down the horsemen advancing up the hill. Muhammad al Mahdi's horse was wounded and fell to the ground. He leapt from it, unsheathed his sword and rushed forward on foot. The other horsemen, some distance behind, followed until he was wounded by several bullets and fell to the ground.[2] Soon the rest fell, including Muhammad wad Bishara and 'Uthman al Dikaym.

As this was going on, Ya'qub stood patiently waiting for Shaykh al Din, or for the arrival of orders from the Khalifa to attack. 'Ali al Julla finally arrived with instructions to hand over the Standard and report to headquarters.

The *amir* Ya'qub was on horseback. He was armed only with a long spear. Directly behind him were the guard of the banner of the Black Standard. He bowed his head for a while, then looked up and turned back to the Khalifa's headquarters. He was about 1,800 yards from the headquarters when he saw a body covered with an *'imma* placed on the Khalifa's *angarayb*. A mule was bearing the load and was heading for Omdurman.

'Who is that being carried away?' Ya'qub asked.

Somebody answered, 'It is the body of al Khalil'.[3]

Ya'qub paused. Then he raised his spear and shouted, 'Ansar, look at us now! Young men like Ibrahim al Khalil have gone to their eternal resting place. Here we are still on horseback. . . . A *tabaldi* tree had fallen. A *tabaldi* has fallen on the infidels. Raise your banners aloft and let your horses charge.'

He turned and galloped on horseback along the whole of the front line repeating, 'A *tabaldi* has fallen, a *tabaldi* has fallen.' The front rows answered him by shaking their rifles and swords high over their heads. Then he returned to his former position and faced north-east towards the enemy. He raised his spear, kicked his horse and dashed out across the wide plain towards MacDonald's brigade. The thousands in the Black Standard dashed behind him along the slope towards the enemy. Thus the second phase began.

Ya'qub set off with all possible speed towards MacDonald. The din was deafening. Dust and splinters were thrown up. His horse paused for a few seconds until the effects of the explosion settled. He was then forced to dash to right and left, and then once more charged ahead with his spear held high and with 12,000 men behind him.

Ya'qub's quick charge led to the division of his force into three groups. On the right was a small group that charged eastwards towards Surkab aiming to take the place of those who had withdrawn in the earlier attack and to face the assault of the brigades of Maxwell and Lyttelton. Another group headed north-east towards the gap between the brigades of MacDonald and Lewis which Wauchope was making haste to fill. The main group on the left set off behind Ya'qub.

The right-hand group crumbled before the fire of the brigades advancing across Surkab, and those who survived among the wounded withdrew to the west. The gap between Ya'qub's group and the others increased. Men at the flank were exposed to fire from the enemy brigades as well as artillery fire from Jabal Surkab, augmented by the arrival of 32 battery and a group of Maxims which had a lethal effect from that elevation.

In fact the Black Standard, when its line was stretched out behind Ya'qub, was exposed to a line of fire more than 4,000 yards long. This line absorbed a great part of the impact of the attack directed at MacDonald. The front-line fire of MacDonald's brigade saw to the rest. Their feet were firmly placed on the ground and they were able to take careful and continuous aim. The firing this time was discharged not in volleys but by individuals and at great speed. MacDonald's artillery fired long range shrapnel, but when the enemy got within 400 yards they changed their ammunition to case shot. In those few minutes MacDonald's brigade alone fired more than 450 shells with devastating effect. Cannon balls, shrapnel, case shot and also the fire of the eight machine-guns soon began to thin out the Black Standard.

A few minutes before 1000 Shaykh al Din's exhausted van could be seen advancing towards the gaps of the Karari hills. His distance from the nearest enemy unit – MacDonald's force – was more than two miles. They still had the whole chain of the Karari hills to cross. When the forces of Shaykh al Din and Abu Siwar were ready to advance and open the second front of the second phase in accordance with the role originally assigned to them the Black Standard was virtually in its death agony. At the same time Broadwood's cavalry was now returning by the shortest route, by the river, after making sure that they were no longer being pursued.

The Sirdar's brigades passed Surkab under cover of artillery fire from the summit. Small groups were the only obstacle that divided the advancing soldiers from the last organized group on the battlefield at that moment – the headquarters and private guard of the Khalifa.

'Abd al Rahman Ahmad waited on horseback in the midst of this group. He was deafened by the explosions and was apprehensive about the fate of the Black Standard as it went off behind Ya'qub. He heard the name of his brother, Ibrahim al Khalil, repeated several times. He turned and asked somebody near him, 'Where is al Khalil?' He was told that Ibrahim al

Khalil had been killed.

'Where is Ya'qub?' he asked.

'He's gone ahead of the enemy.'

'Where are the infidels?'

'They are in front of you.'

He requested that his horse be turned to face them. He then unsheathed his sword and dashed forward only to collide with MacDonald's front ranks. His horse fell to the ground with its blind rider.

The soldiers Ya'qub had spent hours in collecting and organizing were lost in the smoke. Soon bodies began to cover the ground, showing the bloody path the Standard trod.

At 0935 Ya'qub was hit by a stream of machine-gun fire. He fell from his horse, toppling on to his face. He died still clutching his spear. Ya'qub had been at the front of the Black Standard from the beginning of the assault. He fell 600 yards from the front line of MacDonald's brigade. Two horsemen dismounted amid the tempest of bullets, raised Ya'qub and bore him back to the rear, but they too fell victims of machine-gun fire. The same fate befell all who attempted to raise the body and take it back. The rest of the Standard continued to surge towards MacDonald's brigade. In spite of continuous fire from cannons and machine-guns the casualties were mainly not among the front line, but further back. The front lines, mostly horsemen and *amirs*, were able to advance until they were within a hundred yards of the enemy. Then MacDonald's fire stopped most of them. Still the survivors went on until they almost hit the mouths of the rifles levelled at them. Some were even able to plunge their spears into MacDonald's ranks. Many of the casualties in MacDonald's brigade were caused this way.

The second group, a little behind Ya'qub, charged towards the gap between Lewis and MacDonald. Although they were exposed to incessant flank fire, inflicting heavy loss, survivors managed to dash between the gap and wheel round to the back. They then faced machine-gun fire that had changed direction to face them again. Others went to the right and faced Lewis's brigade and the fire coming from the summit of Jabal Surkab. A few even tried to retrace their steps, but Wauchope's brigade now blocked the gap. Soon Broadwood's mounted forces arrived back on the battlefield, and also a squadron of Lancers, completely surrounding these survivors. The British soldiers called out to them, 'Aman . . . aman, you are safe', in broken Arabic, calling on them to throw down their arms.

The men guarding the banner of the Black Standard rushed behind the mounted standard bearer. He stopped and planted the Standard 300 yards north of the Surkab. In spite of bullets whistling around from three brigades at a clear target, its bearers collected stones to buttress the pole of the Standard, rising twenty feet above the ground. The guard began falling round the Standard and were immediately replaced from behind.

The Standard was now exposed to fire raining down from north and east. Holes appeared in the fabric. There were first twenty bearers, then only three who advanced to confront 9,000 soldiers. These three were wounded but continued to cling to it until they fell. It seemed as if the Standard stood by itself, but then warriors from the rear ranks hastened to hold it high. Some soldiers crept back to guard it during the charge. Steady, precise fire was levelled at it from Surkab's summit. As one man fell, another would rally to it. When the last of the Black Standard overtook it, there were thirty men around it. Soon machine-gun fire devoured all around it to the last man. The enemy arrived at the flag. One hundred dead bodies and twice as many wounded were found around the Standard. One of Kitchener's staff took it up and the Sirdar rode in front of it on his way to Omdurman. But the Standard had a final sting for its enemies. One of the Nile steamers saw it from the river and opened fire on it until Slatin became aware of the danger and had the flag lowered to the ground.

By 1000 the battle was well nigh over. The area enclosed by the hills of Karari, by Jabal Surkab and the Nile had become a vast graveyard full of the bodies of thousands of slain men and horses. As they piled up, the bodies showed with deadly accuracy the course the battle had taken. East of Jabal Surkab towards the Nile were the traces of Ibrahim al Khalil's bloody path to the zariba. West of Surkab were traces of Ya'qub's assault. The Black Standard was divided into three. One group of bodies lay immediately west of Jabal Surkab around the body of its leader, Muhammad wad Bishara. Another group, denser and broader, stretched in a line that inclined to the north-east. The third was the one that charged directly at MacDonald. Another group, piled up around a heap of stones, marked the heroism of the guardians of the banner of the Black Standard. About 2,000 survivors were taken prisoner, most of them wounded. Other survivors were seen in scattered groups heading for the desert in the west or towards Omdurman, the road to which was choked by several thousand men bearing their wounded.

The enemy dead were distinguished by their uniform in contrast to the white *jubbas* of the Ansar. Eighty of Broadwood's cameleers had fallen in the hills of Karari, more than one hundred in the *zariba* and twenty-five inside Khur Shambat. The wounded were transported to mobile hospitals whose doctors began at once to treat them.

The Black Standard lost about 3,450 men (1,600 slain, 1,850 wounded). Most of the famous *amirs* fell. Among the slain were the *amir* Ya'qub, al Zaki 'Uthman, 'Uthman al Dikaym, Muhammad wad Bishara, Muhammad al Mahdi, Muhammad wad Nubawi, *amir* of the Bani Jarrar, Sulayman Kusha, *amir* of the people of Omdurman, and tribal leaders of the Fallaita, Bidayriya, Burqu, Jawam'a, Humr, Kababish, Jimi'ab, Zayyidab and Arakiyyin.

The assault of the Black Standard, as a distinct operation, had at first the potential for success, but other factors intervened and led to the dissipation of this potential within a few minutes and in an unforeseen way.

The strength of the Black Standard's position lay in its sudden appearance as a great force armed with swords and spears. For three hours it remained concealed. Its offensive was sprung from a position quite near the enemy. This contrasted with the offensive of the first phase, which was exposed from a great distance, for a long time, to overwhelming fire power.

Three factors weighed in the Black Standard's favour before it launched its attack. The enemy's position was vulnerable in contrast to Ya'qub's. The artillery and the gunboats were remote and ineffectual. The whole of the Sirdar's army lay between them and the Black Standard. Furthermore the assault was directed against the Sirdar's army while it was on the march; even the ground artillery was now on the move. The cannons were not securely based, with ammunition being dragged from afar. Thus the effect of the artillery was more limited than it had been in the early morning attack. Not only that, but the attack would be directed at the right side and the rear of Kitchener's forces. This would oblige him to change direction again. If the Ansar artillery had been effective there was a chance of close engagement with the enemy in hand-to-hand combat. Twelve thousand brave men were not a force that could be eliminated in a few minutes by an enemy on the march, however powerful their fire.

What went wrong and led to the virtual extinction in a few minutes of more than 12,000 men? There are two reasons. The first is that the assault was one with swords and spears without the backing of fire cover. In spite of their numerical superiority, the Black Standard as a firing force was extremely weak, with only 1,000 rifles, mostly antiquated. If they had had ample fire cover, their situation, with their speed and great numerical force, may have been different. For the enemy was defined and the range was close. The Standard's main hope was the *mulazimin* fire.

The other reason lay in the fact that twenty minutes elapsed from the time MacDonald caught sight of Ya'qub until the beginning of the charge. These precious minutes helped to determine the fate of the assault.

We must remind ourselves of the importance of the second factor in a surprise operation: 'speed', as mentioned in the last chapter. Ya'qub had prepared the first factor, 'surprise', or 'a suddenly changing position', by concealing the Black Standard and keeping it quiet. But their quietness, which was a blessing before 0934, became a curse after 0935. Those twenty minutes while Ya'qub was standing transfixed after the enemy had sighted him enabled MacDonald to stop, to rally his forces, to face the enemy, and to fire his first shell as a signal to the Sirdar and to the other brigades. By then the initiative had passed from Ya'qub to the enemy, who became progressively stronger, checkmating any advantage Ya'qub had had.

If Ya'qub had launched his assault the moment he was sighted by the enemy the chance of success would have been greater. The Sirdar's brigades were scattered all over the wide plain, there were wide gaps between them, they were facing another direction; all this would have prevented the Sirdar using his most important weapon – his concentrated fire. The distance between Ya'qub and his prime objective – MacDonald's brigade – was not more than 1,200 yards. It would have been easy for Ya'qub to reach them before he came under heavy fire. The result would have been to his advantage even without the backing of *mulazimin* fire. When the Black Standard finally moved off at 0955 they found not scattered brigades, but a solid line of soldiers more than 4,000 yards long, enfilading them continuously and paralyzing their right flank. Thus the situation slipped away from Ya'qub for one reason of his own making, and for another of the Sirdar's. The causal connection between the two is clear.

The Sirdar's quick manoeuvre and his ability to concentrate great forces in particular positions was what decided the issue in his favour in the end. By moving two brigades to the west as a quick reaction to the right flank attack of the Black Standard as it was advancing, he saved MacDonald. By changing the fronts of the brigades of Lyttelton and Maxwell and ordering them to advance and open heavy fire from the summit of Jabal Surkab on the flank of the Standard, he did much to lighten the impact of the assault of MacDonald. Ya'qub was forced to divert a large part of his Standard to the east to deal with the situation.

Moreover MacDonald's firepower – he had the largest share of artillery or machine-gun fire assigned to one single brigade – enabled him to parry the attack or at least to dilute its concentration with machine-guns from afar and with case shot at close quarters. We must not overlook the stolidity of the Sudanese soldiers in MacDonald's brigade. These men were able to stand firm in the face of the great assault, and not one wavered in his place.

Ya'qub cannot be exonerated from the responsibility of missing a valuable chance. But the main blame falls on the shoulders of Shaykh al Din. Ya'qub was in an acute dilemma. Should he attack at the appropriate moment without the promised guarantee of fire cover? Or should he wait for Shaykh al Din so that the two assaults could be timed as one operation? He waited for Shaykh al Din, but did not know what the enemy was doing, because Surkab stood between them. He was waiting for orders from the Khalifa for the Standard to attack.

However, Ya'qub's reputation is not irreparably damaged. In the west of the Sudan – where the remark 'The *tabaldi* has fallen' has become proverbial – it is believed that Ya'qub's charge was a result of great emotion after he had seen the body of a young man, either Muhammad al Mahdi or Ibrahim al Khalil. It seems on closer investigation that Ya'qub went up and down the front ranks repeating this phrase trying to instil enthusiasm into the others before he led them in the assault.

Ya'qub made a tactical mistake in apparently concentrating on one enemy, MacDonald's brigade, in spite of alternative targets elsewhere. By directing his attack at the gap between Lewis and MacDonald there might have been a chance of eliminating MacDonald and getting through the enemy lines. But a direct bombardment from the artillery on Jabal Surkab changed the situation.

Ya'qub's assault was the last turning point in a battle that seemed to be lost from the beginning, as the Khalifa let opportunity after opportunity slip through his hands. The Black Standard was the last obstacle between the Sirdar and Omdurman. After the assault the Sirdar was able to start the race to the town with a better chance of success than Shaykh al Din or 'Abd Allah Abu Siwar. 'Abd Allah was in the hills of Karari throughout the battle. His standard was completely ready, but was not exposed to battle except during the time they crossed, early in the morning, from Khur Shambat to the hills of Karari. With him was a respectable force of 400 horsemen. What then was preventing him reinforcing Ya'qub's assault with another charge on the flanks to the north? Again, the answer seems to lie in inadequate communication.

The Khalifa's army lacked an effective communication unit, relying solely upon messengers. This hampered the implementation of his plan, the coordination of his forces, and the flexibility of his manoeuvres. When 'Isa wad Ahmad reached 'Abd Allah, asking for his force to take part, the assault of the Black Standard had already been under way for a quarter of an hour, and the vanguard of Shaykh al Din was not far away. Had Shaykh al Din been in the right place at the right time, and had the Green Standard launched its assault to follow up Ya'qub's, there might have been a different outcome.

We must now return to the Khalifa's headquarters. All near the Khalifa on that day say that the men remained firm of purpose, as he directed the battle and sent thousands to their deaths, except for those moments when he lost patience with the absence and irresponsibility of Shaykh al Din. He certainly knew when he launched the Black Standard that there was now small hope of a complete victory. He realized that his plan was in shreds.

When Lyttelton's and Maxwell's men reached the summit of Surkab, they brought heavy fire on the Khalifa's headquarters, which swarmed with over 1,500 warriors. The Khalifa 'Ali wad Hilu was hit in the thigh by a bullet. An emergency operation was carried out to remove the bullet. The old man lay patiently on the ground as the flesh of his thigh was cut with a knife and the ball dug out. The wound was staunched with earth and an *angarayb* was brought for him to rest on.

Lyttelton's brigade then advanced towards them. The Khalifa summoned his personal attendant, Ab Jukka, and ordered him to take the rest of the guard and ward off the attack. When he felt that the situation was becoming critical, he sent an urgent message to Shaykh al Din and to 'Abd Allah Abu Siwar for assistance. He commented, as if to himself, 'Whenever we send anybody to Shaykh al Din, he never comes back.'

The Sirdar's soldiers approached. The accurate fire increased, and the headquarters became an open target. Some around him tried to persuade him to withdraw to Omdurman to avoid being taken prisoner. Shaykh Muhammad al Badawi told him, 'War is a matter of ups and downs. Let us go to Omdurman and die under the *qubba*. Do you want, my Lord, to consume all the armies of the Mahdiya in a single battle?'

Al Sayyid al Makki said, 'So long as you are alive, true religion triumphs. Let us retire from the enemy lest they take us prisoner.' As the fire got thicker and the enemy got closer, they drew more courage from the danger of near death. The Khalifa gazed silently at them all. A little after that a wounded man brought the news of Ya'qub's death. The Khalifa bowed his head, and from that moment lost interest in the course of the battle. He suffered from a shock that was never to leave him. All he wished was to seek martyrdom on his *furwa*. Only now did Osman Digna join them. He came with the Khalifa's great white horse, and the Khalifa's servant 'Abd 'Allah. But it was on to a donkey that he was raised without resistance by Osman Digna and Ab Jukka. Osman Digna walked by him, talking to him all the time, quoting Qur'anic texts and verses of poetry. He grasped him by the hand and said, 'This is not the end of everything.' He spoke of the many times his soldiers had been wiped out, and he alone had returned, with heavy wounds, to begin the struggle anew. Certainly the Khalifa would be able to collect another army with which he could continue the struggle against the invading enemy. 'One day we will both die on horseback, but it is no use waiting here upon your *furwa*.' He went with him for some distance, consoling him. Then he took his leave, promising to join him again in Omdurman, and broke off to return to his men.[4]

The Khalifa's small escort moved towards Omdurman by a route four miles west of the Nile. Soon those around him slipped off, and only Yunus al Dikaym remained. After a while he was lost among thousands who were retiring to Omdurman. He made his way, head bowed, to the northern rest house outside Omdurman. Here he dismounted, rested awhile, and then ordered some *mulazimin* who had joined him from the battlefield to blow the *ummbaya* and beat the drum to rally the rest of the fighters inside Omdurman and to renew the fight within the city.

Only 'Ali wad Hilu joined the Khalifa at the northern rest house. He was brought in on an *angarayb* with his thigh bound after the bleeding had been stopped. The Khalifa sent another message to Shaykh al Din, bidding him come to his house at Omdurman. He then mounted his donkey and, with 'Ali wad

Hilu at his side, made his way to the mosque. He ordered the *ummbaya* to be blown once more. After that he entered his house. Food was brought in, the first he had had all day. He mixed some honey and water and drank it.

Finally the Khalifa went alone, without a guard, to the Mahdi's tomb in the damaged *qubba*.

At 1000, the greater part of the missing divisions joined up with the Green Standard on the hills of Karari. The commander of the *rub'* in the van of the *mulazimin*, Jabir Abu Shilaykhat, met 'Abd Allah Abu Siwar.

As the soldiers were reorganizing themselves, they witnessed the latter moments of the attack of the Black Standard. MacDonald's brigade was nearest to them, so they felt that they too must launch an attack on them, sweep them aside and advance forward to the main concentration of the enemy behind. For MacDonald's brigade, as it faced south-east, was isolated from the rest of the Sirdar's army and there seemed to be a chance to strike a sudden blow on the enemy from behind.

Jabir Abu Shilaykhat and 'Abd Allah Abu Siwar hastened to merge the forces of the two standards. They joined with the *amirs* in organizing more *mulazimin* who had just turned up. The *rub'* of Jabir Abu Shilaykhat was in front, followed by the few survivors of al 'Arifi al Rabi's *rub'*. Then there was a large gap, and then the main bloc of *mulazimin* not in order; behind that was Shaykh al Din's square. Jabir Abu Shilaykhat placed as many riflemen as he could find in front. But their numbers were depleted and most of their ammunition had been used up in the battle against Broadwood's camelmen. In addition to which half the *mulazimin* were still on their way, wandering about in the rear. These never had a chance to join in the assault. 'Abd Allah Abu Siwar himself was on the right. His men were in order from the beginning and were ready to attack. 'Abd Allah spent an anguished time as he watched the Black Standard facing destruction on the plain. With him were the horsemen of the Dighaim led by the *amir* 'Abd al Jalil Ahmad. Their right wing struck out into the farthest desert. 'Abd Allah Abu Siwar was very worried at the loss of time. As the *mulazimin* finally organized themselves, 'Isa wad Ahmad arrived with the news that the Khalifa's headquarters was under attack and that the Khalifa was seeking urgent assistance. Abu Siwar waited no longer. Without turning to the *mulazimin*, he shouted to his standard bearer, 'Get moving, 'Abd al Qayum. Unfurl the banner'. The banner was unfurled and the force set off at speed. As soon as the *mulazimin* saw them moving, they too set off parallel to them, past Abu Zariba and its slopes.

After a short while there appeared a front more than 2,000 yards long. The horsemen of the Dighaim extended to the west; they were more than two rows deep and behind their organized ranks were scattered thousands more who had not had a chance to get into regular formation. Most of these were Shaykh al Din's *mulazimin*, exhausted by battle and the long miles of running.[5]

At 1010 the *mulazimin* and the Green Standard reached the ridge over the Karari hills and began to pour down on to the plain, heading for MacDonald's brigade. They announced their entry into the battle with a hail of rifle fire on the enemy. From a distance of 1,200 yards the riflemen stopped to open fire on MacDonald's brigade, who were busy changing their direction to face the new danger.[6]

The Black Standard's assault was in its last moments. From the huge mass that half an hour earlier had poured down, only a few survivors were trying desperately to reach MacDonald's brigade. Most had been turned into corpses or were in their final death agonies.

As the first bullets were fired by the *mulazimin* and before the main onslaught from over the hills of Karari, MacDonald became aware of the new danger that he was facing. It was his task to transfer the weight of his fire and infantry to another direction, to estimate at each moment the size and concentration of the two assaults, one waxing, one waning, that were being launched simultaneously from opposite directions.

MacDonald decided to turn his front round to the north-west, leaving a small force to deal with the last of Ya'qub's assault. He turned to look for help from the other brigades, but they were far away and preoccupied with their new front as it advanced west. The nearest friendly brigade was that of Lewis and that was still under attack from part of the Black Standard.

MacDonald sent a swift horseman to seek help from the Sirdar. He decided to face the assault alone until help arrived. These were the moments that put MacDonald into the history books. He was able to communicate his coolness and self-possession to his brigade so that they conducted a difficult manoeuvre in a remarkably short space of time.[7]

A squadron of artillery and two Maxims were placed on the left centre, with Collinson's brigade, which was just emerging from the *zariba*, on the right. These reinforcements strengthened MacDonald's position a great deal. When the Green Standard crossed the hills of Karari and came down on to the plain they found before them an enemy on a front 4,000 yards long.

Jabir Abu Shilaykhat's men and the depleted *rub'* of al 'Arifi al Rabi' were over 200 yards apart. Meanwhile the *mulazimin* advanced with gathering momentum over the sloping ground. The regularity of the ranks and the evenness of the pace surprised the enemy. The gap between the front group and the rest varied whenever those in front took aim to fire at MacDonald's brigade as he negotiated his difficult manoeuvre, a manoeuvre that inhibited their firepower and gave the *mulazimin* an opportunity to take careful aim. The losses among MacDonald's brigade during this manoeuvre rose to 200. The rest of the assault forces were able to cross over 1,200 yards without exposure to the direct fire of MacDonald's brigade. But it was exposed to other fire.

The gunboats were the only artillery units of the Sirdar that followed Shaykh al Din in his pursuit of Broadwood. They kept track of his exact position during his return. Their artillery did not have sufficient vision or range until after the *mulazimin* poured down on to the plain. Then they were able to intervene from a position to the north of the former *zariba*, 4,000 yards from the assault force. Their intervention was dreadful.

The *rub's* of the Green Standard charged towards the left-hand corner of MacDonald's brigade. 'Ajab al Fiya was on the far right then 'Abd Allah Barajub, wad Makkawi and Abu Bakr 'Amir. 'Abd Allah Abu Siwar summoned the *amir* 'Abd al Jalil Ahmad, commander of the Dighaim horsemen, and ordered him to set off to the far west, wheel round and challenge

MacDonald's left. 'Abd al Jalil hurried back to carry out his orders.

Meanwhile 'Abd Allah Abu Siwar set off with the Green Standard to confront MacDonald. He was soon within range of MacDonald's artillery. At the latter's strongest point he had three machine-guns and twelve cannons. The machine-guns were the first units to be placed to face the new front.

When the first men of the Green Standard were 700 yards from MacDonald they came under heavy fire, 200 case shot shells and 150 shrapnel shells in less than twenty minutes. The *amir* 'Abd Allah Abu Siwar was one of the first victims, to be followed by other senior *amirs* of the Green Standard. Among MacDonald's men those who made up the right-angle of the pivot on which the change of front was made suffered most casualties. The 9th Sudanese battalion that had been on the far right of the old front became the middle of the new front. The 11th Sudanese battalion was moved from its place on the far left to a new position to the right of the 9th Sudanese battalion, with the second artillery battery between them. The 10th Sudanese battalion that had been on the far right slipped behind the new front to take up position to the right of the 11th Sudanese battalion, with the 3rd Artillery battery between them. Maxim guns were distributed along the whole front. The three Sudanese battalions now faced north-west to deal with the new assault. MacDonald moved the Egyptian battalions to the far left and placed them so that the new front turned back, forming a right-angle. Their role was to deal with the last of Ya'qub's offensive. They did not have much to do for the rest of the Black Standard had already had its share of the fire of MacDonald and Lewis and were reduced to small groups that could be picked off piecemeal. There could be heard the rat-a-tat of Maxim guns, the explosions and whistles of the *mul-azimin's* bullets, and the shouted orders of the commanders of the battalions: 'Right turn', 'About turn', 'Quick march', followed by a flurry of activity.

Meanwhile Wauchope had been racing to fill the gap between the brigades of MacDonald and Lewis during the Black Standard's assault, while the Sirdar's battalions were lined up to open fire on the Black Standard. Then firing was heard again from a northerly direction and Shaykh al Din and his men were sighted. General Gatacre, Commander of the British Division, saw MacDonald's difficult position. He ordered Wauchope's nearest battalion to go to MacDonald's assistance. The first battalion went off to extend MacDonald's front on the right. They were soon joined by Broadwood's mounted forces. The reinforcements were no deterrent to the Green Standard in their forward dash in the face of ever increasing fire. As the *amir* 'Ajab al Fiha tried to stop the assault and turn away after seeing the casualties pile up, a voice rose from behind shouting 'We are people seeking martyrdom. We wish to keep our oath to the Mahdi'. The assault was continued to the end.

MacDonald's new front was completed just as the front line of the *mulazimin* was 200 yards away in small groups of three, four or five. The main body was 500 yards further off. The *mulazimin* fired but the volume gradually lessened and then stopped altogether. Many threw their rifles away and advanced with swords and spears at the ready for they had used up all their ammunition in the earlier engagements.

Wauchope's first battalion arrived to help MacDonald just as his Sudanese battalions were running out of ammunition. Many soldiers had only one or two bullets left. They now prepared to fight with bayonets. The advantage would have been with the *mulazimin* but for the arrival of Wauchope's battalion who now opened concentrated fire.

The qualities of the new rifle, the Lee-Metford, were soon demonstrated. They were able to eliminate almost all the advancing *mulazimin*. Survivors reached MacDonald's men and plunged their spears at them, only to fall to the ground stabbed by bayonets or struck by bullets fired from rifles almost against their bodies.

Concentrated fire gave way to volleys, assisted by shells from the gunboats; it checked the main onslaught and gave enough time to the officers of the three battalions to distribute more ammunition.

Under fire from three directions – MacDonald, Wauchope and the river – the *mulazimin* showed no less courage and resolution than in earlier assaults. Each line advanced and crumpled up before the crushing fire. Before the smoke settled another line was advancing and was similarly mowed down. This happened sixteen times. Sixteen lines went through the same stages one after the other. Not one man turned aside, but charged on hoping to meet the enemy and meeting only the enemy's fire. Some charged with empty rifles with which to belabour their enemy. Others hurled their lances. Standard bearers tried to use their flagpoles as weapons. A few advanced unarmed, their only weapon their white hot fury.

As 1100 approached it became clear that the fate of the third assault was to be the same as its predecessors.

The last tremor of the Khalifa's army that day was the assault of the Dighaim horsemen on MacDonald's left flank. The *amir* 'Abd al Jalil faced west so that he could bypass MacDonald and attack the left flank at the same time as the infantry attack. This had been a reasonably safe tactic in the past when the furthest range of the rifle was 200 yards, and before the appearance of machine-guns and cannon artillery. But in the short time 'Abd al Jalil Ahmad took in making his broad sweep, the main bulk of the assaulting infantry was wiped out, and Mac-Donald's force was able to thwart the offensive when it was still 700 yards away. When the horsemen's attack was launched, MacDonald's men were able to direct heavy fire at them. The charge was desperate with no clear aim but death and glory, for no infantry remained for them to support.

As they grasped their spears and flourished their swords in the charge, the Dighaim horsemen came into the range of MacDonald's fire only to fall one after the other to the last man.

This last assault was repulsed by 1100. Bodies were piled up right to the feet of MacDonald's men. Many had been stabbed by bayonets. Like all other commanders save Osman Digna, Shaykh al Din and 'Abd Allah Abu Siwar had been unable to get within striking distance of the enemy.

Not long afterwards the plain between the battlefield and the hills in the far west was covered with groups of men, trooping to the west towards the hills of al Markhiyat, bearing their dead and wounded.

Among the *mulazimin* and the Green Standard there were

4,000 dead, 2,000 from each. There were about 2,000 wounded among the Green Standard and 2,400 from among the *mulazimin*.

Among the major *amirs* from the Green Standard who were killed were the *amirs* 'Abd Allah Abu Siwar and 'Abd al Jalil Ahmad. Among the *mulazimin* commanders who died were the *amir* Mas'ud and the *amir* 'Uthman Adam.

Thus ended the battle of Karari and with it the Khalifa's state as an independent political city.

The second phase had been conceived as a simultaneous pincer movement. But the half hour separating the two attacks led to a difference in the closing of the two parts of the pincers, thereby making them two entirely separate movements, so the enemy was able to deal with each piecemeal.

The main cause for the delay lay of course in the movements of the *mulazimin*. When Wingate interrogated surviving *amirs* after the battle about the reason for their failure, all said, ''Uthman Shaykh al Din'. Al Tayyib al 'Arabi said to those who suggested after the battle that he rest awhile in the shade of a tree, 'This is the kind of puerile advice that lost us the battle a short time ago.' Shaykh al Din was absent for more than an hour and a half with the strongest part of the Khalifa's army, three miles from the battlefield. It seems that he may have intended being absent for longer had not 'Ali al Julla caught up with him.

Some blame also falls on 'Abd Allah Abu Siwar who did not stir himself during Ya'qub's attack, so that the whole burden fell on the Black Standard. 'Abd Allah's excuse is that he sat waiting for Shaykh al Din, thereby carrying out his instruction to the letter. If he had stayed in one place in readiness for a signal to attack, he would have been able to carry out the role that had been assigned him in the plan. The Khalifa realized, too late, that his son 'Uthman was not suitable to command all the *mulazimin* and tried to lessen the damage by detaching one-third from his command and handing them over to 'Uthman Azraq.

Shaykh al Din was twenty-four years old and had not fought at all before. He commanded the striking force of the whole army, and was hoping to win his spurs on the field of battle. It was he who insisted on an attack by daylight, so that he could show the rest the effect of the rifles of the *mulazimin* and their excellent training. For this reason, too, he seized the chance of attacking the horse and camelry of Broadwood, seeing in them valuable prey; but the pursuit of a mounted force for miles and miles led to disastrous consequences.

The second phase met the same fate as the first and failed for a simple reason. The Sirdar was able to mobilize and concentrate fire against the Black Standard's charge. Then he was able to switch once again to face Shaykh al Din and 'Abd Allah Abu Siwar. This was only possible because of the interval between the two assaults. Many recalled the anger of the Khalifa as he saw the Black Standard's charge at its peak while the ranks of the other front were still forming up.

Would two simultaneous charges have achieved anything? The Khalifa's strategic blunder when he chose Karari as the battlefield and attacked by day was too great for the battle to be redeemed by any tactical success. But the final result would not have incurred 26,000 losses on his own side and a few hundred in the ranks of the enemy. At the right moment for the double assault the Sirdar's brigades were scattered all over the field – facing the Black Standard, rescuing MacDonald, confronting Shaykh al Din and the Green Standard. The latter would have been exposed to quite serious losses, as would the Black Standard, but Shaykh al Din would have drawn the fire of MacDonald's brigades, then clashed with Wauchope and then Maxwell, all while the Sirdar's artillery was powerless to intervene. If this had happened the two sides might have been able to get to physical grips with each other. The technical differences between them would have become irrelevant. This would at the very least have guaranteed a greater number of casualties in the ranks of the invading army.

NOTES

1 Oral tradition, supported by the position of the graves today, shows that Muhammad al Mahdi dashed due east to face Maxwell's squadrons without waiting for Ya'qub's general order to charge. Ya'qub's grave lies exactly on the route taken by the Black Standard.

2   When, a few days after the battle, Muhammad's widow went out to bury him, she found mud still clinging to his feet and shoes.

3   There are three accounts of these events. My account is mainly derived from an eye witness, the *'umda* Adam Yusuf, who was standing a few yards from Ya'qub. I recorded his account on 13 January, 1971, and consider it the major evidence. The second account is that of al Hajj Amin Ahmad Sharfi, who got it from 'Ali al Julla. When 'Ali al Julla reached Ya'qub and told him that the Khalifa had summoned him, he wondered whether it was appropriate for him to leave the whole standard ready to charge. He looked behind and saw a horseman charging. He asked who it was, and was told 'Muhammad al Mahdi'. He said wearily, 'By God, if the Mahdi's young son offers up his life, I, Ya'qub, who have spent my youth and maturity in the good things of this world, now await a life after it. . . . We call upon you, God and His Prophet. We shall meet hereafter.' This story does not differ substantially from the first, though the accounts conflict over the cause of Ya'qub's grief.

The third account is that of Yusuf Mikka'il, who was one of the *amirs* of the Black Standard and also one of the clerks.

4   H. C. Jackson in his biography of Osman Digna says that it was Osman Digna who persuaded the Khalifa to retire. He relied on interviews with the Khalifa's servant, 'Abd 'Allah, and with Muhammad Bilal al Ja'li, Osman Digna's secretary. On the other hand Shaykh Babikr Badri says that Muhammad al Banna persuaded the Khalifa. However, in an interview Shaykh 'Abd 'Allah Muhammad Nur told me that Osman Digna attached himself to the Khalifa's headquarters.

5   Most European authorities say that the whole of the *mulazimin* took part in the last assault – allegedly 20,000 warriors. On the other hand Muhammad 'Abd al Rahim says that 'before Shaykh al Din arrived at the line of fire, a horseman came to him, telling him that the Khalifa told him to make for the hills of al Markhiyat. The deaths of Ya'qub and of Ibrahim al Khalil and the pounding his army had received probably made him indulgent towards his son, who had turned away from the battle, and had done nothing worth mentioning.'

6   It is generally accepted that this is the moment that 'Ali Dinar seized for slipping away west to al Fashir. There is also a local oral tradition which asserts that 'Shaykh al Din did not fight' or that 'Shaykh al Din did not want to fight'.

7   When the commander of the 9th battalion attempted, on his own initiative, to move his battalion into the new position, MacDonald called out to him as bullets were flying all around, 'I want your movements and behaviour to be just as if you were on the training ground.'

CHAPTER NINETEEN

The Wounded City

AMID the carnage of shattered corpses and the tang of gun-powder, the Khalifa 'Abd Allahi spent some time praying before the tomb of the Mahdi.

Meanwhile horses and horsemen were filling the mosque square. The first horsemen were led by Ya'qub Abu Zaynab, Governor of Omdurman. He gathered them from the survivors of the battle, from the Omdurman police, from the small number of wounded and others who responded to his summons. Ya'qub Abu Zaynab was given the task of gathering the horses together and of directing the resistance in the city. He sent all his fighting men and the few rifles he could find to man the walls.

His headquarters was crowded and confused. Hundreds of people arrived from the battlefield, seeking to die in the Mahdi's *qubba*. Among them were older members of the families of the *khalifas* and senior *amirs*.

The Khalifa 'Ali wad Hilu had his *angarayb* placed under the *qubba*. He refused to move to his house. The Khalifa Sharif brought along the Mahdi's sons, and placed them round him so they could die together. Other senior *amirs* were scattered around – Yunus al Dikaym, Osman Digna, and Shaykh al Din, who had arrived from the battlefield.

They faced two alternatives: either to defend the city or to withdraw to the west. The general idea was to defend Omdurman. But the Khalifa was absent from the debate; he was preoccupied in the tomb and none dared disturb him.

Machine-gun fire became louder. Artillery explosions

heralded the Sirdar's approach. A horseman dashed in, dismounted and informed Ya'qub Abu Zaynab that Kitchener had entered the city.

Ya'qub went straight to the entrance of the tomb and stood waiting for the Khalifa, anxious to break the news to him. Finally, when the sun was beginning to sink in the west, the Khalifa emerged with that vacant expression that had clothed his features since he had heard of the *amir* Ya'qub's death. He gave orders to Ya'qub Abu Zaynab to move to the west with all who wanted to go. The *khalifas* were to accompany them and families were told to evacuate Omdurman. Then the Khalifa went to the house of his brother Ya'qub to remove some important documents. His family undertook to meet him outside Omdurman.

When Ya'qub Abu Zaynab announced the Khalifa's orders, many refused to move. 'Ali wad Hilu and Sharif were sitting together. The former placed his sword in front of him. The *amir* Wad Mukhawi, his cousin, approached him, seized the sword, and signalled to two companions to carry the *angarayb* away.

As the sun set the streets and lanes leading south began to fill up with men, women and children on the march.

When the last assault had died away, the Sirdar ordered the whole army once more to resume the march on Omdurman. The wounded were sent back to the rear, the ammunition replenished and the Sirdar's huge war machine turned once more to the south. Meanwhile a few of the cavalry went some few miles west and south to try and disperse the thousands who were striking out into the desert or towards Omdurman.

The battle of standards and *rub's* was now over. The battle of the individual began. The triumphant horsemen as they met the wounded were astonished to find that they offered resistance. Each man waged his own individual battle before allowing the enemy to enter the city. Among a group of piled bodies one injured man would leap up and throw what was left of his strength into a final effort with a spear, sword or knife. Another would suddenly sit up after lying down for dead and hurl his spear at an enemy soldier. The scene was repeated a hundred times. It led finally to another of the features of the war – the killing of the wounded even after their surrender, an ugly feature in which the Sirdar's forces indulged.

Before the Battle of 'Atbara the Sirdar had issued a decree in which commanders and soldiers were told to bear in mind international law in the treatment of prisoners. But he refrained from issuing it again before the Battle of Omdurman. Details of the slaughter reached the British press and caused no little controversy.

One eye-witness, Winston Churchill, said 'I personally record that there was a very general impression that the fewer the prisoners, the greater will be the satisfaction of the commander.' The meaning is clear. He went on to say that the slaughter was the consequence of the vast propaganda that preceded the campaign. 'It had inflamed their passions, and had led them to believe that it was quite correct to regard their enemies as VERMIN, unfit to live. The result was that there were many wounded who were killed.'

Churchill divided the wounded into three categories. The first were those considered dangerous. This class was the largest and was wiped out. The second class was made up of those whose wounds were dangerous and painful. They were slaughtered out of compassion. The Sirdar claimed that he was putting them out of their agony. In the third category were those who, in spite of their surrender and their disarmament, did not fall into either of the other two categories, but were slaughtered none the less. 'About the third class there can be no dispute, how many were dispatched I cannot tell, although they threw down their arms and appealed for quarter.'

At 12 noon the Sirdar ordered the whole force to stop in Khur Shambat and on the banks of the Nile to rest and to take lunch. At 1430 they started to advance once more to music played by the Sudanese battalions. The Sirdar himself was among the first battalions of Maxwell's brigade with a battery of British artillery and a large detachment of Maxim machine-guns.

Soon the Sirdar's party approached the walls of Omdurman, only to receive a hail of bullets fired by the defenders behind the great wall; but the defenders' fire, directed from hastily prepared positions, was soon silenced.

The Sirdar turned to the east, towards the Nile, in search of an opening. A large gap was found, caused by the Howitzer bombardment from the east bank and filled up with wood, doors and stones. They continued eastward until they reached the great gate. This was destroyed and the Sirdar went through it and made his way towards the Mahdi's tomb.

He went along the main street of Omdurman and saw only the dying and the dead. He heard only the cries of the wounded and smelled only rotting carcases, human and animal, male and female, old and young. They were lying in the heat of the afternoon sun. This was the harvest of the 300 50-pounder shells that had been poured upon the city which the soldiers had left one day earlier. No house in Omdurman was without its wounded.

As darkness fell a horseman dashed up to Colonel Slatin and whispered something. Slatin sped off and reported what he had heard to Kitchener. Soon the news spread like fire through the army.

'The Khalifa has left the city.'

'When?'

'Two hours ago.'

'In which direction?'

'To the south.'

The Sirdar ordered Broadwood to follow him with the Egyptian mounted brigade. Broadwood quickly rallied his men. After a short rest they left the city and went south through Da'im Abu Sa'd and al Fitayhab.

The road by the Nile to the south was crammed with hundreds who had fled with their families and furniture. Broadwood struck west into the desert intending to return to the river the following morning, to meet a supply boat that had been sent to follow him.

He soon found himself, with his weary men and horses, in marshy ground. He stopped for the night at 2200. At 0300, he set off to return to the Nile to meet the steamer. They reached the rendezvous but the steamer was not there, and they had to wait all day. When it finally arrived the gap between Broadwood and his quarry had extended and hope of overtaking them faded. He decided, therefore, to return to Omdurman. Thus ended the first of a series of attempts to pursue the Khalifa.

After releasing the European prisoners, the Sirdar set up his headquarters in the Khalifa's mosque square. His brigades were distributed inside the capacious walled area and spent the night there. Intermittent firing in the city did not stop until the following morning.

Next morning a number of important wounded prisoners were brought before Slatin. He ordered their execution. The men, among them the *amir* al 'Arifi al Rabi', were taken to the west of Omdurman and executed in the place now called al Rabi' Square.

The Sirdar issued an order permitting the plunder of grain and of the Khalifa's houses by the soldiers. But soon everything got confused and the pillage extended to people's houses. Some people were killed defending their property and honour on their doorsteps. The Sirdar also ordered the destruction of the Mahdi's tomb.

On the battlefield the piled-up bodies showed exactly the course and development of the battle. The eastern ridge of Jabal Surkab was covered with the bodies of the Kara garrison. Their density increased towards the *zariba*. Two lines of bodies beginning from Karari and Surkab converged at the place where MacDonald's brigade had stood. The path of the Black Standard was stained crimson, with dashes of white for clothes and the tawny colour of horses. As Churchill wrote, 'There was nothing *dulce et decorum* about the Dervish dead; nothing of the dignity of unconquerable manhood, yet those were as brave men as ever walked the earth, destroyed not conquered by machinery.'

Some of the wounded remained on the field exposed to the sun each day for several days. Scores crawled a few yards each day towards the Nile in quest of water. Many failed to reach the river, expiring with glazed eyes appealing for water.

Others lay in the same place under small bushes. Survivors were found a whole week after the battle. They were still alive thanks to the women of Omdurman who busied themselves each evening slipping out after dark to bury their dead, succour their wounded and to bring out food and water. The quiet hills each night listened to the wails of the bereaved digging graves or mumbling through tears that spilt into cups of drinking water.

CHAPTER TWENTY

The Round-Up

THE deposed Khalifa was urging his caravan to go faster. Distraction left him. Resolution and mental energy returned. No longer was he at the head of fearsome armies as he had been yesterday, hopeful of victory. Now he headed an army of widows and orphans. He quickly overcame the paralysis of the shock and the horrors of that storm-tossed day. He resolved to behave like his comrade Osman Digna. Let him proceed to the west and rally his forces once more and start all over again. There was still the army of Ahmad Fadil in al Qadarif, al Khatim Musa in el Obeid and 'Arabi Daf' Allah in al Rajjaf. He would call on them to join him. They would then take Omdurman by storm and enter the city as victors just as he had done with the Mahdi thirteen years before.

He had with him a number of *amirs* and a large number of the *mulazimin* who had returned with Shaykh al Din after joining him in Omdurman. Also with him was a large company of women and children who went on foot.

Silence reigned, unbroken except by the tramp of feet and of the hastening beasts. Suddenly the peace was shattered by the report of cannon and the crackle of machine-gun fire as the whole caravan was exposed to the gunboats.

The caravan carried on its way for three days,[1] during which they suffered great hardship. Women and children collapsed. Feet were swollen from the continual walking. On the Monday afternoon they looked down on Umm Ghunaym where camels, horses and provisions awaited them, guarded by the Zaiyadiya tribe. They remained there for one day until they were joined by the Khalifa 'Ali wad Hilu still borne on an *angarayb*. From there the Khalifa wrote to al Khatim Musa and to Ahmad Fadil asking them to meet him at Abu Rukba.

Another distinguished group that left Omdurman was the group of the Khalifa Sharif who was accompanied by the sons of the Mahdi. They proceeded straight to al Fashashoya and were followed by many of the Fur and Rizayqat on their way back to Darfur to join 'Ali Dinar.

On 5 September a second attempt to round up the Khalifa was made under the leadership of Abd al 'Azim Bey, chieftain of the 'Ababda. This force was made up of a mixture of tribes. They pursued him to Shiqayq but Abd al 'Azim returned because his camels were unable to match the Khalifa's for speed.

After two days' rest the Khalifa left the White Nile and struck west to the area of the Nuba Mountains. He first visited the tomb of his father at Abu Rukba where he was joined by al Khatim Musa and the el Obeid garrison. The arrival of al Khatim Musa was an encouraging moment for the Khalifa, for the el Obeid garrison, though small, contained loyal and valiant soldiers.

When his men had assembled he turned west to Shirkayla where he stayed for two months, all the time waiting for Ahmad Fadil. In November the Khalifa decided to continue his journey to Jabal Qadir. But he left the families behind at the wells of Saisabana and advanced only with his fighting men.

At Jabal Qadir the king of the mountain, King Bosh, gave him a kind and friendly reception which mitigated the physical torment and spiritual bitterness. It is reckoned that he stayed there for three months and then he went back to Shirkayla.

At last Ahmad Fadil arrived, after a series of gruelling adventures. He had responded to the Khalifa's call to join him at Omdurman and to guard the east bank; he was at Rufa'a when the battle took place. He soon learned of the defeat. Two envoys from the Sirdar and Slatin came to him. They bore news of the battle and demanded his surrender. Ahmad Fadil lost his temper and retorted by killing one of the messengers, claiming that he was a traitor. The other returned to Slatin to carry his reply: he would not surrender and he would fight to the end.

After this he changed direction and returned south and crossed the Blue Nile at the point where the River Rahad joins it. He then planned to advance west to join the Khalifa. It was here that he received the Khalifa's letter. But he decided to go back to al Qadarif where his soldiers had left their families and belongings. But the situation there had changed. Colonel Parsons had heard of the outcome of the Battle of Omdurman and had taken the town.

He fortified it and waited for Ahmad Fadil. The latter advanced and made three vigorous but unsuccessful assaults on the city during which he lost a large part of his force. He therefore pitched camp and besieged the city, waiting for hunger to force them to surrender.

News of the siege reached General Rundle in Khartoum. He sent out an expeditionary force. Ahmad Fadil saw that he would be caught between two fires and so raised the siege, gathered his troops together and turned south to cross the River Dindar.

On 7 November he crossed the River Rahad in safety and struck west, reaching the River Dindar at a point opposite Karkuj on the Blue Nile. He stopped there to make further reconnaissance. General Rundle, however, sent another force to reconquer the whole area of the Jazira.

For the two months that followed the pause on the River Dindar, Lewis tracked Ahmad Fadil, who crossed the Dindar and moved steadily southward, seeking a place to cross out of reach of the gunboats. He reached Dakhla, about twenty miles south of al Rusayris, on 18 December, where his vanguard crossed the Blue Nile. With half his men on the west bank and the other half on the east, Ahmad Fadil was taken by surprise. He had set up a defence post on Dakhla Island to cover the crossing. The gunboats *Dal* and *Malik* joined Lewis with a reinforcement of 200 soldiers and an assault began. It turned into a fierce battle lasting all day. In the course of it 117 of Lewis' men were wounded. 500 of Ahmad Fadil's men were killed and 2,700 taken prisoner.

Ahmad Fadil slipped away with the remaining men and crossed the Jazira. But fatigue and suffering had taken their toll. When a large force was sent by gunboat to engage them at

Renk on 22 January, many of them surrendered. Ahmad Fadil crossed the White Nile in stages on small inflated rafts, in groups not exceeding thirty men. He then joined the Khalifa at Shirkayla.

The third attempt to eliminate the Khalifa began on 29 December when a force under the command of Colonel Kitchener, brother of the Sirdar, was ordered to advance and attack the Khalifa in Kordofan so long as the Khalifa's own force did not exceed 1,000 men.

The force left the Nile on 23 January after sending ahead an advance group to occupy the Wells of Jadid, a suitable springboard from which to make forays. The force made its way south-west. As they proceeded they encountered thicker and thicker trees. The progress of the force was extremely tiring and was like the progress of Hicks on the same road sixteen years before.

At Jadid they found that most of the water in the wells was brackish. They resumed their march towards Abu Rukba where they spent the night around the grass huts built for the Khalifa whenever he visited the tomb of his father.

One of the inhabitants was interrogated. He told them that the Khalifa had paid three visits to the tomb of his father at Abu Rukba and that his present base was at Shirkayla to the west. The force set out for Shirkayla on 23 January. When they approached al 'Aqaila they found a well-planned city with levelled streets. All this showed that the Khalifa had lost none of his passion for strict order even in his days of adversity. The city extended for quite a few miles. The number of empty huts indicated that the population was perhaps 10,000, with at least 5–6,000 fighting men.

The force spent the night in the camp at al 'Aqaila and the following morning sent reconnaissance parties towards the Khalifa's camp at Shirkayla, where they found the Khalifa prepared to meet them.

The Khalifa's strength was beyond the size that the force was permitted to take on so it turned east and retraced its steps. The retreat was toilsome and painful, mortifying and frustrating. Colonel Kitchener was relieved when he reached the

Nile again. Thus ended the third unsuccessful attempt to eliminate the Khalifa.

Arrangements for feeding his men occupied much of the Khalifa's time, for they spent most of the year in a state of semi-permanent famine. The number of women and children reached thousands. A survivor of those days told me of the horrors they endured, of the awfulness of the hunger they faced and how sometimes they did not even have a single grain of *dhurra*.

In spite of the many loyal men who remained with him, the Khalifa was haunted by memories of the awful battle of 2 September. His anguish was sharpened by the repeated news of the collapse of his authority, and of the harassments of his own tribe. 'Ali Dinar's presence in Darfur was an insurmountable obstacle to the Khalifa in the west. The continuous patrol of gunboats on the White Nile was an obstacle to the east. He was besieged in Kordofan. Twice he sent for the Khalifa Muhammad Sharif who lingered on Aba Island. The Khalifa wanted him to join him and to bring the sons of the Mahdi. But twice the Khalifa declined. Those who remained with him to the end included 'Ali wad Hilu, Osman Digna, Yunus al Dikaym, 'Uthman Shaykh al Din, Ahmad Fadil, 'Ali al Julla, 'Abd al Baqi 'Abd al Wakil and Ya'qub Abu Zaynab.

When Colonel Kitchener's cavalry were near the Khalifa's camp, they estimated that he had over 10,000 men with him. But that was in January. As month followed month and as hunger increased, large numbers began to desert and return to their homes. He always let people choose to stay with him or to go home. By November, 1899, there remained with him but 5,000 fighting men.

At the end of October there spread among the *suqs* and alleys of Omdurman dark rumours about the Khalifa's movements and about a supply of buried weapons in Omdurman, to be used to prepare the way for a renewed revolt in his support. Reports were repeatedly reaching the Intelligence Department of the preparedness of the men of Omdurman and the neighbouring villages. An atmosphere heavy with rumours hung over the city. The rumours finally took shape in definite news. The Khalifa was on the move, heading for Omdurman.

On 20 October, before he left Khartoum for Cairo, the Sirdar issued instructions for the fourth campaign to march on Kordofan and the destruction of the Khalifa.

Colonel Wingate, head of the Intelligence Department, was put in command of the campaign. His force was made up of one Egyptian cavalry company, two camel companies, an artillery company and a company of Maxims. The infantry brigade consisted of the 9th and 13th Sudanese battalions, one Sudanese battalion of irregulars and a miscellaneous group of tribal horsemen. These troops assembled at Kaka on the White Nile, 380 miles south of Khartoum.

On 21 November, 1899, Colonel Wingate left the Nile at al Fashashoya and headed west at the head of 3,700 men. They advanced by night to Nafisa where Ahmad Fadil was reported to have a camp, having been on a *dhurra* foraging expedition. But they found the camp deserted. Ahmad Fadil had set out the previous day for Abu 'Adil, five miles away. Wingate immediately sent his mounted troops ahead, with a Maxim battery and two cannons. The mounted troops advanced and occupied the high plateau that overlooked the whole of Ahmad Fadil's camp. At first light they opened fire.

Ahmad Fadil hastily gathered his forces together and hid among the trees and grass. He made a number of violent assaults but the fire of the machine-guns and rifles stopped him only fifty yards from the cavalry ranks. He gathered his force for a fourth and final attack, but the infantry had arrived to strengthen the dismounted cavalry and camelry. They were able to repel him with ease.

Ahmad Fadil lost 400 men. After the action he withdrew and joined the Khalifa at Umm Dibaykarat near the Wells of Jadid. Wingate himself set out for Jadid.

The force reached Jadid at 1000 on 24 November after a forced night march. They occupied the wells. A man who had left the Khalifa's camp informed them that the Khalifa was camping with all his forces at Umm Dibaykarat, seven miles away. A quick reconnaissance on horseback towards the Khalifa's camp confirmed this report. After a short rest Wingate ordered an advance.

The Khalifa had been in Umm Dibaykarat for not more than a fortnight waiting for Ahmad Fadil. On the morning of the 23rd he heard a continuous rumble in the distance. He gathered his forces together and waited anxiously. Ahmad Fadil arrived with a party of his men, their clothes soaked in blood. He gave a quick report of the battle, in which he had lost three-fifths of his men, and told the Khalifa of the strength and position of the enemy.

The way north was now blocked by Wingate. The east was closed to him because of the gunboats on the White Nile. As for retreat to the south this was impossible because the enemy occupied the only source of water in the area. The Khalifa decided to make his final stand and to wait at Umm Dibaykarat.

He gathered together all those in the camp and addressed them: 'You have been with me throughout the bloody conflict between the enemy and myself. I lost more than half my army at Omdurman. I have now decided to face the enemy and to seek martyrdom here. I release you all from your allegiance to me. Whoever wishes to leave now, before the enemy's assault, let him do so. I absolve everybody. I am satisfied with you all.'

He then arranged himself in the middle of a circle and spent most of the night receiving allegiance anew. In the background drums and cymbals were beaten, their muffled noise reaching the ears of Wingate at Jadid.

Trees and tall grass covered the land for a mile and a half west of the camp.

More than two hours before dawn the Khalifa moved to a depression near a small ridge a mile long and made his base there. He saw Wingate advancing straight towards him. On the slopes of the ridge the Khalifa ranged a force of 2,000 combat troops and 300 yards to the left of these he ranged a force of riflemen from the *mulazimin*. They deployed over 400 yards. The effective leadership fell to Ahmad Fadil whose position was between the two lines. The command of the rifles fell to the *amir* 'Abd al Baqi 'Abd al Wakil, while the leaders of the hand-to-hand fighters were the *amir* Bashir 'Ajab al Fiya and Osman Digna.

The Khalifa sat on his charger. Round him were the Khalifa

'Ali wad Hilu, Ya'qub Abu Zaynab, Siddiq son of the Mahdi and his own brother Harun.

Meanwhile Wingate placed a detachment of cavalry in front. They were strengthened with mounted Maxim cannons. Squads of camel troops defended his flanks. In spite of the moonlight the force stumbled about on account of the denseness of the trees on both sides of the track. This forced Wingate's men to cut their way through with knives.

The cavalry and Maxims reached the beginning of the ridge. The rest of the force followed, concealed by the long grass. At the ridge they paused to rest. The cavalry withdrew to the rear.

Ahmad Fadil observed the enemy's advance just near the gap between the hand-to-hand fighters and the riflemen. He ordered the latter to move to the right to cover the gap. The move was perceived by Wingate. A few minutes before dawn at 0505 Wingate ordered his cannons and machine-guns and also the riflemen to open fire. The *mulazimin* stood their ground. Indeed they returned fire – heavily and repeatedly – in preparation for a hand-to-hand assault. But the enemy's fire had its effect even in the darkness, especially at close range. At first light they rushed forward. But the unrelenting fire mowed them down. As the light became clearer Wingate directed a devastating bombardment at the *mulazimin*. This halted their advance. He then ordered all his soldiers to advance towards the settlement. Under cover of Maxim fire they forced back the riflemen who had to retire even though they were firing steadily.

Behind the swordsmen and opposite the 9th battalion one group consisting of the Khalifa and his closest advisers could be seen in the light of the dawn. They had dismounted from their horses and each was seated on the ground.

The Khalifa saw the rifle fire destroying his front ranks. As the enemy advanced he ordered all his *amirs* to dismount. They rolled out their *furwas* on the ground, sat on them and faced Mecca. The Khalifa placed 'Ali wad Hilu on his right and called Ahmad Fadil, busy rallying the men, to sit on his left. The rest of his close companions sat behind him.

The Khalifa was wounded in his left arm. He covered the wound and the welling blood with his right hand. As the infantry of the 9th battalion came nearer, 'Ali wad Hilu could bear it no longer. He unsheathed his sword, rose and limped forward to attack the enemy. The Khalifa bawled at him and ordered him to sit down. These were the last words he uttered. He was hit three times in the chest. One bullet penetrated his heart.

At twenty minutes to six on 24 November, with the death of the Khalifa, there died the last struggle of independent Sudan.[2] On that small patch of land were assembled the last of a long line of heroes, who fell after building the state that had been nurtured in their hearts and fashioned by their swords.

One thousand of the Khalifa's men fell, either slain or wounded. 3,150 men and 6,250 women and children were taken prisoner.

Apart from the Khalifa 'Abd Allahi and the Khalifa 'Ali wad Hilu those who died included Ahmad Fadil and Bashir 'Ajab al Fiya. Among those taken prisoner were 'Uthman Shaykh al Din, Yunus al Dikaym and al Khatim Musa.

Osman Digna was able to slip away from the battle of Umm Dibaykarat at the last moment, just before the 9th Sudanese battalion surrounded the Khalifa's group and the whole settlement. With his customary speed he soon reached the White Nile and crossed it at night near al Duwaym. He crossed the Jazira, continuing his journey mostly on foot until he reached the shores of the Red Sea where he remained concealed in a cave in the mountains, waiting for a boat to take him across to Arabia, but was betrayed to the new authority and taken prisoner.

'Uthman Shaykh al Din was taken to the prison at Rosetta and died in 1900 of gangrene, the result of a wound received in the battle. Other prisoners with him have maintained that the wound was not serious and was healing, but that the treatment was deliberately careless. Mahmud wad Ahmad died in 1906 after a long illness. Most of the prisoners from the tribe of the Khalifa Abd 'Allahi died in Rosetta prison. Thousands died of pulmonary tuberculosis as a result of the cold weather and bad food. Yunus al Dikaym returned to Omdurman and lived to a great age, dying in 1936.

After he withdrew from Omdurman the Khalifa Muhammad Sharif made his base on Aba Island for a while. He was later allowed to settle at Shukkaba, a village near Sinnar. False reports reached the occupation authorities that he was stirring the embers of revolt once more, and that his followers were gathering arms. Colonel Lewis, Governor of the area, moved in and surrounded the house. There were no grounds to substantiate the truth of these reports. They were in fact leading an ordinary peaceful life. But Lewis ordered the death of the Khalifa Muhammad Sharif and all the sons of the Mahdi. Only two sons got away.

NOTES

1   Sayyid Musa Ya'qub who was thirteen years old at the time, told me that he did not have a single morsel of food during those days even though he was in the front group with the Khalifa.

2   Wingate's official report, written only a few minutes afterwards and sent at once to Khartoum describes the last moments and the death of the Khalifa as told him by Yunus al Dikaym.

BIBLIOGRAPHY

A. *BOOKS*

1 H. S. Alford and W. D. Sword – *The Egyptian Soudan – Its Loss and Recovery* (London, 1898)
2 'Ali al Mahdi – *Jihad fi Sabil Allah* (Struggle for the Cause of God) (Khartoum, 1965)
3 A. H. Atteridge – *Famous Modern Battles* (London, 1911)
4 Babikr Bedri – *Hayati* (My Life) vol. I (translated as *Memoirs* by Y. Bedri and G. C. Scott, Oxford, 1969)
5 R. Bermann – *The Mahdi of Allah* (tr R. John) (London, 1931)
6 Wilfrid Scawen Blunt – *My Diaries 1888–1914* (London, 1919)
7 A. B. Brassey (ed) – *The Navy Annual* (London, 1899)
8 Neville Brown – *Strategic Mobility* (London, 1967)
9 Bennet Burleigh – *Sirdar and Khalifa* (London, 1898)
10 Bennet Burleigh – *Khartoum Campaign* (London, 1899)
11 Central Records Office, Khartoum – *Daftar Waqa'i' 'Uthman Diqna* (Register of Osman Digna's Battles)
12 Central Records Office, Khartoum – *Manshurat al Mahdi* (The Mahdi's Decrees)
13 Winston S. Churchill – *The River War* (2 vols) (London, 1899)
14 Winston S. Churchill – *My Early Life* (London, 1930)
15 Carl von Clausewitz – *On War* (3 vols) (tr) (London, 1873)
16 S. E. Ellacott – *Guns* (London, 1955)
17 Charles George Gordon – *Journals* (London, 1885)
18 B. Liddell Hart – *The Strategy of Indirect Approach* (London, 1941)
19 G. F. R. Henderson – *The Science of War* (London, 1905)
20 Richard Hill – *Biographical Dictionary of the Anglo Egyptian Sudan* (London, 1951)
21 Richard Hill – *Egypt in the Sudan* (Oxford, 1959)
22 P. M. Holt – *The Mahdist State in the Sudan* (Oxford, 1958)
23 Michael Howard (ed) – *The Theory and Practice of War* (London, 1965)
24 H. C. Jackson – *Osman Digna* (London, 1926)
25 E. F. Knight – *Letters from the Sudan* (London, 1897)
26 H. A. Macmichael – *A History of the Arabs of the Sudan* (2 vols) (Cambridge, 1922)
27 Philip Magnus – *Kitchener* (London, 1958)
28 Muhammad 'Abd al Rahim – *Al Nida fi Daf' al Iftira'* (Call for Repudiation of Slanders)

29 Musa al Mubarak – *Tarikh Darfur al Siyasi* (Political History of Darfur) (Khartoum, 1971)
30 Anthony Nutting – *Gordon* (London, 1966)
31 Anthony Nutting – *The Scramble for Africa* (London, 1970)
32 'An Officer' – *Sudan Campaign 1896–1899* (London, 1899)
33 Joseph Ohrwalder – *Ten Years in the Mahdist Camp 1882–1892* (London, 1892)
34 G. N. Sanderson – *England, Europe and the Upper Nile 1882–1899* (Edinburgh, 1965)
35 Mekki Shibeika – *British Policy in the Sudan 1882–1902* (Oxford, 1952)
36 Mekki Shibeika – *Al Sudan 'Ibr al Qurun* (Sudan across the Centuries) (Beirut)
37 Mekki Shibeika – *Al Khartum bayn Gordon w'al Mahdi* (Khartoum between Gordon and the Mahdi) (Khartoum)
38 Na'um Shuqayr – *Jughrafiya wa Tarikh al Sudan* (Geography and History of the Sudan) (Beirut, 1967)
39 Rudolf Slatin – *Fire and Sword in the Sudan* (London, 1896)
40 G. W. Steevens – *With Kitchener to Khartum* (Edinburgh, 1898)
41 Lytton Strachey – *Eminent Victorians* (London, 1918)
42 A. B. Theobald – *The Mahdiya* (London, 1949)
43 A. B. Theobald – *Ali Dinar Last Sultan of Darfur* (London, 1965)
44 J. Weller – *Weapons and Tactics* (London, 1966)
45 Harold F. B. Wheeler – *The Story of Lord Kitchener* (London, 1916)
46 F. R. Wingate – *Mahdiism and the Egyptian Soudan* (London, 1891)

B. *ARTICLES*

1 (Brigadier) 'Abd al Rahman al Faki – 'Ma'raka Karari min wajha nazar al Khalifa' (The Battle of Karari from the Khalifa's Point of View) in *al Qalam*, February, March, April and June 1967, Khartoum
2 *Daily Telegraph*, 28–30 August 1898; 1, 3, 5, 8–10, 23 September 1898; 12 December 1898. London
3 B. R. Mitford – 'Diary of a Subaltern on the Nile in the Eighties and Nineties' in *Sudan Notes and Records*, vol XVIII, part 2 (1935), pp. 167–193 and vol XIX part 2 (1936), pp. 199–231
4 J. A. Reid – 'Story of a Mahdist Amir' in *Sudan Notes and Records*, vol IX part 2 (1926), pp. 79–82
5 Al Tijani Yusuf Bashir – articles in *Umm Durman*, 30 September, 1936, 31 October, 1936, 15 December, 1936, 1 January, 1937. Omdurman
6 *The Times*, 12 December, 1898
7 F. R. Wingate – 'The Siege and Fall of Khartum', in *Sudan Notes and Records*, vol XIII, part 1 (1930), pp. 1–82

C. *THESES*

1 'Abd Allah Ibrahim – 'The Battle of Atbara', University of Khartoum

2 Gasim Y. Bedri – 'British Writings on the Sudanese Mahdiya', American University of Beirut
3 'Development of the Army of the Mahdiya' (in Arabic), Staff College, Omdurman

D. *DOCUMENTS*

1 Central Records Office Khartoum
   i Papers of the *amir* Ya'qub: lists of soldiers and materials of the army of the Mahdiya, kept in eight boxes, 2.43–50. Unsorted
   ii Correspondence of the *amirs* from A.H.1314–1316
     a. The Khalifa to 'Uthman Adam, 12 Rajab 1305 1.11.32
     b. Muhammad wad Bishara to the Khalifa
       14 Safar 1314 1.2.3.287
       18 Safar 1314 1.2.3.289 and 1.2.3.290
       23 Safar 1314 1.2.3.294
       last day of Safar 1314 1.2.3.297 and 1.2.3.298
       1 Rabi' I 1314 1.2.3.300, 1.2.3.302 and 1.2.3.303
       3 Jumada I 1314 1.2.3.337
       10 Jumada I 1314 1.2.3.340
       11 Jumada I 1314 1.2.3.343
     c. Mahmud wad Ahmad to the Khalifa
       20 Jumada II 1314 1.15.4.270
       23 Muharram 1315 1.8.1.2
       24 Safar 1315 1.8.1.3
     d. Commanders of the *rub's* to Mahmud, 22 Muharram 1314 1.8.3.2
     e. The Khalifa to Mahmud wad Ahmad, 2 Safar 1315 1.28.4.3
     f. The Khalifa to Ahmad Fadil
       15 Muharram 1316 1.12.4.326
       29 Rabi'I 1316 1.12.4.342 and 1.12.4.343
       8 Rabi'II 1316 1.12.4.443
     g. Al Khatim Musa to the Khalifa
       17 Muharram 1316 1.14.7.23
       19 Muharram 1316 1.14.7.34
       last day of Muharram 1316 1.14.7.32
       3 Rabi'I 1316 1.6.10.240
       29 Rabi'I 1316 1.6.10.235
       7 Rabi'II 1316 1.6.10.244
     h. 'Uthman al Dikaym to the Khalifa, 20 Muharram 1316 1.18.9.427
     i. 'Adlan Muhammad Surur to the Khalifa
       8 Muharram 1316 1.6.16.289
       19 Safar 1316 1.6.16.34
     j. 'Abd al Baqi 'Abd al Wakil to the Khalifa
       7 Safar 1316 1.6.12.274
       1 Safar 1316 1.6.12.275
       2 Safar 1316 1.6.12.276
       12 Muharram 1316 1.6.12.279

18 Safar 1316 1.6.12.287
4 Rabi'I 1316 1.6.12.296
17 Rabi'I 1316 1.6.12.301 and 1.6.12.302
19 Rabi'I 1316 1.6.12.303
20 Rabi'I 1316 1.6.12.304
21 Rabi'I 1316 1.6.12.306
23 Rabi'I 1316 1.6.12.309
24 Rabi'I 1316 1.6.12.310 and 1.6.12.311
25 Rabi'I 1316 1.6.12.312
26 Rabi'I 1316 1.6.12.313
1 Rabi'II 1316 1.6.12.314 and 1.6.12.315
2 Rabi'II 1316 1.6.12.316
6 Rabi'II 1316 1.6.12.317
7 Rabi'II 1316 1.6.12.318
9 Rabi'II 1316 1.6.12.319 and 1.6.12.320
10 Rabi'II 1316 1.6.12.321
11 Rabi'II 1316 1.6.12.322 and 1.6.12.323
13 Rabi'II 1316 1.6.12.325

  iii Papers of Muhammad 'Abd al Rahim, including the manuscript History of the Mahdiya, Dictionary of Personalities and History of the Turkiya

  ivPapers of Yusuf Mikha'il

  v Papers of 'Ali al Mahdi

2 University of Durham

  i Wingate Papers Box 17

  ii Manuscript memoirs of al Zubayr Pasha

3 Private Collection of Sayyid Muhammad al Sayyid al Khalifa

4 Private Collection of Sayyid 'Izz al Din al Mahdi

5 Private Collection of Sayyid 'Abd Allah al Amir, manuscript papers of al Nur Anqara

E. *ORAL TESTIMONY*

1 Conversation 21 January, 1971, with the *'umda* Adam Yusuf, who took part in the assault of the Black Standard

2 Conversation, 27 May, 1971, with *Shaykh* Husayn wad al Zayn, who was among the *mulazimin*

3 Conversation, 29 June, 1971, with *Shaykh* 'Abd Allah Muhammad Nur, an attendant of the Khalifa 'Ali wad Hilu who was at the Khalifa's headquarters throughout the battle

4 Conversation, 13 June, 1971, with *Shaykh* Ahmad al Nur, who took part in the operations on the east bank

5 Conversation, 8 July, 1971, with Sayyid Musa Ya'qub, then aged 86, son of the *amir* Ya'qub, who was present at the battle of Umm Dibaykarat

6 Conversation, 11 May, 1971, with *Hajj* Amin Ahmad Sharfi, then aged 88, nephew of the *amir* Ahmad 'Abd al Karim

7 Conversation, 26 December, 1970, with *Shaykh* Babu Nimr, grandson of 'Ali al Julla

8 Conversation, 1 June, 1971, with *Shaykh* Ibrahim, then aged 84, of Sabaluka

9 Conversation, 2 February, 1972, with *Hajja* Zaynab bint al Amir Mahmud, then aged 83, who accompanied the Khalifa to Shirkayla

10 Conversation with *Shaykh* Ahmad al Kabashi 'Arafi of al 'Ijaija, son of the man who met the Khalifa and Slatin on the eve of the battle

INDEX

(References to Khartoum (the city), Omdurman, Karari, to Kitchener and the Khalifa 'Abd Allahi are so numerous that no useful purpose would be served by mentioning them all in the index.)

253

al Halfaya (Halfaya al Muluk), village north of Khartoum, 17, 40, 100
Hamad Ruqay'at, Mahdist intelligence officer, 118
Hamdan Abu 'Anja, *amir*, 4, 12, 14, 23, 99, 138, 139, 154, 181, 182
Hamid Sabun, Mahdist officer, 170
Hamuda Idris, Mahdist commander at al Firka, 56–7, 59, 60, 64
Harum, brother of the Khalifa, 24, 245
Hasan Husni, ammunition workshop supervisor, 40
Hasan wad al Nujumi, Mahdist officer, 66
Hasan Zaki, Egyptian doctor and armaments manufacturer, 40, 106
Hasan al Da'in, Mahdist officer, 170
al Hawsh, village north of Khartoum, 118
Hicks, Col William, British soldier and commander of ill-fated Expedition, 15–17, 85, 91, 97, 99, 101, 108, 135, 138, 152, 153, 154, 182, 241
Holt, P. M., historian, 24
Hunter, Major-General Sir Archibald, British commander, 51, 55, 56, 69–70, 77, 113, 125, 198, 205

Ibrahim 'Ali Sabir al Maghrabi, clerk, 22
Ibrahim Farah, Sudanese officer with Kitchener, 124, 142, 144
Ibrahim al Hajjaz, 123
Ibrahim Jabir, Mahdist officer, 170, 177–8, 179
Ibrahim al Khalil, *amir*, 36, 47; character, 87–8; 95, 102, 113, 114, 115–16, 121, 151–3, 156, 157, 160, 161, 163, 164, 165; attack in the battle, 169–72; death, 172; 174, 176, 179–80, 181, 182, 188, 189, 190, 207, 213, 214–15, 216, 220, 231
Ibrahim Malik, Mahdist officer, 174
Ibrahim Sa'id, companion of Osman Digna, 190, 195
al 'Ijaija, village north of Omdurman, 149–50, 155
'Isa wad Ahmad, Mahdist messenger, 221, 223
'Isa Zakariya, commander at battle of 'Atbara, 76, 141–4, 148
Isma'il, Khedive of Egypt, 3, 4, 5, 49, 50
Isma'il Pasha, Egyptian invader of the Sudan, 2
Isma'il Ahmad, brother of Ibrahim al Khalil, 87, 214
Isma'il Aiyub, Governor General, 4

Jabal Abu Zariba, hill on the battlefield, 160, 162, 174, 182, 183, 202, 224
Jabal Daham, hill on the battlefield, 182, 183, 184, 185, 186, 202
Jabal Qadir, hill in the Nuba Mountains, 10, 12, 13, 14, 84, 189, 239
Jabal al Shaykh al Tayyib, hill near Omdurman, 130
Jabal Surkab (Surgham), hill on the battlefield, 114, 141, 147, 151, 157, 160, 161, 165, 169, 170, 171, 172, 173, 174, 175, 176, 188, 191, 193, 194, 195, 201, 205, 206, 207, 208, 211, 214, 215, 216, 219, 220, 221, 236
Jabir Abu Shilaykhat, Mahdist officer, 174, 223, 225
Jabir al Tayyib, *amir*, 149
Jackson, H. C., administrator and writer, 155, 231
Jackson, Sir Herbert, soldier and administrator, 155
Jadid, village in Kordofan, 241, 243, 244
Jaqdul, wells in Bayuda Desert, 20
John, King of Abyssinia, 30, 136
Jubayr, Mahdist *amir*, 57

Mustafa al Amin, merchant, 31–2